TO LIVE IS TO FLY
My Life in the Fast Lane

Tizi Hodson

CHAPLIN BOOKS

www.chaplinbooks.co.uk

Chaplin Books
75b West St
Titchfield PO14 4DG
www.chaplinbooks.co.uk

ACKNOWLEDGEMENTS

I would like to thank Kathy Peyton and Linda Lawrie for all their help, time and advice with editing, ideas and suggestions. More thanks to Ken Pankhurst for helping to get this book on its final way. Special thanks to Ray Barnes, Robin Voice, Amanda Field and Dave Thomas for all their help at the final end.

INTRODUCTION

Life is good: it's a phrase you'll hear from me all the time. Sometimes I've even said it when I've just crashed my motorbike, fallen with my horse, or had to make an emergency landing when flying an aircraft through thick cloud. I just pick myself up and try again – even if that means discharging myself from hospital in order to do so, which has happened a few times.

I firmly believe that you should seize every opportunity that life offers you: and to seize it today. That's why, when I was on a pleasant motorcycle holiday in Germany with some fellow members of a bikers' club and saw the Wall of Death at a fairground, I asked to try it. I became a Wall of Death rider, and my friends went on the rest of their holiday without me. It's why, when I was first at the solo controls of an aerobatic aircraft, I thought I'd try to loop-the-loop (what could possibly go wrong?). It's also why I instantly accepted every job offer that came my way, whether it was as a stunt rider, real-estate seller, saddlery maker or snake hunter, sometimes accepting three jobs on the same day, and worrying only later about how I could fit them all in.

I've never really given much thought to the things that more 'sensible' people like my sister Toto worry about, such as where to live (surely I could kip down in the aircraft if I removed the tail-fin?), what to eat (a block of cheese could sustain me for days), or what clothes to wear. Major world events just passed me by because I never watched TV, listened to the radio, or read the newspapers: they were a distraction from whatever goal I had at the time – whether it was competing in the Trans-Kalahari motorbike race or gaining my commercial pilot's licence.

Life is short, so I'd say that anything you want to do, you should go ahead and do it – preferably today. It's how I've lived my life: I hope you enjoy reading about it.

Tizi Hodson

PART ONE

ANIMALS RULE THE ROOST

Chapter 1

THE SILVER GHOST

It was 25 July 1970. 'Life is good' I remember thinking. How lucky I was to have Spook – such a special partner in life! Spook was a dapple-grey thoroughbred cross Connemara pony and, at just over 14 hands, was an inch short of being a horse.

The fact that I was walking my little horse along the road was unusual: normally we would canter on every patch of grass verge and sometimes trot on the tarmac, but this was a special occasion. We had just finished a week of intensive training to improve our dressage, jumping and team skills: we'd been among the lucky few to be chosen to represent our branch of the Pony Club – the Essex Farmers Hunt.

Ann Playle, our instructor, was a knowledgeable horsewoman who had bred and trained horses for many years and had also taught young riders like me. Short with dark brown hair cut sensibly short, she had endless energy and patience and had instructed me to take the next few days at a very steady pace so that Spook and I would be on top form.

Thud.
Silence.
A car passed by and the driver, Captain Luke Nicholson, stopped at the horrendous scene. He saw a horse pushed into the ditch with two legs badly broken and dangling and its young teenage rider tangled up in the bumper of a van, her hard-hat smashed and her skull obviously broken. One of her legs was half embedded into the tarmac with the van's body crushing it.

Luke flagged down the next car and sent them for an ambulance, a vet and a policeman, then tried to assist the young rider in disentangling her from the van.

The emergency services arrived. The vet dispatched the horse. The ambulance took the rider to the nearest hospital at Broomfield where she spent five days in intensive care, waking in bouts but not coherent. The police tried to take details from two hitchhikers who had been travelling in the back of the van, as to what had happened.

It emerged over time that the van driver – who died five days after the accident – had been on the road for 12 hours without a break. He had fallen asleep at the wheel. The van had hit the kerb, bounced across to the opposite side of the road and pushed the horse into the ditch, catching the rider's leg in its bumper. After rolling over three times, the van had come to a rest upside-down in the middle of the road.

Before the crash I had been thinking that to be selected for the Pony Club Team was the greatest honour I had ever been given, especially as I had bought Spook from a dealer's yard as a green youngster, fresh from Ireland. He was a new page on which to start writing: no faults, no blemishes. Any faults he might develop would be mine alone. So handsome, it was love at first sight for me, so – despite being slightly over the 'allowed for' price bracket – my dear mother Anne agreed he was perfect. With no name, but having a glorious colour of a silver dapple-grey, I named him Silver Ghost, or Spook for short.

Since then, I'd spent every hour with him that I was not at school, and some hours when I should have been. I groomed him, hacked him, jumped him, trained him and took him hunting to improve his forward movements. We attended many shows and regularly won showing, hunter trials, jumping and cross-country events. He loved me as a dog loves his master and followed me everywhere. I rode him with a saddle or without, with a bridle or without. On the occasion of our local hunt's 50th anniversary meet, I rode – as we were requested to do – side-saddle and he was the perfect gentleman, understanding that I was precarious and taking the jumps carefully as though he were trying to balance me on his back.

A packed season of contests would follow this week of ease. It was certainly going to be the most exciting summer of my life.

*

"Hello Tizi, how are you?" my mother was asking, bending over my bed. Her brown eyes looked worried. She was a tremendous mother, not least because she had given up all her friends in London and moved to Purleigh in Essex, where she knew nobody, to enable me and my sister Toto to keep our ponies – Filou, Candy and Spook – after our father died of Hodgkin's Disease, four years earlier. The small house she bought had a one-acre field and some old stables, instead of a small courtyard, which was the only garden our previous house in London had had.

"I'm fine," I replied in typically British fashion. "Where am I?"

"You're in hospital. You got knocked down by a van. I'm afraid you're in quite a mangled state, but you'll be better soon," she said reassuringly.

"How's Spook?" I asked in terror.

"He's fine, don't you worry about him," she said, helplessly lying. "The Nicholsons are looking after him." The Nicholsons ran a local riding school.

"Will I be out in time for the competitions?" I asked, thinking what lousy timing this was.

"There are quite a few bits broken but I'm sure you'll catch at least the end-of-season contests. You have been right out for five days, so you're going to need a little time to recover."

I dozed off again to wake the next time in a proper ward, out of intensive care. The buttons to push were explained, especially the emergency button and I was introduced to neighbouring patients. My immediate neighbour, Mrs Joan Potter, was a lovely, cheerful but frail 75-year-old with curly grey hair. She told me she had been knocked off her bicycle by a 24-ton truck which had then driven over her, removing half of one leg and caused considerable other damage. That was seven years earlier. She was now in for 'top-up surgery', as she called it. The only thing she recalled at the time of her accident as holding her head clear of the wheels: she had been determined not to die.

Compared to her, my injuries seemed minor; in fact I still had no idea what had happened. The nurses also seemed unclear. On questioning them, it was always, "well, we don't know the full extent yet, we shall have to wait."

The following day, when my mother returned, I asked her what had been damaged. She told me my head was fractured on both sides, and so was my jaw, which was why people were finding it hard to understand me.

There were sixty stitches down my back from where they had extracted fragments of windscreen glass. My right leg from the knee downwards was sliced, battered and scarred, as were the toes.

However, the worst damage was to my left lower leg, which they were still trying to save and if they managed to, would require extensive grafting and rebuilding. The other option was to remove it.

"It sounds heck of a time-consuming business," I said with all the confidence of a 15-year-old. "Strikes me if they take off the leg, then I can get a false one, and be back riding Spook next week and still be ready for the first competition."

"No, dear," said my mother. "It's not that straightforward. "You'd have to learn to walk all over again with a false leg and there are 'phantom pains' to consider."

The doctor came on his rounds at that point, so I asked him how soon I could expect to be riding again.

"You've suffered severe injuries and there's no chance that you'll ever ride a horse again," he said. "We are only hoping you may be able to walk eventually, but a great deal will be up to you."

My mother looked distraught.

"Don't worry," I said to her. "The day I'm out of here, I will ride and jump. There'll be no problem getting on – Spook has learned to bow, so I can step on while he bends down." I was now pleased I'd taught him his latest trick.

When my mother left, I pulled back the bedclothes to look at the 'damage' and saw a horrible purple mass of swellings and blotches through the bits of bandage I pulled away. I certainly did not want any part of that ugly leg. I called the sister and asked when I was due for the next operation.

"That will be tomorrow afternoon," she told me.

"I've decided I want the leg removed below the knee," I told her. "And you can have it from me in writing, with my signature. I'll miss out on the whole season's competitions if they try to patch up this mess. I'll get the hang of a new leg in no time – there's no changing my mind."

Strangely enough, I found myself looking forward to the operation as I was wheeled down to the theatre. I wanted to go home, with a new leg, to walk and be with Spook again.

On awakening a few hours later, I looked down to my legs. They were both still there. I double-checked. I was furious and pulled the emergency bell for the first time.

"What's going on?" I shouted to the sister, Janice. "I told them I wanted that ugly bit of leg removed!"

"I'm sorry but you're not yet 16, so your mother had to sign the agreement for removal of your leg, which she wouldn't. She'll be along soon." Joan had warned me that Janice had a vicious streak in her and not to expect any kindness from her.

My mother arrived. As soon as she saw me, she said,

"I'm sorry Tizi, you can always have a leg removed later, but you can't glue one back on. Please be a little patient. Everyone is trying to help you."

I tried to resign myself to the situation.

"But please tell me Spook is alright?"

My poor mother. She had to speak the truth some time.

"No, he had two of his legs cut clean off in the accident, but he didn't have to endure the pain for too long; the vet was very quick."

Suddenly my leg didn't matter.

4

"Look Tizi, you must still fight to get better. Poor Filou and Candy are missing you. They need you. I want you home and so does Toto."

My sister, Toto – a year older than me – had been to the hospital many times to talk and joke about everything. The two of us were similar to look at, both around six feet tall and slim with fair hair although Toto had inherited brown eyes from my mother Anne whereas I had blue eyes from my father, Mark. My mother thought the names Tizzie and Toto sounded good together, though I changed the spelling of mine to 'Tizi'. We were both given the middle name of 'Jane' and later, when Toto started her career, she used 'Jane' instead of 'Toto'.

Toto was sensible, dressed well, talked slowly and thought before she opened her mouth and was not reckless. She worked hard at school, intending to go ahead with a secure career after college. In contrast, I tended to wear jeans or shorts and T-shirts, spoke rapidly – like all my father's side of the family – and only opened my mouth to change feet. I was totally reckless, thinking I would never get hurt and found school an irritating waste of time. I had only ever wanted to be a saddler or farrier, so I felt schooling was an expensive waste of time.

Candy was our shared first pony that we had both outgrown and who was now a family pet. An ideal, bombproof first pony she now taught our family and friends to ride.

Filou was Toto's horse, a nine-year-old scatty dark bay thoroughbred. He had a lovely temperament, but spent a lot of time waving his fore hooves in the air and looking terrifying to anyone who didn't know him. As Toto was at boarding school, I looked after Filou for her during term time.

At hospital, so many friends came every day. I remember one day having 21 visitors. Although it was tiring, it certainly passed the time so much quicker. Three months sped by. My mother came every day, sometimes twice, with anything I could possibly want. Of course the only thing I could possibly want, no one could give me. He was gone: the best little horse ever created.

The skin grafts continued. Once, before another trip to the operating theatre, I asked the doctor if he could take the skin from the right leg, as the donor area on my left leg was terribly sore, sensitive and painful. He agreed. To make doubly sure, I wrote in pen on the left leg 'do not remove skin from here' and on the right leg, 'here is OK'.

Awakening this time, there was more pain than I could ever envisage. I looked down. The left leg was heavily bandaged yet seeped blood already. I used the normal buzzer. Stern-faced Janice arrived and asked what was wrong. I told her I had requested the skin be taken from the other leg; why had they not done so?

"Oh, they decided you should have one normal leg since the left one is messed up anyway, there was no purpose in disfiguring the other one as well." She seemed to enjoy giving the bad news.

"How long will this pain continue?" I enquired pathetically.

"At least 10 days," she snapped viciously. "Would you like a pain killer?"

"No thank you, it's actually not that bad," I lied.

When Janice came round for the night checks, she asked how the pain was. I told her it had gone totally. I even let my friends and visitors believe there was none. I did not want Sister Janice gloating over the fact I could not tolerate the pain, so I pretended to everyone, including myself, that it was not there.

As the pain eventually subsided, I was getting fidgety and wanted to dispel some excess energy. I had the idea of continuing to make the watch-straps, belts and chokers that I had started in my spare time at home. I asked Anne if she could bring in my leather, cutting board and tools. I reasoned that if I sold the watch-straps I could buy a small bike or moped when I got out.

The poor cleaners complained bitterly that my bed was the worst on the ward, with all the scraps of leather to be vacuumed or collected up. Nevertheless, the time passed swiftly. Whenever my schoolfriends came to visit, they would bring their order books: I made my friends a free watch strap for every 10 belts or 20 straps sold. It certainly provided an incentive and soon my watch-straps became the 'in thing' at school.

On 28 August I 'celebrated' my 16th birthday. The nurses were wonderful and treated me like a celebrity. My mother and Toto came in with a cake for me and so many friends came in with gifts.

Finally I progressed to a wheelchair; the next step was to try to walk. It was hell. The right foot was now more painful than the left leg. I complained regularly but was told to be quiet, as there was nothing wrong with it. It should be the left leg which hurt, I was told repeatedly.

Having mastered crutches, the day finally arrived for my release. My mother helped me into her car and started slowly. It was the most terrifying drive of my life.

"Slow down, please!" I begged.

"But Tizi, we are only doing 10mph."

I apologised for being so pathetic and gently dug my fingernails into my palms for the rest of the trip.

On arriving home to a welcoming cup of tea, which was the best one I'd had in three months, I wobbled and hobbled over to say hello to Filou in his stable then went to the field and called Candy. She trotted up, apparently pleased to see me.

"Hi love, mind taking me round the field?" I asked her as she put her nose through the halter.

I thought I could hold a bunch of her mane and swing myself up onto her back as I used to just a few months ago.

No chance. I hadn't expected this. I was now a pathetic cripple. I led Candy to the front lawn by the coal-bunker, thinking I could use it to climb on board. I could not get onto the bunker.

My mother watched nervously from the kitchen. Finally she came out and told me she would help me get on, as I was only going to break something if I carried on unaided.

Between us, we aligned Candy sideways to the coal-bunker. I used a chair to get onto the bunker, and then climbed onto Candy. With my mother leading Candy, we walked round the lawn. Unexpectedly, I felt unsafe and terrified.

The next day, I took Candy into the garden again and this time managed to get on unaided (using the chair, still there, by the coal bunker). I rode poor Candy round and round the little garden for over an hour. Finally I felt at ease and more comfortable. I returned her to the field and told my mother I would ride Filou the next day.

"Is that wise? He hasn't been ridden for a few weeks now."

"That's settled then. He'll need the exercise."

While hospitalised, I had spent a good deal of time wondering how best to ride effectively with half of the inside bottom left leg missing. I would not be able to grip astride but as there was not much damage to the outside and zero feeling, it should be possible to ride side-saddle on the 'wrong' side. Although side-saddles were hard to come by, the one I used on Spook happened to be reversible.

The saddle fitted Filou a treat. Mounting was a little weird, but since ladies in the past were either helped up by a gentleman or used a mounting block, this would mask my lack of balance in the mounting procedure! I still had the skirt my mother had sewn for me for the Anniversary Meet. So, everything was ready.

The next day, was the same rigmarole to get on, using the chair and the coal bunker, with my mother's help in positioning Filou.

"Where are you going?" she asked.

"Only round the block," I said, going out of the gate toward the quiet country lane. The block was about six miles and there was very little traffic as it was winding, country lanes all leading nowhere in particular, with few neighbours.

The first car that passed had me involuntarily bunching up in absolute terror. 'Pull yourself together', I reprimanded myself, or you'll get Filou worried'.

After the third car, I was still in a state of terror. With the passing of the fourth car, Filou now danced a little. I was conveying to him that something unpleasant might happen from the passing of a car.

We were now halfway round the block and had there been a short cut home across the fields, I would have taken it and not gone on the roads again for a long while, but I had to make sure I wouldn't ruin my sister's horse by making him traffic shy.

There was no option. I had to cover my fear, so I started singing at the top of my voice. Then a car appeared. I continued singing and paused to pat Filou and tell him he was a good boy. The car passed and I hadn't flinched. Filou hadn't danced either. I knew I could do it again.

Sure enough, another car came by with no problem, and then a real test as a lorry appeared behind us. I waved him past and continued singing at the top of my voice. The driver must have thought I was celebrating something and he honked his horn as a friendly sign. Filou didn't bat an eyelid.

The tremendous feeling of relief made me want to go round the block again, just to prove I could. I thought I should tell my mother what I was doing or she would be worried about how long I'd been away. On reaching home, the car was missing. I wondered where she had gone, and then she appeared behind me and guiltily explained that she'd followed at a distance in case I needed help. I couldn't help laughing and told her if I'd known she was behind me I would probably have admitted defeat and stayed a pathetic wimp all my life.

My mother asked if I would like to buy another horse, as Toto would be returning from school and might like to ride Filou. I thought this was sensible, especially as I could not return to school; the blow on the head had not just affected my balance but also movement on the right side of my body. I couldn't hold a pen with my right hand and found myself scrawling illegible notes to people with my left. While in hospital, my Uncle Alec had given me a portable typewriter, so I learned to type with my left hand.

Mother took me to a couple of horse dealers: at the second, there was Thora: a perfect replica of Spook. She was the same dappled grey but two hands larger, an Irish Draft crossed with Thoroughbred.

"She is the one," I said.

I rode her around bareback and then asked someone to pop her over a small jump and decided she was what I was looking for. I hadn't yet tried a conventional saddle, so Thora was loaded into our trailer and brought home to inspect her new surroundings.

The next morning, I put the side-saddle on her and took her round the block to see her new home ground. She was a lovely ride, not quite as lively as Filou but that was nothing a generous amount of oats wouldn't rectify.

The following day I tried her over a few very low jumps, which she popped over happily.

Toto returned home the next day. I told her Filou was quite fit and asked if she'd like to jump him in the field?

"You mean you'd like some help putting some jumps up?" She knew me too well.

She set up the jumps for the height she would use with Filou. I gulped and thought, well why not try?

Toto went first with a clear round. I then aimed Thora at each jump, concentrating on staying on board, side-saddle, and achieved this as well as a clear round. I was delighted.

After we had finished riding, Toto searched for a show we could both attend before the end of the year. My first show, at Southminster, would be exactly six weeks after being discharged from hospital. We sent off the entry forms.

The day and the horse-box came. My first class was the Novice Class, as Thora hadn't been ridden in a show before. I had also entered the Open Class.

I was in my usual hyped-up state and trotted Thora round the collecting ring, waiting my turn. We entered the arena on the bell. I rode very determinedly, but unfortunately sat too far back on the second-to-last jump and caused poor Thora to rap the pole, which fell off, giving us four faults.

I apologised to Thora for letting her down. Then my number was called into the ring, which was futile, as there were too many clear rounds for me to have gained a place.

They were awarding me a special rosette, for 'a brave try, jumping side-saddle'. I felt patronised and humiliated. I did not want to be treated like a cripple and allowed handicaps or given special privileges. I wanted to be on equal terms with everyone else.

Two classes later came the Open. Filou went before me and did his usual trick of stopping three times at the first fence. This was crazy as he jumped beautifully at home or over any height of practice fence, but he seemed to lose his nerve in front of a crowd.

My number was called. The bell went and I rode poor Thora hard, making no mistakes. Thora was foot-perfect for a steady clear round. There were five others, also clear. I stood a good chance.

Finally, my number was called for the jump off, against the clock. I rode the hardest round of my life, determined to prove I could be on the same terms as the others, not a pitiful cripple.

We were the fastest and were called in as winners. Now I knew I could do anything alongside my friends and with no preferential treatment.

*

About this time, I felt the need for some means of transport. At sixteen I was not old enough for a motorbike or car, but there was nothing stopping me looking for a moped.

My mother leafed through a women's magazine and saw an ad for a ladies three-wheeled moped, an Ariel 3. It was the perfect answer, though at £117 the price tag was rather high.

"I can sell something to raise the money," she said. Would you like to go and see this machine?"

"Of course. But I have the money. I made £140 in hospital with the watch-straps."

We arrived to see this spectacular machine. It was the most ugly vehicle I had ever seen, but I could ride it. My penance for buying it was that I had to ride it 12 miles home, which at top speed of 35-40mph, was barely faster than a horse.

"I'm freezing," I said when I got home. "Think I'll pop out and brush a horse to warm up." My mother laughed and said she would boil the kettle ready for my return.

Having spent all my savings, I needed to start a new hobby that would be useful and perhaps bring in some spare pennies. Having messed around with leather for a while, I thought the next step was to try making a bridle. I visited some craftsmen to pick their brains. A friendly saddler in Halstead showed interest in taking me on as an apprentice. He showed me how to get going, which tools to buy and the type of leather to look for.

This was exciting. Making and mending saddlery would occupy the dark evenings: it would also mean I could now mend our broken tack and make new pieces. I progressed and advertised my business, Tizi's Flying Repairs, locally. It was certainly more profitable than making watch-straps and very interesting. Everything made or repaired increased my knowledge.

The next event on the calendar was the Golden Horseshoe Ride, (a 75-mile ride over two days); I had never tried endurance riding before. To take part, a rider must prepare by completing a 40-mile qualifying ride at a minimum average speed of six miles an hour, basically a brisk trot most of the way. A 40-miles trot would be tough enough, but torturous on a side-saddle.

On the day, Thora and I were as ready and fit as we could be. With the start signal, I set off at a gentle trot, hoping to maintain the pace. After about ten miles I dismounted, leading Thora up a very steep hill. She needed a break from a weight on her back and I needed a rest from the pommels.

Then the problem arose of getting on again. One of the riders who had decided to stop at this stage, very kindly gave me a leg up. I cantered the next couple of miles to make up for the lack of speed on the hill.

The entrants had now developed into groups. I joined those who were careful not to waste energy but were aware of the time limit. The trail was well marked all the way and we were all provided with a map of the route. As we neared what should have been the last few miles, there was a very clear marker pointing in what seemed to be the wrong direction.

We checked to make sure we were to finish where we started. We were, so we followed the sign. We were getting close to the time limit and thought we must have all miscalculated our gentle trot speed. There was no option now but to move up to a fast trot.

With two or three miles remaining, I was aching, sore and rubbed beyond belief. Some of the riders had dismounted and were running; I wished I could, but nothing would make me quit now.

Our group was the last over the finish line, with three minutes to spare: I had qualified! I later learned that our group had covered an extra ten miles as some lousy people had turned the signs round to make the journey longer.

The following day, as a special concession from my mother, Thora was allowed on the lawn where the grass was sweeter. She nibbled a little and then lay down; I lay snuggled up against her neck and chest, soon dozing off with her sleeping soundly. Toto came out at lunchtime with a plate of food for me and a bowl of carrots for Thora. Toto gently pointed out that in the Golden Horseshoe Ride, Thora and I would have to do the same 50 miles on the first day and 25 miles on the second.

"Are you going to manage?"

"Yeah, no problem. I'll start training, from tomorrow."

It came home to me that the next stage could not be taken lightly, especially with the side-saddle: I'd sustained heavy bruising to both my legs where the pommels had rubbed through the layers of clothing. This was despite my precaution of wearing tights under my jodhpurs, beneath the skirt.

A solution came via a kind lady called Mrs Gee. She had heard I was riding side-saddle due to injuries and contacted me through a friend of my mother's. She offered to lend me a full-size side-saddle, designed on the 'wrong' side.

Mrs Gee explained she had also been injured and had lost a leg. She could ride perfectly well in this style on the reverse side but there was no hope of her riding astride again. She had given up riding many years earlier and although she had received many offers for the saddle, she would not sell it.

She was keeping it to lend to anyone who needed it. She reckoned I was in need. I could borrow it for as long as I still used it.

My life took a wonderful turn at this stage. Gone was the pain of squashing into a tiny saddle, similar to wearing shoes a size too small, and running for 50 miles. My jumping improved, as did my confidence.

Toto was finishing school and moving away to go to college: to become intelligent, unlike me. Our four-bedroom house would be too big for two of us, so my mother had been trying to sell the house but with no luck. Unexpectedly, an offer of 'immediate possession or no sale' came. My mother hadn't found anywhere else to buy, so decided to take the offer and move in with her mother, my grandmother Ilma.

"I'm afraid you'll have to find homes for the dog and cat and perhaps a home for Thora, until I get somewhere for us," she said.

I was dumbfounded. I couldn't even think of a life without Finn, my Alsatian-Collie cross, and Tiger, a tabby cross Siamese – and of course Thora.

"There is another possibility," said my mother. "Ann Playle would happily take you all for as long as you like."

Ann Playle was a knowledgeable horsewoman who had bred and trained many of her own horses and ponies. She was a small, stocky woman in her late twenties: as a farmer's wife she usually worked twelve-hour days, seven days a week and never complained about being tired. She was married to Ken, who apart from farming a small arable farm in Latchingdon, was also a Whipper-In to the Essex Farmers Hunt. Ken was quite a few years older than Ann, well built, fit and incredibly strong. Apart from farming he also worked as a farrier and had shod our ponies for a while.

"That's fine then. When do I go?" I decided straight away that this was the only option if I was to keep Tiger, Finn and Thora.

"It looks like being about three weeks' time."

"I'm looking forward to a new life on a real farm with the Playles," I answered cheerfully, sounding far more confident than I felt.

My mother seemed relieved I had agreed to the only option. We celebrated with a cup of tea.

I was still limping around on one crutch – I could not yet walk unaided – so felt useless when it came to helping pack. The one benefit was that I now limped rather than hobbled. On the regular check-up trips at the doctor's, I always said "the right foot gives more pain than the left leg" but they reckoned I couldn't tell the right from the left. My mother got upset and had a private doctor examine my right foot. It turns out I had three broken toes, one of which would have to be re-broken and fused back together, which would affect my balance even further.

"Well that explains the pain; now it can go!" I shouted excitedly.

Within a week, I was out of hospital and almost comfortable. Except now the left leg hurt more. I finally found the real meaning of the Shakespeare expression, 'one pain lessens another's anguish'. Pain and fear had to be ignored in order to get on with life.

Chapter 2

LIFE ON A FARM

The two weeks before uprooting passed in a flash. Ken arrived with his horsebox to collect Thora, Finn, Tiger and me to start our new life. The drive was barely an hour and Ken had a wonderful habit of making everyone feel at ease. I was nervous, in the same way as a kid starting a new school, except I knew both Ann and Ken well.

On arrival I settled Finn, who was to live with the five dogs already there. They had all met before, so no problems were encountered. Tiger was not so keen on suddenly becoming an 'outdoors' cat, since he had been used to the comforts of laps and fires, but he was soon purring contentedly in an empty stable. Later he slept on the rug covering Roetan, a lovely bright bay, kind-tempered horse. Thora inspected her large stable, decided it was perfectly adequate and happily settled to munch on the hay net tied in the corner.

I hadn't brought my crutches with me. I was too embarrassed to look disabled in public. Around our local village it had been OK as everyone knew me, but this was a fresh start. I was determined to walk without a limp, even if it meant going very slowly.

The next morning I went to muck out Thora. Since Roetan and Yussoff were also in the adjoining stables, I cleaned them out as well. Yussoff was a dark bay, a former point-to-pointer, with a lovely temperament.

I then took Thora out for a lovely ride along the sea wall at Burnham. The air was so fresh and salty. I couldn't resist the urge, so I removed the saddle, my skirt and jodhpurs and took Thora in for a refreshing swim.

After lunch I asked Ann if she would like me to exercise Roetan and Yussoff.

I tried my saddle on Roetan: it fitted like a dream. At 17 hands, he was the largest horse I had ridden sideways; his strides were long and comfortable, and even his trot was less bone-jarring than normal. I led Yussoff and we rode round the block, which was about six miles.

When I returned, Ann saw me trying to open the gate and rushed up to get it for me.

"I didn't know you were taking the Toe Rag side-saddle," she said, using her nickname for Roetan. "How was he?"

"An absolute gentleman."

''We shall have to get you to take him hunting. He does look elegant."

From then on, I was in charge of the stables. The day started with grooming, which I loved, then mucking out, which warmed you up when you went out on a cool early morning, and exercising, which I adored.

Soon, more people were asking Ann if she would look after their horse, but she would ask me each time if I could cope with another. She knew the answer would always be 'yes'.

Soon the seven stables were full, as were the four stalls round the back in the big Dutch Barn. I was in my element. I no longer felt like a cripple and was rapidly getting fitter than I had ever been before. With eleven horses to exercise, groom and muck out, it was certainly a full day's work, seven days a week.

I was concerned about how much my mother was paying, as I knew boarding out a human, horse, cat and dog was not cheap. No price was ever disclosed but, after the first week, Ann shoved three pounds into my hand. I asked what it was for.

"You've been working so hard – you can't expect nothing in return," she told me firmly.

"But I'm only helping out towards my board and lodging. You can't call it work because I'm loving every minute of it!"

I tried to return the notes but Ann insisted I kept them and warned it would be the same each week.

'If this is work, why do people grumble about it?' I wondered. 'After all, anybody could work with horses rather than go into a cooped-up office and work in a big town.'

At sixteen years old, I had no idea about mortgages, pensions, family life or travel.

Back in the Yard, I found Thora had developed a sore spot on her withers. I blamed myself for putting the saddle on with the salt still in her hairs after swimming, so decided to rest her for a few days. Ann knew I had qualified for the Golden Horseshoe Ride and was keen to take part. She wasn't going to let me miss out.

"Take the Toe Rag, Tizi. You said he's the most comfortable horse in the stable. Besides, he's hard and tough, so he'll have no problem doing seventy-five miles."

"But Ann, he's Ken's hunt horse," I replied.

"He won't want you to miss the ride either. I'll tell him tonight. You can step up Roetan's exercise – take him out two or three times a day."

So Roetan had his exercise doubled, then trebled. Then with one week to go, he also developed a sore wither. I discovered it first thing one morning and rushed inside to tell Ann the terrible news. I had ruined the number one horse in the stable and there was no way I could put my saddle on him until it cleared up. Ann suggested I try riding astride – and chose Goldie, a white-grey hunter belonging to Colonel John Cramphorn.

Sadly, although I could feel no pain and had an enjoyable ride, when I returned and inspected my leg under the bandages, there was blood everywhere.

"Right," said Ann. "That's obviously out of the question. I'll think of something else."

The 'something else' was suggesting taking Goldie to a local show the coming Saturday, even though Goldie had never jumped over coloured poles before.

It was a perfect day with blue skies and warmth that occasionally comes in late autumn. Goldie behaved perfectly, a gentleman in every way. When his turn came to jump, he popped over as though it was really beneath his dignity to leap over poles left lying around, not blocking the way to a field, with hounds running full cry. Having always done as was asked of him, he jumped each fence to a perfect clear round.

In the jump off I asked him to go a little faster – in fact flat out. He seemed to think this was more like the hunting field and made more sense, feeling the urgency from his rider. He jumped a faultless clear in the fastest time to win the 'open class'. I was over the moon. How could life get better?

Soon, a new acquisition to the yard came, in the form of Prince Yari. He was technically a strawberry roan, but the strawberry colouring was bright pink. He looked like a dappled pink horse. I thought it was the most beautiful colouring I had ever seen in my life and immediately nicknamed him Pink Horse.

Ken arrived in the yard with Prince Yari and unloaded him into the stable.

"Now you be careful with this one," Ken told me. "He bites, kicks and chases horses, people, anything. He is a good ride but a savage character."

When Ken had gone into the house, I went to make friends with this new arrival. He vaguely tried to snap, but it seemed to be out of habit, not viciousness. He tried to kick as I brushed his hind legs; again, it seemed from habit rather than ill intent.

"You and I are going to get on well. You will look good against a blue skirt with your pink coat," I told him affectionately.

As the days went by, we became the best of friends. He did not object unless anyone tried to do something in a hurry. His strides were as good as old Toe Rags, and at 16 hands, he was nearly the same height. He carried the side-saddle beautifully and never stopped at a fence or knocked one in all the years I knew him.

One of my treasured memories was taking him hunting when the meet was at Burnham. Ken was Whipping In on Roetan and offered me a ride in the box. It was the best day's hunting I can recall. Pink Horse behaved perfectly. There was only one occasion we opened a gate, with low trees over it. With the rest streaming through to gallop off into the distance, he remained stock still while I remounted in my somewhat clumsy fashion. Then we tore off at top speed to catch up with the front-runners in a couple of minutes. The rest of the gates, tiger traps and ditches, he took in his stride.

By the end of the day there were barely a half dozen followers remaining.

"Well dear, I knew you'd be here to the end or I wouldn't have offered you a lift," said Ken with a wink. I felt pleased and proud to be on such a superb steed; yet, when he was at home, he offered teeth and heels to any stranger.

Just after my fabulous day with the hunt, a new arrival came in the form of Soldance Queen, a 16-hands dark bay, fine-boned thoroughbred known as Dancer, since she perpetually danced around. She had a failed Pointing history: she had been either pulled up or had fallen at every Point-to-Point in which she had started, so Roy Jones had bought her for a modest sum as a hunter. To look at she was perfect, a bright bay with lovely large eyes, a terrific turn of speed and a gentle mouth. She was ready to gallop flat out at any excuse.

Roy made it clear she was not to be ridden side-saddle. I was sad as she had a perfectly shaped back, a good wither for the saddle and long sloping pasterns (part of the leg between fetlock and hoof) to give a comfortable floating ride. The first time Roy took Dancer hunting was a memorable sight. Roy was always impeccably dressed and especially so in the hunting field. He wore his pink coat, top hat, hunting boots and breeches, astride Dancer, who shone in the sun with her mane plaited and tail neatly pulled.

George Peverley, the Huntsman, blew his horn and everyone moved off. On hearing the horn, Dancer immediately took off with Roy hanging on, while she galloped flat out, covering several fields. Roy finally managed to get her back under control and rode back to the horse-box and then drove her back to the stables, asking Ann if her oats could be dropped and her exercise stepped up. Ann told Ray that Dancer would benefit more from being ridden than led but that I was the only person available and I could only ride side-saddle. Roy firmly told Ann that Dancer would be led.

The next fortnight Roy again took Dancer hunting. She looked splendid once again, but as soon as the horn was blown, she took off at top speed and headed straight for a six-foot hedge, accelerating as she approached it. She had the bit between her teeth and there was no stopping her.

Roy bailed out before she reached the hedge, hitting his head on landing. Someone caught Dancer after she had sailed over the fence with room to spare and she was reunited with Roy, who led her back to the box and left her there. She was then returned to the stables in disgrace. Seeing me, Roy said, "You can put your saddle on that brute and even take her hunting if you want to. I don't care any longer. She is now up for sale. I'm not riding her again."

I thought this a strange attitude: to buy a horse and not even ride her or get to know her before going to a Meet, where for the first time most horses go scatty with excitement. Inwardly however, I was delighted.

Dancer recovered and was superb, every bit as comfortable as I'd expected and so responsive. Ann asked me if I'd like to take Dancer to the Boxing Day Meet: I did not even need to answer because Ann could read me like an open book.

Boxing Day finally arrived with a hard frost. No snow, but a gentle breeze – a perfect day. Dancer was impeccable at the Meet. We moved off and she settled into a slow gentle canter, while the others were going at a flat-out trot. Then the pace quickened and her canter simply extended, until we were at full tilt with the rest of the field. I thought she was trying to make amends for her misbehaviour earlier. Dancer gave me one of the best days of my life to that day.

As life was a daily delightful 12 hours, seven days a week, I rather lost touch with my mother, sister and my friends. I was far too shy to ask Ann to use her phone just to call friends and family. Even with Christmas coming up, I hadn't really given it a thought.

*

It was a glorious winter, but then a sad event happened early in the New Year: the death of my cat, Tiger. I hadn't seen him curl up on Roetan's back for two days and had searched the place and called frequently, but he was nowhere to be seen.

The person to give me the news was Haydn, who was Ken's son from a previous marriage. He lived at the farm too, along with Ann and Ken's own two children. He was a few years younger than me, equally slim, with lovely manners but very quiet and gently spoken. He had no real interest in horses or riding. I knew he wanted to tell me something. He acknowledged my greeting with a shy smile and a "Good morning, Tizi, how was your ride?"

I told him it was a lovely day and the ride good. He then blurted out he had found Tiger. I was so relieved. Then he told me Tiger had died. I immediately asked where he was. I was concerned his body would be given to the pig they were fattening. I was not keen on the pig as it emitted a horrible squeal if you tried to touch it and seemed to have no purpose other than eating and sleeping, while it was waiting to be eaten.

Haydn seemed to read my thoughts. He said: "Let me help you put the horses away, and I'll show you where I've buried him."

I was touched. He then took me to a grave he had dug, adjacent to the back stalls. He had even put some flowers on it. I thanked him and thought what a special person he had suddenly become to me. When he left, I broke down into uncontrollable tears, feeling racked with guilt. I had taken my poor cat away from a comfortable indoor life to live outside, forced to gain his place in the pecking order with the other tabby cats.

I saddled up Dancer, telling her: "I'm taking you out by yourself, love. I want to be alone."

We rode to the sea wall. I got off and sat down watching the waves, oblivious to the world and anyone's problems. The sea and waves always had a wonderful calming effect. After a few hours I seemed to wake up from a trance. Dancer was nudging at me, as if to suggest we go back before being washed up with the waves. Now I tried to jump up and found I was stuck, squatting down. I had almost frozen solid; I was only wearing a T-shirt and this was a cold day in January. Looking at my watch, I realised four hours had passed. I needed to hurry back or people may get worried, but it took a while to remount in my frozen state.

Not a word was said when I returned. Haydn had told Ann about Tiger and she knew I was a hopeless case with animals. Tiger was not mentioned and after finishing stables, I came indoors and started repairing some broken pieces of tack. Ann never did manage to make me understand that death, being a natural process, shouldn't be mourned, but that life ought to continue as before for the living. She loved her animals and children but never spoilt them and would not have what she called 'soppiness' around her. I was fortunate that she put up with me. All Ann's horses, dogs and children were impeccably behaved, a joy to have around and have all gone far in their own directions. I was so lucky to have had the few months with her influence and her very special friendship, which continued throughout her life.

Before staying with the Playles, my mother had applied for a position for me to train and study for my BHSAI (British Horse Society Assistant Instructor) exams, at Jenny Lorriston-Clarke's training establishment: Catherston Park Stud. A letter arrived to tell me I had a start date in two months' time. The extra good news was that I could ride side-saddle there as Jenny specialised in showing side-saddle.

"You will be dearly missed," said Ann, "but this is an opportunity that you cannot throw away. Besides, you can come back and help improve my dressage when you have finished there!"

"Are you taking Thora and Finn with you?" asked Ken.

"Yes, I'm lucky – they've agreed that Finn can come on trial and said that Thora is welcome."

I found myself happy and sad at the same time. Excited to be going to Jenny's, but sorry to be leaving behind the farm life I had come to know and love so well.

Chapter 3

RUNNING ON EMPTY

My first day at Catherston Park Stud at Brockenhurst in the New Forest was terrific. There were some 40 horses in stables and many more brood mares in the field, which I was taken round and introduced to. The whole establishment was immaculate; not a blade of unclean straw, hay or any dirt in sight. All the paint was fresh. The horses were all gleaming and were a picture of health.

There were 13 of us 'working pupils' with the Head Girl, Penny Longden and a deputy head, Penny Fowler, known as Penny 2 or Fowler.

Penny Longden was older than all of us, short and slim with long straight dark brown hair that she tied in a ponytail. She was short-tempered with us, the student grooms. She had her own horse called Walter, who was an impressive looking, very dark brown, thoroughbred stallion.

Penny 2 was very friendly but a little shy. She showed me round, proudly introducing a lovely old pony.

"This is Loppy Lugs," she said, "named for his lop ears. You may know him as Our Nobby."

Everyone had heard of Our Nobby: he'd won a Silver Medal in the last Olympics.

"What's he doing here?" I asked.

"He belongs to Jenny's sister, Jane Bullen. She's kept him here since she bought him."

She then told me a 'secret', which everyone heard when he or she arrived. Our Nobby was too small to take part in the Olympics, as he was a genuine pony of 14.2 hands: only horses were allowed. He grew an inch when the vet measured him – with a drawing pin placed under his belly!

With 15 people attending to 40 horses, this was going to be a working holiday, I mused, reflecting on how enjoyable the sole duties of looking after 14 or 15 horses back home on the farm had been. Penny 2 showed me the brood mares' yard with foaling box, the covering yard and teasing box and lastly the indoor school. The school was built to Olympic measurements, complete with gallery and full-length mirrors at top and bottom of the arena to be able to see exactly where horses placed their hooves. Adjacent to the arena were 25 indoor stables with sliding doors and automatic water feeders. The tack room was also among the stables. This was the Top Yard.

The Bottom Yard had open boxes, with an extended roof, next to the cottage that we – the grooms – occupied.

The Bottom Yard housed the stallions with celebrities like Xenocles (Tammy), a champion event horse and proven stallion. The world-famous Bubbly was there: a brilliant bright palomino over 20 years old who had won almost every top showing class in the days of White City, Harringey and Wembley. He was still serving mares and used as a teaser – a stallion that tests whether a mare is in season – by the newcomers as he was small and so gentle to handle.

A recent addition to the Bottom Yard was Double Bubble, another impeccable palomino, and a son of Bubbly, winning prizes already, despite being not yet two years old. Around the back of the Bottom Yard were more quality horses, with an outstanding bright bay who had so much presence I was almost bowled over just looking at him.

"Who is this?" I interrupted Penny as she listed the sires and dams of the previous horse.

"I was just coming to him. That is Kadett. He is our Olympic hope in Dressage for the coming Games," she told me.

I was then shown the dumper trucks we took turns in driving for mucking out. The yellow one was hard to start, but idled forever, the green one was temperamental in starting and prone to stall but was the fastest and more fun to drive. Penny showed me how to start it, by winding it up at the front with a large iron bar.

"Hey, it's just how we started the oat crusher back home!" I exclaimed. Penny gave me a strange glance. She had never heard of anyone crushing their own oats. Ken had always bought oats whole and crushed a quantity daily, as they were fresher and contained better protein value.

After evening stable duties, everyone went back to the cottage for an early meal then did whatever they liked until 6am the following morning, when the yard again came alive. As we entered the cottage, I asked Penny if I would be able to make and repair saddlery in my evenings and spare time. That was welcomed and I was given an area to use as a workspace.

The 'list' allocating horses to us, appeared during breakfast, making it the most exciting time of the day. On my first day I was given Thora – my own horse – and Maid, a show hack with a low wither. A long hour mostly at a fast trot on Maid concerned me somewhat as it was her first time carrying a side-saddle. I found it quite strenuous using a sitting trot and occasionally used a rising trot to take a break.

I then lunged Thora, receiving instruction from Jenny. Lunging is having a horse walk, trot or canter in circles on command, at the end of a long rope called a lunge line, held by the person lunging the horse. A long lunge whip, when shown behind a horse, encourages it to go faster; when shown in front, it encourages it to slow down the pace – but the whip is never used to hit the horse. I had earlier prided myself on my abilities and now found they were all wrong. But it felt wonderful to make improvement on my first day. Jenny was a delightful person to work for. A hard taskmaster, whether on herself or the people she was teaching, she aimed only for perfection.

Sally Trickett, a former 'lad' in racing stables, lunged Kadett: he was her charge. He looked terrific at a gentle trot; he didn't seem to touch the ground. At lunchtime I asked Sally what Kadett was like. She told me he was OK but didn't have much personality, also that he did not do anything exciting when ridden.

"So why do you do him?" I asked.

"No one else wanted a third horse. I said I didn't mind as I was doing three in my previous job."

"Well if you don't want three, I'll happily take him from you as a third."

"Sure, ask Penny. I wouldn't mind at all." This was the musical answer. Kadett became my third horse.

I rushed out to say hello again to my new idol and told him he was to be special from now on.

The following day, Maid had developed a tiny sore on her withers. I told Jenny, who agreed Maid was not an ideal shape for the side-saddle. She asked what the exact problem was that was stopping me riding astride. I showed her my damaged leg.

"How would you feel about riding something tomorrow on a conventional saddle without stirrups, so nothing rubbed your leg?" she asked.

"Well, I'm game for anything."

The next morning, heavily bandaged, I was joining the first ride, astride Maid. It was harder work, rising to the trot for long spells, but there was no damage and at least I didn't feel so out of place. My second ride was Whitsun, an American quarter horse, bred for the quarter-mile races. He was a short, compact, very dark bay gelding. My third task was to lunge Kadett. Jenny supervised me very carefully while I lunged him the way she had demonstrated the previous day.

By the following week, I was listed to ride Kadett, along with my other two charges. I took him out first, in the school, under Jenny's watchful eye. He was so hoof-perfect and faultless that I thought he must be the best horse in the world. The aids given were unseen, yet as clear to Kadett as if I were kicking his sides or pulling his mouth with the reins.

The exercising took place in the morning, with the grooming, mare covering and stables after lunch. Being new, I led the mares into the teasing box. If the mare showed interest, she was taken outside to the covering area where she was hobbled (just in case she should kick and damage the stallion), then covered by another stallion. She was then walked for fifteen minutes to ensure retention of the semen. With the first mare successfully covered, I asked if I could sit on her while she walked. Penny agreed: there should be no reason not to but no one else had asked before.

This gave the covering a whole new excitement for me, as some of the mares we covered were old faithfuls like Desert Storm, a beautiful black thoroughbred, Wembley winner in showing classes. More exciting was when a mare had been covered that had never previously been ridden. There could be fireworks when I jumped on, as she would often try to buck me off. Fun! But when Jennie saw me being bucked by a mare, she told me: "if you insist on getting on unbroken mares, please take them to the sand school first in case you fall off." Which I did.

As the Olympics were approaching, I decided to make Kadett a special present to wear at the Games. I stitched him a beautiful leather head collar with his name on one side and on the other side, five circles representing the Olympic symbol. For the cheek-pieces and nose-band, I cut several small holes and wove a very thin band of leather in criss-crosses in and out of the holes. I was very proud of the finished product. Jenny was delighted with it. Kadett wore it proudly to the Games, and even when I visited the stables 15 years later, I was shown my old head collar, still in perfect condition and very well cared for.

Prior to the Games however, Kadett was short-listed as the first reserve, pipped to the post by Detective, who was a good horse with a better piaffe (a stationary trot) than Kadett. Detective was a bright chestnut, temperamental stallion with three white legs. Kadett, having been gelded, was more predictable whereas Detective was liable to 'explode' in the middle of a dressage test. I was surprised he had been placed ahead of Kadett for that reason.

With just three weeks to go before the Games, Jenny came to the cottage during breakfast.

"I have some terrible news," she said. "Detective has died of twisted gut overnight."

"Then Kadett is in the team!" I exclaimed excitedly.

"Yes, Tizi, but at least sound sad and show some respect for poor Detective."

"Sorry. I *am* sad."

At the end of the evening, having finished the repairs for that day, I went upstairs, took a bath, then picked up my sleeping bag and a blanket and went outside. Someone asked where I was going and I told her I was sleeping with Kadett.

Jenny got to hear of this: just as I was dozing off, snuggled up against Kadett, who had also lain down, she appeared, shining a torch at us both and asked what the heck I was doing there.

I told her I wasn't taking the chance that he should get colic overnight.

"You'd better get out of there," she retorted. "Kadett could roll or get up and trample you."

"Look at him. Do you really think he would?"

I was lying against his neck and chest. Although he had looked up somewhat startled when Jenny appeared with the torch, he had now settled down again resting his head protectively on my chest.

"Besides, I am very comfy and sleepy," I added.

"Really, I give up with you, Tizi. Just don't get trodden on."

If anything, Kadett seemed pleased when I joined him in the late evenings. Each night he would rest his head gently on me as though to let me know he would look after me.

Earlier in the year, Jenny had suggested I pass Thora to someone who would take her on in eventing and jumping and perhaps get a horse more suitable for dressage. Jenny preferred Dutch blood in horses, or thoroughbreds. Sally Roome, my best friend from schooldays, heard about Thora and said she would like to have her.

The next horse I bought was called Princess Colleen, nicknamed PC, appropriate as I purchased her from a policeman. She was a dark bay thoroughbred by Prince Arthur who was stabled near my old home in Purleigh. My mother took me to see the horse, then as it was local to the Playles, Ken agreed to bring PC down to the New Forest. It was great and nostalgic to hear all the news from the Playles and see their horses.

There was one big advantage to having your own horse at Jenny's. When Herr Rockavanski, (known as Rocky), former director of The Spanish Riding School in Vienna, came to 'fine tune' Jenny, riding Kadett, he also helped us with our own charges. On one of Rocky's later trips, after I had been working hard with PC on her dressage, he got her performing a very passable piaffe. I was delighted.

My new love for dressage had long since replaced my desire for jumping and cross-country. One of my ambitions for many years had been to ride in a Point-to-Point, but if no one had seen you win, there was no hope of being offered a ride. The only other way to get started racing was to buy a suitable horse. As I was still riding astride without stirrups, or with the side-saddle on higher withered horses, I decided using the side-saddle would be easier and safer. I wrote to Weatherby's, the main go-to for all professional horseracing, for permission to Point-to-Point, riding side-saddle. They granted it almost by return of post. I had not expected that and wondered if writing from Catherston had made a difference. It had always been not what you know, but who you know, that mattered.

I registered my colours of purple and lilac and dyed everything I owned to suit. Then I took PC out with the New Forest Hunt half a dozen times to 'qualify' her as a genuine hunt horse. Life was exciting and good.

*

My daily expression was still 'life's good', although it irritated many people who had personal problems.

Each day one of us, rostered in turns, would be exempt from stable duties. The nominated person would set out the breakfast, do the washing up, then make up a shopping list to give to Anthony, Jenny's husband, who bought the ingredients for the rest of the day. Lunch was a simple sandwich. Dinner was where an individual's popularity scored by making an appetising evening meal on 25/6d (in 'new money' that was £1.27 and a ha'penny, but decimalisation had only just happened and I still thought in shillings and pence) for thirteen hungry working girls.

Lucy was the daughter of a butcher and on her day off, she went home and returned with a large joint of meat. She was always rostered to cook after her day off. Her popularity was high!

I remember my first day when the cooking arrangements were explained; I felt a rising panic. My mother had always cooked for me. My sister Toto was gifted and loved cooking. I had never bothered with food or cooking and had never cooked a meal in my life. There seemed no need. I ate enormous quantities if it was there, but never bothered if it wasn't, as a chocolate bar would do. At the farm, Ann always cooked for everyone.

On my early attempts, I usually cooked whatever we had had the previous day, as that was about the only thing I could remember we'd eaten. I also found 25/6d did not go far. Eventually I found I could cope with cauliflower cheese; this became my only dish. If that was served the previous day, I was stuck. So I added a vegetable and cheese dish to my new-found skill. My popularity was deservedly at the bottom.

With one day off a week, there was not enough time to go home or visit anyone. Brockenhurst was a long ride from my mother in Purleigh and the Ariel 3 moped was limited in speed. So I decided to stay at Jenny's on my day off, where I could ride PC and Kadett, filling in the remainder of the time making and repairing saddlery. The finished products were improving and I was able to make anything that was needed.

When my mother discovered I stayed without a break, she thought this would not be beneficial in the long run. She bought a secondhand camper wagon and drove down to Jenny's to collect me after the evening stables, prior to my free day. She would drive us down to a picnic area in the New Forest where we had a meal, strolled around the beautiful forest and chatted for hours before going to sleep. We would then take a generally easy, relaxed day, doing nothing in particular. Anne then returned me to the Stud, complete with a large bunch of venison sausages or some such treat she had bought. How my popularity soared!

I later learned the reason the small meal allowance was deliberate, in as much as we were supposed to be learning how to budget. This was supposed to prepare us for the outside world. It backfired, however, when we all brought food back after our day off.

Life was getting quite demanding. I wanted to buy many items for PC and pocket money was not available. As we were all working pupils, this meant working for our instruction, board and lodging.

Jenny could not afford to pay for 13 full time grooms, as she had to remain a true amateur to be eligible to ride in the Olympic Games. Catherston Stud was a non-profit making organisation. By using the working pupil arrangement, Jenny could run the establishment without horrendous staff bills and in return she gave us all instruction in equine matters and teaching abilities so we could take the Instructor exams.

Most of the other girls came from wealthy backgrounds and just asked for anything they wanted. I knew my mother was struggling and going without many things to send me to Jenny's. There was a nominal fee charged for keeping your horse there, although I never did find out how much. Money was a subject never discussed at Catherston.

The saddlery was a hobby and I would not have dreamt of asking for payment for the repairs. It kept me occupied and I enjoyed it. While the other girls were engrossed in hobbies that cost money, I always felt that I was the lucky one: I enjoyed far more satisfaction from making a noseband or a pair of reins and feeling proud of the finished product. The alternative was to go to a movie then spend the rest of the evening discussing it. I have always held a total dislike for time-wasting television and only ever wished to see a movie if it had a very good reputation; the sort that come round every few years.

One evening Sarah, one of the girls, mentioned there was a sign outside the local hotel asking for help in the kitchen, washing up in the evenings. Sarah was a lovely looking, petite girl with long, straight, pale brown hair but she was very shy.

"I wouldn't mind going, but I wouldn't go alone," she said understandably, then added, "I think you get a proper restaurant meal as well as a wage."

"I'll go with you." I leapt in before she'd finished, thinking the meal would be a change from our cooking.

The following evening, after stables were finished, Sarah and I wandered down the road to the hotel. We were warmly welcomed and asked if we could start that evening and then we were shown the vast kitchens and told where to put the scraps, which went to a local pig farm. We both thought what lucky pigs they were, as we threw the luxurious food remains, some hardly touched, in the bins. We were told to have a break halfway, when we could have any meal on the menu with as much as we wanted.

To this day, I am sure that was to stop us eating the delicious 'scraps'.

The hours were 8pm to midnight, the pay 2/6d (12 and a half pence) per hour, making a vast ten shillings (50 pence) for the evening. I was keen to go every night, more for the meal than the cash. If no one else came, as was often the case, I went alone. I was welcomed at the hotel now as one of their regular staff.

After the first full fortnight of washing up, I realised I was getting way behind on the saddlery repairs awaiting my attention. I had got myself into a corner: I couldn't let everyone down, but as there was now reluctance from any of the girls to join me in the washing up, I didn't want to let the hotel down either. I'd agreed with them they would always have at least one of us daily.

The only way out was to work through the lunch break on the saddlery, but repairs soon piled up. The main reason for this entire backlog was doing all the repairs by hand. I never obtained, or wanted, a machine, as hand-stitched work is far superior. When a rug got ripped, it would have been a five-minute job to run it up on a machine. With careful hand stitching, it would take some hours, but the finished product lasted forever, so I always gave a ten-year guarantee on everything I made or repaired.

Soon, on arriving back from the hotel, I would treat myself to a couple of swift hours of saddlery repair prior to going to bed. I had so much spare energy; it was just another way of using some surplus. But as time went on, the two hours stretched up to five.

I kept saying to myself that after this last piece, I'd go to bed, then I'd glance at my watch and see it was 5am. Where had the time flown? It seemed pointless retiring to bed for one hour, so I went ahead and mucked out the top stables alone. Cleaning out 25 stables using deep litter sawdust bedding – shavings for those with an allergy – ought to have been quicker than mucking out the 15 full straw beds on the farm.

If nothing but to prove a point to myself, I raked out the beds then drove the green dumper along the long narrow corridor, shovelling the soiled bedding in as I went. The final piece de resistance was to sweep the corridor.

Single-handed, the whole operation took exactly one hour. As the girls arrived at the top of the top yard, I shouted, "It's all done!"

"That's impossible," said Penny. "What do you mean?"

I explained, then suggested we gave the others a hand with the bottom yard and the brood mares, so we would all be quicker to breakfast. Strangely that day I had more energy than ever, shaking slightly and feeling slightly hyped up: a new experience. I liked the feeling. I was probably running on empty but I had no idea at the time.

The following day I went to the hotel but slept soundly on returning after midnight. The day after, however, I did the same routine as I was intent on catching up with the backlog of repairs, plus some new orders I was dying to get started on. The following day I did the same. My popularity rate soared. It was wonderful: having always been very much a loner, I was not very good in groups. There was one drawback. The girls now expected to find the stables done before 7 o'clock. So even when I was very tired, I felt almost obliged to work through the night, just so I could get the stables finished before anyone woke and were disappointed.

There is only so much a body will take, I eventually found out. In the earlier days I had no idea there would be any harm done to a normal, healthy, young, fit, body just by working it a little harder. I found I was losing my appetite.

I was still working the lunch hours on saddlery repairs but didn't bother with a sandwich – it was less hassle to skip, since I would talk to the others while eating, wasting a precious half hour. Still desperately trying to utilise more hours of the day, I now found myself only eating a small part of the hotel meal and working faster, to finish earlier. The result was that I lost a vast amount of weight, which neither the girls nor I noticed; we were all lean and fit.

Jenny, however, did notice and called me to the house for a talk. She asked if anything was wrong. I said no, just that I was short on hours in the day. She then told me that since Penny 2 had given in her notice, she would like to offer me her position, but only if I worked less and ate more, as she thought I was wasting away.

Both Pennys had worked for the Stud for a few years and were the only girls on a salary, as they already held the exams we were all working toward.

I felt honoured; I couldn't believe I could be so lucky. How could I now work less? If Jenny was prepared to offer me Penny's position, I felt I had to justify her faith in me and work harder than I did already. At sixteen years of age, I could not have known I was slowly destroying my poor over-willing body.

A few weeks later Jenny came to the cottage at lunchtime and told me to pack a suitcase with some clothes for a few days. She was taking me out. I figured we were going to an overseas show, so packed my riding clothes, nightwear and saddlery tools. She drove me to a hospital. I wondered who we were visiting, hoping it was no one I knew, then found out she was leaving me there.

"When you're better," she said, "give me a call and I'll come and pick you up."

"But there's nothing wrong with me," I called after her as she jumped into the car and drove off.

A nurse led me to a room and instructed me to put on my gown and asked me if I would like a book or a magazine, to which I sulkily answered that I couldn't read. I was brought a comic. Which served me right.

I was taken to an operating room and given my first dose of EEG, the electrode treatment that everyone is now familiar with after 'One Flew Over the Cuckoo's Nest'.

I awoke not knowing who, where, or what I was doing there. I knew I didn't belong, so waited until midnight, dressed quietly and crept out, thinking I could find my way back somehow to the Stud. Bits of memory came nagging back in drifts; it had only been a short trip. So I headed for the nearest railway station and without money tried to talk my way through the barrier without a ticket.

The hospital alerted the police who caught up with me in minutes and had me swiftly escorted back to my 'prison'. The following morning it was explained I was suffering a fairly common teenage 'breakdown' and my weight, at six stone, was dangerously low for my nearly six-feet height.

"What can I do to get back where I belong?" I asked.

'When you weigh 8½ stone, you can go."

I felt totally deflated. How had it happened? How could I possibly be having a breakdown? I was the happiest person on this planet.

This time there was no chance of escaping; my street clothes had been taken away. I was in total disgrace. My improvement continued gradually although it felt as though I was locked up forever. My mother visited me, so did Ann Playle and Jenny, although I begged Jenny not to come again and not to let any of the girls come. I felt humiliated and guilty at having caused everyone so much trouble.

I started eating three helpings of every meal including breakfast, despite having no appetite. The meals were awful, like cooked cardboard. But if I were not to be allowed out until I weighed 8½ stone, then I'd get there by force-feeding myself. I soon began to dread mealtimes. They became a chore, having to force food down into a perfectly happy, overfilled belly. We were weighed daily: the weight wouldn't go on.

After a month my mother looked very worried. I asked what the problem was. She told me that keeping PC at livery prices without me being there to look after her was getting hard to cope with and no one knew when I would be coming out. I asked what could be done.

"Well, to sell PC would be the only reasonable option," she said. "Since she is going so well with her all-round training and has qualified to Point-to-Point, plus her good breeding, she would fetch more than you gave for her. You would be able to buy another, perhaps a Dutch-bred horse, like Kadett, when you get out."

She had offered the carrot that Jenny had suggested.

"OK," I replied.

PC fetched a good price. I didn't even care. Finally after three months, I made the targeted 8 ½ stone and was allowed home with my mother to her new house in Dorchester, Oxford, to recover prior to returning to the Stud. I could not have kept up with the pace of life back at the Stud if I'd returned immediately. I could see the sense in this although I didn't look forward to life without a horse. My mother knew I wouldn't last long without a horse, so she had searched desperately for a local horse which needed exercising.

Chapter 4

MEETING REXTON

The first morning I awoke at home in my mother's new semi-detached house in Dorchester, I was wondering how to get fit as soon as possible and how to pass the rest of the day. The room I woke up in was clean and comfortable but seemed crowded and lifeless, with people outside but no dogs or horses inside. My mother asked how I'd slept and then told me there was a horse two miles away that desperately needed exercise but couldn't be ridden as it had a bad problem.

"What sort of horse is it and what's its problem?"

"It's a Pointer with a fabulous turn of speed, but it can't be raced because it won't go on any ride without another horse for company. There are no other horses in the yard so there is no way he can get fit enough to race. The owners are called King. They are lovely people and desperate to get this horse, Rexton, exercised."

"Well I've finished breakfast," I said, rapidly swallowing a banana, apple and an orange almost in one. "Can I go now?"

"Only after your piece of toast as well," joked my mother, passing me a buttered slice as I darted through the door to her car.

"You must keep this weight on that you've struggled so hard to get back," she said firmly.

"Yes, mother."

When she dropped me off, I wanted to go straight to the stables but my mother insisted I met the Kings first, to be courteous. I had to suffer another cup of tea politely, while dying to see my new friend, Rexton.

Eventually, after the ordeal of our 'British manners', I was introduced to Rexton. He was a fabulous bright bay, compact little gelding with perfect conformation and a white blaze. I fell in love at first sight. I turned shyly to Mr and Mrs King asking if I could have a brush and get to know him alone for a couple of hours.

"That's just what I had in mind," said Mr King. "Why don't I show you his grooming kit and tack then you can brush him before riding, if you feel like it?"

"Thanks," I blurted out and followed him to the tack room.

"Give me a shout before you go out riding and I'll give you directions."

"Sure." I returned and shut myself in with Rexton to brush him, chat and sympathise with him.

"They all say you won't go out for a ride by yourself, Rexton. Is that true?"

He nuzzled me as if wanting me to understand what he was trying to say. I felt he wanted to go out but didn't know how to explain it. He probably only reared because he was confused about what he did want. I had been told he stood on his hind legs and wouldn't go anywhere, so he couldn't be exercised, resulting in being unfit to race.

When his coat gleamed, I saddled him up and then tapped on the door to say I was ready to go. Mr King suggested going round the block and cutting through a field where I could have a canter if I wanted. Then he said:

"Mind you, this is all a maybe. So far, he has never gone past the end of the drive. He just naps whatever we do to him. Would you like me to follow behind with a lunge whip, to try to get him past the end of the drive?"

"Oh no, thank you sir. I'll just wait. I'm in no hurry. We have all day. You don't mind how long I am, do you?"

"Of course not, but that sounds a funny way of getting a horse to do as it's told. But I've heard you can ride anything, so do whatever you like. Treat 'ole Rex as if he's yours."

When a horse naps, he refuses to continue walking: some riders will whip them or kick their sides, but often the only result is that they rear up on their hind legs. Napping is quite common with many horses, especially if they are allowed to get away with small problems in early life – usually it's a mental problem that causes them to nap, so the worst thing you can do is to hit them or hurt them.

When we arrived at the bottom of the drive, Rexton decided that was far enough. I pushed him forward and he dug his toes firmly in. I pushed him again and he rose gently on his hind legs. "No lad, that's silly," I told him, giving him a free rein, whereupon he spun around to return up the drive.

I forced him to about-turn to face the road and the oncoming traffic. He refused to budge. Luckily it was a warm spring day. I sat comfortably on top and played his waiting game. When he tried to turn around, I wouldn't allow him to. I no longer pushed him forward: just sat and waited … and waited.

After three long hours he gave in and walked a few paces onto the road. I stroked him and told him what a wonderful friend he was and that he had just given me the best present he could. Two miles later he stopped and stated plainly that was enough. The wait this time was two hours. Then all of a sudden with no warning he just went forward and completed the rest of the trip without any problem. We finished with a lovely exhilarating canter with a few high-spirited bucks for good measure.

"What a fabulous ride, thanks my love," I told him as we returned up the drive. I brushed him down as much to warm myself up, as to restore his circulation.

Mr King came out and asked how he had behaved. I told him what had happened.

"If you want to come again tomorrow, that would be terrific," he said, enthusiastically. "We saw you having some trouble at the bottom of the drive, but I forgot to mention if you managed to get past the drive, then the following bend was the next place he has not passed before."

Mr King insisted on another cup of tea when I had finished Rexton so he could call my mother to pick me up. He suggested I leave my saddle in the tack room.

The following day, Rexton took me to the bottom of the drive and stopped as if to say 'this is where I stop and mess around'.

"That's up to you entirely," I told him, "but we'll both have a better ride if we just get going and keep going." Since I had not forced him or pushed him forward, he must have thought this was to be another game of who had the most patience. He walked straight on, continuing round the block and through to the field, ending with another spirited canter, with a couple of gentle explosions to show he still had some energy.

Two weeks later, he was getting fitter. We were exploring different rides most days. I asked Mr King if I could jump Rexton in his field as there were some jumps out.

"You can try. He hasn't been over coloured poles before; there are some rustic ones to start with. You can try some coloured poles if you like. They are only out there for a friend who comes over to use them."

I put my side-saddle on as it felt more comfortable than Rexton's little racing saddle. I presented Rexton at the rustic poles, which he leapt like a stag. It was the same with the coloured poles. He acted like a professional show jumper, not a young novice Pointer. Then I set to give him the go-ahead, pointing him at a fairly high gate. We took off together but I continued through the air, still firmly attached to the saddle, while he continued cantering round the field. I got up and saw the two smaller safety straps had snapped. There was no main girth; as it had been too long, I had left it off. I called Rexton. He looked round as if to say, 'what are you doing on the ground?' and trotted back to me. I apologised to Rexton for being so dumb, whereupon both the Kings burst into laughter. I asked why it was funny, falling off with the saddle.

Mr King said they weren't laughing at the saddle falling off, but at the fact I apologised to the horse.

In another two weeks, Rexton was showing some muscle and getting toned up. Mr King said his son, Roy was going to race Rexton at the next Point-to-Point and Roy had asked his father if I would care to lead Rexton around the paddock. Roy was a tall, strong, good-looking lad with short brown hair. Although I would have liked to talk to him, I was too shy to start a conversation.

The race, in two weeks' time, was well timed as afterwards I was to return to Catherston. The day before the race I noticed a slight swelling in Rex's near foreleg. I called Mr King into the stable to look.

"It'll go down if you take him round the block," he said, looking at the leg.

I mentioned that rest would be more beneficial than riding on the swelling, adding that he should get the vet to give the go-ahead if Rex was supposed to race the following day.

"We'll get the vet in if it makes you happy, but Rex is going to race tomorrow anyway. We couldn't race him before as we couldn't get him fit or even exercised, and as you are going, this may be our last chance."

I felt terrible. Perhaps it would have been better if I hadn't ridden him; then he wouldn't be forced to race on an obviously dicky leg. The vet looked at the leg and suggested hosing it down but said that Rex would be fine to race.

I had to stop him racing but could think of nothing. I groomed him until he gleamed, pulled his tail and plaited his mane on race day, then took a photo of him as he looked so well. Then I rugged, bandaged and loaded him into the box; I jumped in the back with him. Mr King and Roy travelled by car. Mr King asked if I wouldn't prefer to ride in the car, as it would be more comfortable. I answered that I'd stay with Rex.

Leading him around the small ring awaiting mounting orders for the jockeys, I couldn't help feeling proud of my charge. He stood out among the runners as the best conditioned and best turned out.

He was walking completely sound; perhaps I was being silly, I found myself thinking. Mounting orders came; I led Rex in and gave Roy a leg up. What a picture of magnificence – both horse and jockey looked great. Roy wore black and gold silks; Rex gave a sideways dance and a couple of playful kicks. Roy, unperturbed, sat still; he was an excellent rider.

"He's never looked so good, you should feel proud of yourself," said Mr King as I watched them canter down to the start. "Are you going to join us at the finish? Have you backed him?"

"No, I never have any luck with betting but I'd love to join you; I just wish his leg was OK."

Under orders and they were off. Roy sensibly held Rex back in midfield for the entire four laps. With five fences to go, he asked for a little more speed with no use of the whip, which was wonderful to watch. Four fences remained; he had gained two places. There were now only three horses in front. Already he looked like a 'place' for sure. Two fences to go, and he had taken another. This was better than the fastest National. With only one fence left, he was neck-and-neck with the leader. This was unbearable. Approaching the last fence side by side, the other horse fell over slowly – what we call 'pecked' – on landing and Rexton shot into the lead. I couldn't believe it. This had to be the most fabulous day of my life. I could handle anything the world threw at me now. Just round the last corner and a 500-yard dash to the finish post. He had already as good as won.

Suddenly he pulled up and stopped. Roy had dropped the reins and wasn't asking at all.

"What the ..." I shouted, tearing down to where they stood. Totally ignoring the rest of the world, which no longer mattered, I ran up to Rexton and took his reins from Roy, who had already dismounted some 200 yards from the finish post. Rexton stood on three legs. The near fore dangled back and forth as he held it up in agony.

"Get a vet immediately, I'll hold him," I shouted to Roy.

I started crying into Rex's mane, hugging his neck as hard as I could.

"Hold on love, they're going to help you," I cried to him. Hopefully he was feeling nothing – perhaps in shock? I had no idea. He stayed motionless with his leg dangling.

The vet arrived, took one look at his leg and removed the bridle, asked me to stand back and, with a humane killer, put poor Rex out of pain – forever.

I was numb, with my new-found love gone from my life as quickly as he had entered it. My world shattered. Still holding his bridle, I slowly walked back to the paddock.

My mother appeared, Roy having summoned her. She took me home and we did not talk at all about Rexton until the following day. She told me that apparently a previous injury had surfaced during the race and Rexton's leg had literally snapped taking the last bend.

She knew what I was thinking.

"Look, Tizi, you can't blame yourself – you did everything in your power to stop him racing. Now you'll have to forget him and get on with your own life, or you'll be straight back in hospital."

"I won't think of Rex any more," I said, lying. "And I won't go back to hospital. I'd like to go to Jenny's if that's possible."

She arranged that I returned directly.

I had been away too long, Penny 2 had left; Juliet had taken her position, which I felt she deserved as I thought she was the better rider, better at organising people and nearly as good at stable management. I was surprised that Jenny had even considered me in the first place. Juliet was an extrovert and fun to be around.

I could only describe myself as a loner, desperately shy, and as totally introverted as I was dedicated to my charges. I was a complete workaholic, not liking going out or socialising, whereas Juliet knew when to stop and socialised with the others. She was a 'people person' and popular with everyone, without having to buy extra food or bring treats from her home visits. She was also a beautiful blue-eyed blonde, incredibly bright and hard working.

After a month, I realised I should move on. With the BHSAI exams taken, I felt now was the time to get a proper paying job. I was offered a position looking after Junker, a lovely dressage horse owned by Sarah Whitman. He had been shortlisted, after Kadett, for the Olympics, but he had no character. His stables were fantastic – no expense spared with a private indoor school and beautiful living accommodation for his groom. He was a good-looking dark-brown horse of 16 hands, part thoroughbred with some Dutch blood in him and a Roman nose, which detracted from his looks. Somehow, though, I couldn't communicate with him so I thought it would be a mistake to work with him as my only charge.

Another couple of offers came my way, but I had been badly spoilt, working with the absolute cream of England's dressage horses, and variety of eventers, hunters, mares and stallions.

Chapter 5

A FLICK-KNIFE IN MY POCKET

Sally Trickett at Catherston had recalled so many stories about exercising strings of racehorses, falling over sheep at flat-out gallop on the misty gallops, that it had sounded like a fairy tale. Since I had not worked in a racing yard, I thought it was time to try one.

Much to Jenny's horror, I wrote off to a couple of yards in Lambourn, receiving an immediate phone call from both.

"What a waste of your training, to go and throw it all away to work in a rough racing yard!" Jenny complained.

Rough? What was she talking about? The finest quality thoroughbreds ever to grace the turf, and she was calling it rough. On my day off, I rode on my poor tired moped for an interview with Barry Hill's Yard. On seeing my height, at nearly six feet, I was told I would be too heavy as they only had horses that ran on the flat.

"But I can make any weight," I said, stupidly. "If you want seven stone, you can have it in a few days."

"Sorry. Why don't you try Dave Hanley? He's only 300 yards away. He has jumpers, so your weight won't matter."

I was still only eight-and-a-half stone. That was a knock-out.

Dave Hanley was a typical countryman, dressed in tweeds with a flat tweed cap with a peak. He was tall and well built with a lovely laid back, relaxed attitude.

"I nearly always need someone; if you're good, hard working and can ride anything. But I never need anyone who isn't," he said.

"Well that's me; when can I start?" I asked, surprising even myself. I couldn't have returned to Catherston now that I'd told everyone I had 'gone'. I had a little pride left.

"You could start today or tomorrow. You don't seem to have any luggage or clothes with you."

"I could go back now, pick up my belongings and be back tomorrow."

"What are you planning to do about accommodation?"

"I hadn't thought of that. Have you got any?" I felt dumb, then added quickly. "I have a dog who would need to come with me."

"I have six cottages, but they are all full. I'll ring around and find someone to put you up in a B&B until I can give you a cottage. Can you bring your dog after you've settled in for a few weeks?" I answered in the affirmative and returned to Catherston for my belongings.

Life was turning around again. I didn't even stop to think about what I was letting myself in for. I knew the girls at Catherston would be happy to look after Finn for a while, as he loved everyone and everyone loved him.

I loaded up the poor moped, which was really showing signs of overuse, said a temporary goodbye to Finn, Jenny and the girls who wished me luck and insisted I kept in touch, then I set off for my new life.

On my first day, I was given two horses, Hooky Boy and Mr Darling. Hooky Boy was a small compact all black stallion, breathtakingly handsome, as though he had come to life from a George Stubbs print. Mr Darling was a lovely, gentle, affectionate, young hurdler. Although not so striking as Hooky Boy, he was a big generous up-to-weight, bay gelding.

I wondered why I had been allocated Hooky Boy, then found that although he was very keen, fidgety and a wonderful ride, he had no speed at all when he was flat out. Mr Darling had only just arrived and was untried, so he naturally went to the newcomer, me.

After the morning exercise finished, I was talking to Hooky Boy and wondering what everyone did at lunchtime when Spindle appeared and asked if I was joining them all down at the pub. Spindle was tall and spidery, thin with a gaunt face and short black hair. He looked like he had walked out of Oliver Twist. I agreed to and joined the bunch going the same way. Taffy asked if I swore at all.

Taffy was a Welshman through and through, although he always wore a tartan flat cap to ride out. I told him I didn't swear, but it did not bother me when others did. He told me I'd be swearing like the rest of them in six weeks – everyone did.

I told him, no way.

"Betcha ten bob you'll be swearing in six weeks."

"You're on," I said.

At the end of the first week, I asked the Guvnor if I could fetch my dog. He agreed for an initial trial period – his greyhounds were not to be chased or frightened. The tri-ped finally breathed its last. No chance of starting it, even when filling to the brim with petrol and oil and trying a new spark plug. I left it to languish in the overgrown garden of the B&B I was staying at, five miles from Hanley's yard. I now had to use Shank's Pony. I comforted myself by thinking that Finn would prefer walking to work with me than running behind a slow, three-wheeled machine.

I hitched back to Catherston, which was very straightforward, needing only four lifts. Luckily, no one noticed that I'd walked up the drive, or Jenny would probably not have allowed me to hitch back to Lambourn, complete with a dog.

For the return trip, I walked quite a way before offering my thumb, as I wanted a straight road that would only lead in one direction – preferably the right way. I soon started thumbing and in less than half an hour a car stopped and the driver asked where I was going. I said Lambourn. He told me the chance of getting there with a dog was remote, why didn't I jump in and he'd work out something.

I squashed in with Finn at my feet. The back was full. The driver then explained he could pass my way provided I didn't mind waiting while he stopped in at his home and had his tea on the way. The sun seemed to be shining again. This was a good omen to the new start.

Late that evening, I arrived in my new home with Finn. Within a week he was allowed to follow our string onto the gallops. When we rode a hack canter, he could easily keep up. When we were told to run a pipe opener, or a 'fast gallop', he was left behind, but he always ran on the gallops rather than cut across the grass and join us with a shortcut.

On my first arrival I had noticed a particularly striking horse, called Saldez. He stood out from all the others, even head and shoulders from my Hooky Boy. He had tremendous presence, more like Brigadier Gerard, Red Rum or Arkle. He was a five-year-old dark bay with a large muscled neck, big hindquarters and a small white star.

I had my eye on him when I arrived but was too shy to ask for him. Taffy was doing Saldez; he was the only lad in the yard with three horses, rather than two like the rest of us.

After another four weeks I decided to ask Taffy why he did three. He replied he was the unlucky one landed with a third.

"I don't get paid no more for 'aving a third," he added.

"If you'd prefer to do two, could I take Saldez from you?" I didn't think he was particularly struck on Saldez.

"Which one of your 'orses would I 'ave to 'ave? S'pose you want to give me your slow running fucking Hooky Boy."

"Excuse me, he is not fucking Hooky Boy. He is Hooky Boy, and I wasn't offering you one. I would take Saldez as well as my two!"

"Hey, you said a swear word! Did you all hear that? She owes me ten bob," he shouted in excitement. "'Course you can 'ave Saldez. I don't want to do three anyway, but you'd better tell the Guvnor."

Needless to say, I was not popular. I didn't drink or smoke and had not sworn since and sometimes Dave would talk to me as a friend rather than order me like a servant. Sometimes his daughter would join me on a quiet exercise ride, which I took as a compliment as she never rode out with a string on the gallops. Naturally, I was accused of sucking up to the boss. I ignored the lot of them and busied myself with the horses.

I gave Taffy his ten shillings, which he neither acknowledged nor thanked me for.

I liked Dave and had a lot of respect for his training. He knew what he was doing, which was more than could be said for some of the trainers in Lambourn. The horses were well fed, well exercised and well looked after. Dave would notice if their coats didn't shine, and you couldn't get by with washing them down after a gallop; it told on their coats, as some of the lads found to their cost.

After a few weeks, Dave told me I could move into a cottage adjacent to the stables. I was overjoyed. This doubled my wage as half of it was going to the B&B. I was to move in with Jan, a new girl starting the next day. The news was extra well received as I would no longer be the only girl. Perhaps I wouldn't be picked on any more?

Jan had worked for Dave before, leaving a year earlier to join another stables. All the lads were looking forward to her return, but my hopes were flattened as soon as I met her. She smoked and drank like a fish and her language was worse than the whole team put together.

One morning, trotting up towards the gallops, one of the lads behind me gave a hard wallop with a whip onto Mr Darling's rump. He took off and I lost control as he belted flat out straight up the remaining distance towards the gallops, to a chorus of laughter from the remaining lads.

I wasn't particularly concerned as I thought he would turn left at the top of the track onto the gallops, then naturally pull up at the end. But no, he was possessed. He didn't follow the natural left turn but headed straight for a barbed wire fence. I couldn't stop him. I couldn't turn him.

Dave galloped up behind me.

"Bail out and save yourself!" he cried at the top of his voice.

I thought, if I shouted 'hup' loudly as we reached the wire, Mr Darling might jump it and then run out of steam. Not a chance. He didn't see the wire. He didn't even try to jump it. He ploughed straight on. The wire broke and he went down on his shoulders with the wire ripping his chest flesh. I got up and saw him disappearing into the horizon. At least he was going at a good speed, so he hadn't broken anything. The rest of the string arrived and there were jeers and laughter.

I was still calling Mr Darling at the top of my voice. Then, an incredible thing happened. He stopped, looked back, and then trotted straight back to me. I picked up his broken reins and inspected his chest; he was sliced up and bleeding profusely.

"Don't worry about that, Tizi," said Dave. "It's only a flesh wound. He'll soon be as right as rain. Just walk him back slowly."

Mr Darling was patched up and left to stand in his stable for six weeks, on the vet's advice. Bran mash and hay substituted his oats, to reduce his energy level, so he was fairly contented.

Finally the day came when he was to be exercised gently. Dave asked me if I wanted to ride or would prefer one of the other lads to ride him out. He suggested that if I insisted on riding, I should take him along the road into the village rather than anywhere near the gallops which would probably excite him.

So we set off on a quiet, gentle walk in the opposite direction to the gallops. Mr Darling wanted to go towards the gallops. I told him no firmly and pushed him in the opposite direction. Every 20 or 30 yards he would stop and try to spin round to return to the gallops. I kept insisting he had to go toward the village. It was a long fight, but finally we were through the village and about to return. Mr Darling suddenly jumped at something in the opposite bushes I didn't see and reared up releasing some of his pent-up energy.

I was taken aback and tried desperately to lean forward, to prevent him toppling. It was no use. With my weight past the aft centre of gravity with him in the vertical position, he toppled over backwards. Unfortunately, there was a small stone wall behind us: he cleared it but I was caught beneath him and the top of the wall. He got straight up, then proceeded to gallop right through the centre of the village in the middle of the road, back toward the yard.

I could see a car approaching, so I jumped out, right into its path. The driver screeched to a halt. I went to the passenger door, got in and incoherently told him what had happened. All he heard was that the horse had gone in the direction I was waving. I had to catch him before he returned home.

"Hey, you're covered in blood!" said the driver.

I hadn't noticed, but on looking down I could see the mess and it was all over the car. I apologised as I tried to cover the accessible parts. Then to my relief, just a few miles later, there was Mr Darling standing at the side of the road being held by a lad I didn't recognise. The driver pulled over and I got out. I later realised in my relief that I'd forgotten to apologise for the trail of blood I'd left in the man's spotless car.

I thanked the lad for catching Mr Darling. Apparently, he had been galloping straight toward the stables. The lad, Jim, from Barry Hill's yard, had been walking to the pub for a packet of cigarettes. Seeing the loose horse, he'd flagged him down and caught the trailing reins.

"Want a leg up?" he offered.

"I dunno, is he OK?"

"He seems sound, just some grazes on his hind legs. What happened? Buck yer off?"

I explained what had happened but decided to lead Mr Darling the mile home. He might have an injury that did not show, which would be hindered by added weight on his back.

I put him away, brushed him down then hosed his hind legs. Dave came over and asked what I was up to. I explained. He didn't seem unduly worried about Darling Boy, but he did ask if I was OK. Then he noticed the blood that couldn't be hidden.

"Give me the horse and go and get yourself washed down," he ordered.

Suddenly I felt tired, drained and worried about my damaged leg. On removing my trousers I found that all the new skin from the last graft had been ripped off. It must have been sandwiched between Mr Darling and the wall.

Mrs Hanley, a kind woman who worked with Dave but had no interest in horses or racing, came to my cottage and told me the governor had told her to take me to hospital.

On arrival, I was inspected and shown straight into a private room. The news was that I would have another skin-grafting operation the following morning. Afterwards, I'd be in for a week and no riding for at least a month.

Dave and his wife came to visit, which I felt was a lovely gesture. I asked after Mr Darling, Hooky Boy and Saldez and who was doing them.

Dave told me not to worry about any of them. Doug, the Head Lad, had taken on Mr Darling and Saldez, and Spindle was doing Hooky Boy as a third until I returned. He said not to be in a rush to get out.

A week later I called the yard and Mrs Hanley came to collect me and asked what I had been told I was allowed to do. I happily told her 'anything' as long as I was careful. Poetic licence.

The next morning, back at stables I found Saldez's box empty.

"Where's my horse?" I asked Doug. He told me he had been going so well that the owner wanted to race him in America.

"You would have gone with him, but you weren't here, so he went alone. They'll take a lad from over there." He broke the news gently.

"Well fine, as long as he comes home OK."

Saldez never returned. He won a magnificent flat race, and his owner sold him for £10,000 on the strength of the win. That was a higher price than the best horses went for in the early '70s. I was gutted; my best horse gone. Hooky Boy and Mr Darling reassured me with gentle nuzzles when I told them of my sorrow.

I soon amassed a small fortune working in the yard; since not liking alcohol, I couldn't find anything that cost money: a happy state of affairs that was not to last long. I decided to buy an old car. Taking Finn in a car would be easier than on a bike. I started asking around in the local pub if anyone knew of a cheap car and the first evening I found a real bargain. I was told it was the sort of opportunity that couldn't be passed by. I was led up to Fred Winter's Yard with five other lads. Someone showed me an old Austin that looked like it had been sitting in a field for quite some time.

"Can I try it?" I asked.

"S'pose so," someone replied.

So I climbed in and asked how to start it.

"I'll give you a hand, but make sure it's in neutral."

I wondered vaguely where neutral was. One of the others, called Tom, had got in next to me. Tom was short and lean with short fair hair. He wore a flat tweed cap as seemed to be a uniform in the racing yards.

He shoved the gear stick until it wobbled freely.

"That's neutral, when it wobbles," he explained. Someone was winding the handle in front of the car. Suddenly it made a coughing noise.

"Hit the accelerator," shouted Tom.

I looked around for a hammer.

"You fool, I meant step on the pedal on your right," he replied patiently, while the engine gently died. It was wound up again. This time I pressed the accelerator pedal, while Tom grabbed a lever he explained was a choke.

"You've driven this before?" I asked, wondering how else he had known what to pull and where it was. Yet, the car looked as though it had grown into the grass surrounding it.

"No, not this car, but others."

I tried ever so gently to move forward. I didn't want anyone guessing I'd never driven a car before, but it stopped when I moved the gear lever away from neutral.

"Let me show you how to drive," said Tom coming round to my side, as another lad wound it up again. I moved across and watched the procedure.

"OK I've got it!" I said and jumped out to change seats. This time we went forward without stalling. It was getting very noisy. Tom mentioned that it had more than one gear and suggested I should try the next one.

After a half hour round the poor field and removing half the grass, I felt I'd got the hang of it enough to try it on the roads.

"This is where I'm getting out!" exclaimed Tom, opening the door.

"Please don't get out yet, I'll need some petrol but I'll probably hit the pumps if I try driving into a garage. Would you take it to the pump?" I pleaded pathetically.

When the car had been filled, Tom got out and walked away, toward his hostel.

"Where are you going?" I called after him.

Tom turned around and told me the deal was that I drove after filling up. He hadn't agreed to sit with me.

That's fair enough, I thought and wondered how I was going to start it. I put the handle in and wound it up as I'd seen the lads do. The car groaned, jumped into life and lurched toward me then stopped before running me over. The garage owner ran over and said the car was not in neutral.

"Oh, of course," I answered as if I should have thought of that. I got back inside and moved the gear lever until it wobbled. Just as I was getting out to wind it up again, the car started moving of its own accord. I moved back to my seat rather clumsily, thinking it was safer than chasing a runaway car.

The car took off and went onto the road while I was wondering what had happened. Luckily, there were no other cars around. The last thing I heard was the garage owner shouting something about a handbrake. I wondered where it was. I also found myself wishing my tri-ped had not been an automatic; then it would all have been obvious. Perhaps.

I went back to the field: Tom was nowhere to be seen but I recognised Nick and gave him the £35 for the car.

I drove home and parked outside the cottage. I felt proud of my new car. It was a little tatty, full of rust and a horrid faded green colour, but it was my first car and I now had my own dog transporter. It was a good two weeks before I would allow Finn in with me though, as I trusted my driving even less than the lads who had seen my hopeless first attempts had done. Small matters like a driving licence, tax, or insurance never occurred to me: nothing mattered to me apart from the horses I looked after.

I did not like any form of alcohol. As the whole stable life, off duty, was spent at one of four different pubs, of which Sam's and The George were the nearest and most frequented, I had to think of something else to do while there. Betting was a regular hobby for all the lads so I took a chessboard to Sam's and offered one of the lads a game for half a crown (12 and a half pence). He took me on and I lost. I then asked him to be fair and play another for 'double or quits'. This never failed. I then 'just' won the game, and offered a third and final game, which was not usually refused as the lad was still buoyed up with the first easy win.

Perhaps this was a trifle unfair, as I spent much of my hospitalised time playing chess with visitors, patients, doctors and nurses, with four chessboards in various stages of play.

After a short series of eventual 'wins', I could not find anyone keen to play me for money, so I would pounce on a stranger who walked in and offer them a game. The other lads preferred this idea as it left them free. The stranger usually refused (after all who comes to a quiet country pub for a game of chess?). The lads would start taunting the stranger with jeers of 'what's the matter with you, then, frightened to take on a pathetic little female?' At which point the stranger usually accepted.

The lads had decided to rectify my distaste for alcohol. Once we were at the pubs, the different stables didn't matter; we were all one team. Mick, an Irish lad, offered me an aniseed ball to eat. After I agreed that it was nice, he said,

"If you like that, why don't you try an aniseed juice for a drink?"

"Sure, so long as it has no alcohol."

"No, there's no alcohol at all," he lied. "Look, I can prove it to you." He took the bottle from the barman who was also in on this game.

"There you are," he said triumphantly, "it says 40 % proof – which is proof it is all aniseed juice and no alcohol."

"OK, I'll try some," I said reaching for the bottle to have a sniff.

"You have to have it with water, it's concentrated like cordial," Mick informed me.

The barman poured a glass quarter full of Pernod and added water to the top. I must have missed the grins, which were obviously going around.

"Well it's better than coke but I'm not sure I like it," I replied after a cautious sip. Then we carried on chatting and I took the occasional sip, as one does if you hold a glass for too long. Eventually the glass was empty.

"Here, I'll get you another," Mick offered.

"I'm still not sure I like it."

"It does improve as you get to know it, I swear."

Strangely enough it did. Of course, I was steadily getting drunk but having not been drunk before, I had no idea what the experience was. Eventually I felt tired and unsteady on my feet. Thinking perhaps I had been working too hard and sleeping too little, I gave my apologies and drove home. The little car went better than usual even though it was barely half a mile from the pub to my cottage. On arriving home, I realised I had left Finn behind and drove back for him.

The following morning, I was very thirsty. I drank a large glass of water, then soon after felt wobbly again. My first ride was on Nyswith, a lovely chestnut mare with a white blaze who had a mouth of silk, with lovely, even, gentle, long strides. She was later to win a few flat races for Dave. I returned feeling better and after the third ride-out was back to normal. I was pleased it wasn't a virus.

That evening, I had another 'aniseed juice' and found it tasted better than the first one had. It was a couple of weeks before I found out I'd fallen for a practical joke. On the other hand, it was better to drink in a pub with the others than to be the only one not drinking.

*

Despite Hooky Boy having no speed, his owner wanted him to race at Newmarket. There was no joy in his finishing fourth in a Maiden Race – there were only four runners. I consoled myself by shopping in town for an electric guitar, amplifier and mike. I had decided to start trying to sing in the pubs to pay for the drinks, having discovered that aniseed juice cost more than beer.

Going round the shops and trying out all the guitars took longer than expected. By the time I had walked back, Hooky Boy and the horse-box had gone. So, laden with new guitar, amp and bits, I struggled down the road and tendered my rather worn-out thumb, wondering how I was to make it for morning stables.

I was walking down a quiet back road. It was getting dark and starting to rain. After fifteen minutes a sports car stopped and I was told to get in. I obeyed, piling everything on top of my lap, then apologised for being wet.

The driver started off, and then asked where I was going. I told him Dave Hanley's in Lambourn. He remarked that I was many miles and different roads away, which meant several lifts. Why was I doing something as dumb as that? I explained buying my guitar meant missing the transport, but I had to get back for morning stables, even if it meant walking most of the way.

"Well, I have no choice, but to take you the whole way. I only stopped because I knew there would be very few cars on that road. Why didn't you go to a main road?"

"The load was getting heavy. I didn't think I'd make the main road. I honestly never thought the box would go without me."

Arriving back well after midnight, I thanked the driver profusely and offered him a drink. I only had a miniature Pernod in the house but didn't think it necessary to tell him. I had bought it because the bottle was so cute, not intending to drink it. He thanked me but suggested I needed sleep more than he needed a drink. Besides, he was heading back to London. He drove off. I never asked his name. I wished I had thought of taking his number to trace his address and send him a thank you card.

The next evening I tuned and strummed on my new guitar. It sounded better LOUD, with the amp turned up – well, it sort of covered the slight bits where I missed placing a finger correctly. I'd learnt to play at school and enjoyed it, so I'd continued playing regularly at home in my bedroom. I practised a few Beatles numbers, then went down to Sam's and asked him if I could sing in his pub with my new guitar.

"You can give it a try," he said, "but I won't agree a price until I see how the regulars take to it."

The following evening I piled everything into my car and drove the half-mile to Sam's. After a couple of songs, some of the lads were offering me drinks. Being nervous, these were drunk too quickly, so it wasn't much longer before some of the chords were wrong.

"Think I'd better stop. I've had too much of your juice. It's stronger than usual." I told Sam.

"The lads all told me you were drinking it neat now – that's why it's stronger. Anyway, if you want to leave your kit here and come back tomorrow, you'd be very welcome. No one objected to your performance."

My luck was in. He had called my junk 'kit'. It had a professional ring to it. I felt pleased. As I left, Charlie – a lad from the Winter's stable – called after me. Like everyone he was small, thin and wore jeans, a T-shirt and a flat tweed cap. He had shoulder-length fair hair.

"Now you have that new electric guitar, what have you done with your old one? Do you want to sell your old one and what sort is it?"

"I hadn't thought about it but I could do with some cash. That new one set me back and I want to get a motorbike for the coming summer," I replied absent-mindedly, adding the guitar was a classical.

"That's what I'm looking for – can I see it?" I happily agreed and we walked back to my cottage.

After trying it, he agreed he would buy it for £30. He asked if he could take it and bring the cash down to the pub the next night. I agreed.

The next evening, after a few more songs and a few more drinks of my favourite juice, I spotted Charlie, sang a song directed at him and beckoned him over.

"Got my dough?"

"Yes, it's back at the hostel. If you want to walk back with me, I'll get it for you."

I was cross at myself for walking down to the pub or I could have driven. His hostel was five miles out in the sticks, along a quiet back road with no lights. When I collected the cash, I would be walking back alone with, to me, a small fortune. It was the equivalent of two weeks' wages. I was only going to ask £10 for the guitar but Charlie had offered £30. There was no way round it. To walk home to pick up my car would take longer, so I agreed.

Three miles later as we passed an old bus shelter, Charlie stopped and turned toward me.

"What's wrong?" I asked.

"C'mon, Tizi – you don't really think I've got £30 back at the hostel do you?" He moved closer.

"Well what *do* you want?" I asked, getting annoyed. I was not in the least worried as I had a flick knife in my pocket. Before I had started working at the yard, my mother had told me to look after myself as the life may be rough, but there hadn't been an occasion to even think about protection, until now.

"I think you know what I want," said Charlie somewhat menacingly and put his arms round my neck. In a nervous state, trying to appear cool, I put my left arm around Charlie's neck. With my right hand I reached for the knife in my pocket. I opened the blade as I freed my left arm and tried to push him away and told I him to let me go or I would put a knife in him.

He laughed and stated I couldn't go anywhere, so I may as well enjoy what he had planned and he tried to undo the zip on my trousers. I was furious and thrust the knife into his back.

He screamed and yelled, "You bitch!" while he tried to push me down in the road. Luckily I was now ready and held the knife toward him. I told him quietly that I had used it before and would use it again and suggested he left me alone. Then told him he could return my guitar the following day.

"You're not getting that back, you f---ing bastard!" He turned to walk home holding his back. As he wasn't dead, I didn't really think I'd hurt him, but there was blood on my knife. I was concerned now. In my protected life I had trusted everyone, until now. I was so glad my mother had warned me to look after myself.

I'd bought the knife because it had looked so beautiful, but had only ever used it to spread sandwiches and peel oranges. The blade was very sharp. I had never expected to ever need it in self-defence.

The next morning no one said anything so I thought Charlie had kept quiet, but at lunchtime, the atmosphere in The George felt strange. Spindle came up to me and chatted about his horses and mine. Then he asked quietly, "Did you really stab old Charlie last night?"

"Only as a last resort. He must have got the wrong impression about me. I never planned it, honest."

"He was always bragging that no girl had ever turned him down. He told us all last night he was 'going to tame that little stuck up new one'. We all knew who he meant. Serve him right, but his Guvnor may have a word with ours. Charlie needed stitches in his back. He missed morning stables."

"I thought he was a genuine nice, quiet lad. He never fights in the pubs."

"Tizi, nobody is quite the same when they've had a few drinks and they think you have too. No one would have made an approach when you stuck to your little orange juices." Spindle was the kindest lad in the yard: he was married and his wife Linda had just given birth to a baby daughter.

So, that was the plan in getting me to enjoy drink. I returned to orange juice immediately. I stayed away from the pubs for a few days and busied myself with repairs needing attention that I found in the tack room. I never got my guitar back. It would just take a little longer to get the motorbike I was after.

The weeks flew by. I had been quietly repairing the broken bits of tack and replacing them from where I had found them when Doug, the Head Lad, saw me returning a rein.

"So it's you that's bin getting all the stuff fixed up," he said. "Why don't you give me the bill – where are you taking the stuff?"

I explained it was a hobby. I didn't needed paying as I had a load of leather off-cuts that were given to me.

Doug said it didn't seem right then called Dave over to see what he made of it.

Dave picked up the rein, inspected it and asked where I had learned to repair saddlery like that.

I told him I had picked it up, that I was still learning and improving. He asked how much I'd done. I told him I stamped everything I made or repaired with a design containing a bird with T I Z I at the bottom, but that you wouldn't see it if you didn't know it was there.

He then said, "The lads were saying you are saving for a motorbike. Is that true?"

"Yes."

"Tell you what. I'll buy you a bike. I know you've got your eye on one and I'll deduct £2 a week from your wages for the next year and you can continue to repair the broken tack as repayment. How does that suit?"

"I'd love it!" I cried in joy.

Dave and Doug left. I went to tell Hooky and Mr Darling with a kiss to both of them. Heck, life was good.

The next day, after exercise, I called the local bike shop and asked them to deliver the beautiful, bright green 250cc TS 250 Road/Trail Suzuki they had in the showroom.

Dave wrote a cheque as promised when it was delivered. Peter, who delivered it, had a bike of his own and went through the gears with me. "Isn't it a bit big for you, miss?" he asked.

"I've been told the larger the bike, the less likely it is to give trouble and break down. Besides, there's more power to overtake in safety."

Being impatient, I wanted to take the bike down the road. After several kicks, it still wouldn't start. Peter kicked it once and it fired up immediately. Now I had to ride it – what a sound it made!

It would give 35mpg at speeds Finn could keep up with, but I was warned not to ride it too slowly too often or the plugs would foul. Over the weeks, I found the bike was only happy going flat out. So was I.

A few months without anyone trying anything had me feeling totally safe once again. I still carried my knife, but it didn't show in my work jeans. I didn't think Charlie would go to the police: after all, I'd only used it in self-defence. One afternoon at the stables I had a message that he wanted to return my guitar after all: I could pick it up from his hostel. I drove there and asked the first lad I saw for Charlie or the guitar. He pointed to the room at the end and said,

"He's in there. We'll come with you if you like."

Five other lads joined us. Nobody answered my knock, so I opened the door and looked inside. I couldn't see Charlie, but more to the point I couldn't see my guitar.

When the last lad entered behind me, he shut the door and turned the key, putting it in his pocket. I thought 'thank goodness I have my knife' but it didn't stop me being terrified.

"So, where's the guitar?" I asked, trying to stop the tremor that must have been obvious.

"There's no guitar," said one, "and no Charlie to help you either but we'll keep you entertained."

Not knowing what to do, I backed away from them and grabbed my knife as I moved. I flicked it open.

"I suggest you let me out of here and I won't say a word to your governor."

"Not a chance."

They started closing in. I panicked, shoved my knife out in front, and then whirled around, slashing the air and at everyone in range. I felt contact on a few objects and there were a few whimpers. Then at last I saw one lad unlock the door and slip out. Soon the rest followed.

*

As the warmer weather arrived, Dave decided to put Mr Darling out to grass for the summer to let him 'grow on a bit', as he said. That left me with just Hooky Boy. If your horses disappeared, you were not usually kept on until another horse arrived. Lads generally were 'easy come, easy go'.

I rode my bike up to London on my half day. I saw so many bikes dashing in and out of the traffic at breakneck speeds; I wondered what they were up to. At a red traffic light, I asked a rider what he was doing.

"Delivering letters," he replied, but was gone in a flash when the lights began to change.

I noted the panniers either side of his bike and a box on the back, which had a company name on it: Arrow One. It looked fun so I thought I'd find out more about it. I called the number I had written down and enquired if they were looking for more riders.

"Every company is always looking for riders if you know London, have a bike and can ride it," they said. I was told I could start immediately if I wanted. I had said I would have to give a couple of weeks' notice from politeness, even though I was only paid weekly.

That afternoon, back at the yard, I told Dave I would like to leave as soon as he could spare me.

He told me any time would be fine as he was low on stock in the yard. He asked where I was going. I told him I was going to try dispatch riding, as I wanted a break, but had I repaid him for the bike?

"You've well paid your debt on that," he said. "I was worried about you when you came. To be honest I didn't think you'd last a week the way the lads treated you. I heard about the incident at the hostel. My daughter will miss riding out with you, but we managed before you came so we'll manage again." He was apologetic but so kind.

PART TWO

GOING FLAT OUT

Chapter 1

RIDING FOR ARROW ONE

Leaving the Lambourn yard, I packed a small bag and rode to London. It was my longest ride so far on a motorbike. Eventually I located Arrow One.

Entering the office, I felt somewhat nervous. My boats were well and truly burned at Lambourn. I had no contract to start here and nowhere to stay. I walked into what looked like the control area and told the first person I saw, who turned out to be called Trevor, that I had come to start work. Trevor had brown hair and an unmemorable face; he wore a pinstriped suit and looked bored.

"Just fill in this form. Have you ridden before?" he asked casually.

"Oh yes," I replied. "I've just ridden down from Lambourn." I thought that would impress him, as it was only my second long ride on my road-trail machine. He would soon see what a fast machine I had, as I filled in the second question 'what bike do you have?'

"No, you idiot, I meant have you ridden despatch before? I guess I can assume you haven't."

What a put-down. I was trying to get away from all of that. But everyone starts at the bottom in a new vocation. Trevor asked if I knew London, explaining the job would not pay very well if I had to use a street map to get around.

Another blow. I was hopeless at reading maps. I only vaguely remembered a half-mile square of London around Primrose Hill, where I had gone to primary school. Worried that I was not going to get as far as delivering even one letter or package at this rate, I casually replied:

"Oh yes, like the back of my hand. I was born in London and went to school here too."

"Well you should be OK, but you'll be disadvantaged with your bike. The guys that earn the most have road bikes of 125 or 200cc. They are nippier round town and easier to get through traffic. Plus, of course, it is easier to pick up when you drop it." He said that as though it was a regular occurrence.

"I don't plan on dropping my bike," I answered stupidly.

"The only riders who don't fall off are the careful ones that don't make much money – to be honest we'd be better off without them. Anyway, if you want to start now, here's an address. It's only round the corner. They have two 'drops' in the City. Call me when you drop the last and I'll give you your next pick up. As you get better, you can pick up in the same area before you drop the ones you're collecting, but I'll start you gently. Oh, by the way, you'll earn more if you get yourself a two-way radio – saves using the customer's phones or looking for boxes."

I'd thought there would be a bunch of letters to pick up and deliver in your own time.

"Can I leave my backpack here?" I asked, as I was about to rush out to my poor spotless, gleaming, green machine that was not designed for despatch riding.

"Yeah sure, leave it under the desk there. Oh, we lock up at six."

I'd figured on finishing early, as I needed to find somewhere to sleep.

I jumped on my bike and headed down the street. Having lied about knowing where I was going, I could hardly spend ages trying to find it on a map. I stopped at the first red light and asked a taxi driver, beside me, for directions. He pointed behind me giving quick clear directions.

"Thanks," I muttered as I turned around and raced back past the office, hoping no one would look out of the window. How could anyone miss the sound of a noisy two-stroke 250cc machine, going over 60mph outside their window. It was a 30mph limit, but I needed to look the part.

Finding the company, I went in and said 'Arrow One' as I'd been briefed.

"Oh good, there's four for the City and one to Croydon – you are going straight there, aren't you?" the receptionist asked accusingly.

"Of course."

"That's what they all say."

Hours later, around midday, after finding each address and getting very lost in Croydon, I called the office to say I had finished and spoke to a man called James.

"Well there's nothing here at the moment, so you may as well RTB."

"Where's that?"

"It means return to base. Sorry, are you new here?"

Ouch.

Consulting my A to Z took too long, so I used my original taxi driver idea. The helpful taxi drivers of London were the sole means of getting around.

They knew every side street there was, plus they seemed delighted to give me directions.

Returning at lunchtime, I discovered it was a race of first in, first out. Everyone was waiting for a pick-up. There were seven other riders sitting on the carpet, all in Barbour motorcycling suits.

Someone mentioned I might as well take a leisurely lunch break, as there were seven ahead of me. That suited, as it had already been a long day. Taking my sandwiches from my backpack I sat on a piece of carpet and joined in idle conversation with my neighbour, Matt, who was munching a pie. Matt was four feet 10 inches, stocky and weather-beaten. I asked him if there was any local accommodation.

"There's a hostel 100 yards from the building that does nightly accommodation for about ten bob [50p]. There's no food or cooking facilities, or even sheets. But you get a bed and blanket and a kettle if you have your own milk and tea bags."

That was music to my ears. I was tired already. Since there was a while before I could expect a pick-up, I popped round there straight away, munching my sandwich as I went.

At the reception areas, I was asked if I wanted to see the room.

"No, I'll take it anyway. I have no option," I explained, handing over my crisp ten bob note. I was told to pay the morning before I would require a bed. No cash, no bed. Standard rules, if you had a bed when you left in the morning and gave that night's fee, it was yours until you left without paying for the night. No notice required. There was usually a free bed.

I walked back to the office, thinking life was good and it would get better as I learned my way round London.

During the first two weeks, I took longer than anyone else finding addresses. The company didn't mind, since I was the one losing out in wages. I didn't get given anything 'red hot urgent'. That suited me fine, yet I still went everywhere (usually in the wrong direction) flat out. I had to. I never saw a despatch rider going anywhere less than flat out, even if he was going home.

After the second week, although I was still asking taxi drivers for directions, I was getting more letters delivered and enjoying myself tremendously. I met another girl, Anita Costello, who was the only other female. We got on well almost as soon as we met. Anita was five feet tall, slim and athletic, with long black hair, which she tied under her helmet. She asked where I lived. When I told her she exclaimed, "You can't stay in that flea trap – why don't you share my flat? If you paid half the rent, it would help me anyway. It's a council flat and the rent is only £3 a week."

That evening, parking the bike at the bottom of the stairs in Clerkenwell Road, Anita skipped up the five floors (85 steps) without a break. I panted up after her.

"After a week you won't even notice the stairs," she said.

The flat was beautifully decorated, warm and cosy. Two bedrooms, each the same size, a lounge, small kitchen and a small bathroom.

"This is perfect. I can't believe my luck in meeting you, Anita. Who owns these, your boyfriend?" I pointed to various certificates and judo medals round the room.

"No, they're mine," said Anita unassumingly. She was a Black Belt in Judo. I was instantly in awe.

"It must be wonderful knowing no one can hurt you," I said, knowing nothing about Judo.

"Actually it's pretty useless as self defence, unless your attacker fights by the rules, but it keeps you fit and it's fun."

The second evening Anita asked why I was using a rather difficult bike, which must be eating my earnings in petrol. I agreed it was but said I enjoyed riding it. Anita pointed out that she probably earned double my salary by using a 125cc Honda. I thought carefully and on the next Saturday she had me visiting a bike shop in Croydon looking for a more sensible machine.

I had arranged an overdraft with my bank, which had merely asked what I did for a living. On saying I was a despatch rider but needed a smaller, more economical, bike for the job, there was no problem at all.

I looked at a few bikes but then I finally saw a bright gold Kawasaki triple two-stroke, 750cc. It was love at first sight – plus it had terrific acceleration.

"That's nothing like as economical as a smaller one or even a four stroke 500cc," said Anita, trying to dissuade me.

"Well, no, but it will be a lot more fun."

"You're hopeless," Anita said as I handed over a cheque and got on my new toy. We diced with each other on the way home. My Kawasaki was obviously much quicker off the start at the lights and whizzed along the streets. Arriving well ahead, I said I thought a fortune could be earned with this new machine.

"OK," replied Anita. "Shall we keep our petrol receipts and compare the incoming with the outgoing at the end of the week?" She knew she'd be ahead.

"But you've been working longer than me. You know London better."

"You should get a Street Finder and chuck away that A to Z. Haven't you noticed every rider has a Street Finder?"

I hadn't, but did as she suggested. What a difference! I found eventually I could look up addresses, mark them all off, then deliver and pick up, in a sensible order. Until now, I had searched for one address in a pile of letters, then looked for a second, third etc often passing one of the earlier drops getting to a later one.

With the Kawasaki I was earning more money than ever before, although not actually, as Anita pointed out, when the fuel costs were allowed for.

One day when I was riding rapidly up Clerkenwell Road, going home, a car pulled straight out from a small side road, in front of me without looking or stopping. I had no chance of stopping in time, even with full brakes applied. I was going much too fast.

My bike stopped as it ploughed into the car. The bike's front wheel impacted in the space behind the car's front wheel. I was shot forward over the handlebars and hit my nose on the car's mirror, which then forced me back, temporarily unconscious. The hospital discharged me the same day and informed me that my broken nose would heal unaided. A bus took me to our flat. Anita rushed in looking worried, seeing my battered machine at the bottom of the staircase. I never discovered how it had arrived there.

The bike was repairable but would take time and money. The wheel, forks and frame were bent. There was no option but to get another bike. I called the bank explaining my bike was in for repairs but I couldn't work without one, so I needed a further overdraft to buy another until it was repaired, when I could sell one of them.

This time I bought a lovely lime-green racing Suzuki T200 from a newspaper advertisement. It was complete with clip-ons and rear sets: made to go faster with the riding position more horizontal. It looked fabulous.

Anita's expression when she saw it was priceless.

"But Tizi, you can't use that for dispatch riding. Look at the lock – you'll never be able to U-turn it, never mind nip through the traffic. Why didn't you tell me what you were getting?"

"It was in the paper. I fell in love with the colour. Besides, it's smaller than my Kawasaki. It's only 200cc."

"Think that's academic."

At the end of the first week riding my new pride and joy, with several letters in my panniers, another despatch rider came up beside me and tried to overtake. He was on a larger bike, but my little racer did go, so I opened up the throttle and was soon reaching 100mph, leaving the other bike well back, zipping through the traffic. I felt so chuffed with myself and my new purchase, thinking how good life was, that I was unprepared for what happened.

The screw on the front mudguard vibrated loose and the back of the mudguard dropped into the back of the front wheel, just as I was leaning over to take a corner. The front wheel locked up and the whole thing skidded for yards. I was shot off the bike and slid at high speed under a parked car; where my helmet wedged, trapping me under the car.

Luckily, two passers-by helped pull me clear. Unhurt except for bruising and badly damaged pride, I picked up the bike. Apart from scratches, it seemed undamaged but it refused to start. On closer inspection I found the engine casing had been scratched off. It was definitely not my day.

The bike was a write-off. I called Arrow One saying I was out of transport – could they think of anything?

"No, it often happens. Drop in to collect your wages," they said.

I should have listened to Anita's advice about a sensible bike. There was no point in using my lovely Kawasaki again (even when it got repaired) – the fuel costs swallowed all the profit and I couldn't afford fully comprehensive insurance for that size of bike with my age and lack of experience.

I called the bank again with the same story. However this time I got a very friendly 'no'. Well, I could hardly blame them.

Checking advertisements in a local newspaper, I found Easy Riders were looking for despatch riders with previous experience – bike supplied. 'That's me', I thought excitedly.

The next day with my new company-supplied MZ (equivalent to a Skoda) I set off at high speed to prove I was going to be worth employing.

At the end of the first week, the boss, Jeff, congratulated me on a good week's riding. Jeff was tall and slim with a cheerful disposition; he was an ex-dispatch rider having damaged his knee in an accident.

"You certainly fit in here," he told me, which was music to my ears after struggling so hard with Arrow One.

I considered I had settled into a new lifestyle. It was time to collect Finn. I had left him with Dave Hanley and had called each weekend to check that Finn was OK and the stables were still happy with him living there. Finn was popular, enjoying life and still joining each string on the gallops, usually three times a day.

"Will you be able to exercise him enough in London?" Dave asked with genuine concern. "He's welcome to stay here. He gets on with my greyhounds and my wife and I both enjoy his company."

I thanked him, assured him exercise would not be a problem and that I was planning to collect him at the weekend.

First thing Saturday, I rode to the yard. Finn gave me such a welcome, as if it had been years not weeks, removing any doubt I had about a large dog in the city. Dave greeted me and asked how I was getting him back.

I said he would come with the rest of my bulky items I'd left earlier, in my car, and then I'd return by car to pick up the bike. If I left the car there, perhaps the lads could use it to learn to drive, as I had. Dave gave a shout for everyone in the yard.

"Anyone here wants to buy Tizi's car for a tenner, speak now or lose your chance!"

"I'll have it for a tenner!" said Spindle.

Life was good, and it only got better. I was so glad still to be on such good terms with everyone there.

After settling Finn into the flat with Anita, who was more than happy to take him with her on her long regular training run, I returned to Lambourn.

Dave was embarrassed to take the large bouquet of flowers, I presented to him in thanks for all he had done. When I pointed out I couldn't take them back on a bike, he insisted I stay for a cup of tea before setting off back to the Smoke.

When I returned to London, Finn and Anita made a firm friendship. She encouraged me to join her in a run at weekends, later carrying small weights while running. Finn loved it as he got a walk to the park and a run several times round the track. During the week, however, I would run down the stairs in the morning with Finn, get on my bike and ride slowly round the block with him at heel on the left side. I always stopped once or twice during the day, popped up the stairs, ran down with him, jumped on the bike and repeated the morning exercise round the block. He would have another run when I returned and again before I changed for a bath. He remained easily as fit as at Lambourn.

After a couple more months with Easy Riders, where the pay 'on paper' was far less than with Arrow One, I was actually earning far more as I wasn't paying for fuel, repairs and written-off bikes. I did have a bad prang on an MZ, skidding on a patch of oil, colliding with another car in the process and writing off the poor bike. It was nonetheless repaired, with the in-house workshop and put back in service, albeit with poorer handling.

I enjoyed being appreciated and having a bike supplied. The one company, however, that I held in highest esteem was Mercury Dispatch. They rode company Suzuki GST 250s, in orange and black livery, with some of the riders in orange and black leathers. There were more Mercury bikes around London than any others. I heard you had to be really good to get taken on by the boss, Sammy. Moreover, they paid the best of any despatch rider company in London. This was my goal, to be a Mercury rider.

Whenever two despatch riders came alongside, from whichever company, it was 'instant burn off' against each other. Even when I'd started riding my 750 Kawasaki, the Mercury riders always rode me off, on their little 250s. Whenever I was getting beaten, I would peel off down a side street with a wave, which meant I had a drop and the 'burn' was incomplete.

After the third month with Easy Riders, I finally managed to hold my own and stay ahead of a Mercury rider, on my MZ. I felt so proud I decided I could probably handle riding for the famous Sammy. I called up Mercury and asked to speak to him.

"Hi, my name is Tizi," I said when I got through, in as firm a voice as my nerves allowed. "I'd like to ride for you."

"You sound female. We don't take females. Sorry."

He was about to hang up, so I shouted:

"I can ride-off any of your guys and I know London like the back of my hand, so you may as well give me a try."

"Come and see me tomorrow at 9 o'clock." He hung up, giving no directions and I had no idea of where the headquarters was.

I was so excited. Would I really get to be a Mercury rider?

Chapter 2

'IT HURTS' IS NO EXCUSE

The following morning, nine o'clock found me at Mercury's office in a little mews on the west side of London, near Shepherds Green. Sammy occupied the entire Mews with offices, workshops and garages. There were over 50 Suzuki 250cc bikes and nearly 20 Sherpa and Transit vans. It was an awe-inspiring sight on late evenings and early mornings when they were all temporarily present.

I knocked somewhat nervously on Sammy's door and went in with a brave face. I was determined to get this job.

"So, you're Tizi," the big man said, looking at a piece of paper with nothing but my name and the comment 'SAYS SHE CAN RIDE?' scribbled on it. He was tall and well built, with very long curly black hair. He had a round, unlined face and I reckoned he was about thirty years old. "Well, I know I said in a mad moment that I'd give you a try, and I keep my word. You can have a bike for a week, but don't expect to stay. We have had girls before. They don't ride fast enough or last a full day when the weather gets cold. When a girl falls off, they go running home to mummy expecting sympathy – we expect you to get back on a spare bike if necessary and carry on with your deliveries – and at the same speed. No excuse of 'it hurts' or 'it's broken'- if it's broken, get it fixed. If the bike's broken, we fix it. If it happens too often, you're out. Now, d'you still want to work here?"

"Yes, sir."

"OK. Go downstairs to the workshop and give them this chit – they'll give you a bike with a radio. Can you use a radio?"

"Yes, sir, they had them at Easy Riders," again the 'sir' slipped out.

"They're a bum bunch with unreliable cheap bikes. And leave out the 'sir' – I'm Sam to all here. If you're good to me, I'll be good to you in return but …" he paused, "don't expect to last the week. That's all. You can go now."

"I won't let you down."

"Life's good!" I shouted then whistled down the stairs hunting for the workshops – the place was vast.

At the workshops, I met Richard and Duncan, two of the Australian mechanics. Both were welcoming and friendly and put me a little more at ease. Both were tall and slim, Richard with short dark hair and Duncan with blond shoulder-length hair. They could see I was nervous and they chatted with me for a while as Richard kitted my bike out with a two-way radio. Richard told me not to worry about Sam.

"He comes across as frightening and threatening, but he wouldn't hurt a fly and has a heart of gold," he said, reassuringly. "He looks after all his staff and will back them in anything they do, as long as it's honest and legal. Most of the radio and telephone staff are riders who have temporally lost their driving licences. Now this bike may look old and tatty and it's been round the clock, but don't let that deceive you. This is one special bike – it was mine when I was on the road. It goes like the Devil – you'd better look after it. You'll get a new one if you work hard."

"I plan to work hard, but sounds like I won't be wanting a new bike," I answered, thinking how smart the bike looked in the orange-and-black Mercury livery. The registration UJD 72M was also to become memorable much later.

"What's the next step?"

"Go to reception, ask for a number, then get out on the road and ride like hell! Tell you what, you could have my number – it's special, but I won't be riding again; they pay me better in the workshops. Tell them Richard says you can have his 15, which should bring you luck."

I couldn't have known what terrific friends both Richard and Duncan were to become. First-class mechanics, they fixed, repaired, built and raced anything and everything.

I was duly given my number of 615, shortened to 15 in conversations, which I later discovered had not been issued since Richard was called 'Killer 15', having killed a pedestrian on a zebra crossing when his brakes failed. Maybe not the luckiest number, but everything seemed lucky to me at that stage of life. That was the reason for his loss of licence and a job in the workshops. All riders, if they lost their licences, were offered 'inside jobs': radio controlling, manning the phones, reception, anything they could do.

Needless to say, I rode as fast as I could and I rarely used a lift – only stairs, with my personal cut-off at 20 floors (running worked out faster than waiting for the average lift). I kept my sandwiches in the pocket of my newly acquired Barbour jacket. A nibble while running down the stairs or a bite at a red light would make the sandwiches last all day. If a letter was not ready, the usual 'would you care for a tea while you wait?' received my response of 'hang on a tick' as I rushed out to the radio with the expected delay. I was always given either another local pick-up or told to drop the letters on board and return within 10 minutes. We were not allowed to break for tea.

The day started at eight o'clock and finished whenever the wonderful sound of 'RTB' came over the radio It could be any time from six to eight in the evening. Sometimes it could be as late as ten o'clock, which was good news as the commission was better.

Friday arrived so quickly; it seemed I hadn't drawn breath from that first Monday. We all waited at the bottom of the stairs. The first rider to finish the last drop was the first back to base. He was also the first to go upstairs for his pay packet and the first to be issued a large can of lager – Fosters, at the insistence of Richard and Duncan. I thought this was a lovely gesture.

When my turn came I crossed my fingers and went in to Sam. I couldn't have ridden faster. There had been no pauses throughout the days, but my London knowledge was still lacking.

"Well done," said Sam. "Looks like you can stay. I'll eat my words – you're the first rider to earn commission in your first week."

"Thank you, Sam!" I cried in joy. I felt like giving the guy a hug but would never have summoned the guts. I skipped down the stairs, showing my envelope to reception, which was the pass for the can of beer. I could hardly admit to all these tough looking guys that I didn't care for beer, so I opened it and took a sip. Anything would have tasted like nectar with the mood I was in.

"Cheers," someone said, touching my can.

"Cheers," I replied enthusiastically. "Life's good!"

The chap next to me asked if I was new. I told him it was my first week. He said his name was Spock and he introduced me to Ian and Quasi. I explained I was hopeless at names and faces and asked them all to repeat their names when I saw them, until I could tell them apart.

"It's being on the same colour bikes and everyone wearing Barbour," I explained, although I had never been able to remember a name or recognise a face.

"Well you should be able to recognise me by my hair," Spock said, almost offended that I'd forget him. He had shocking long yellow locks, which looked permed, as they were so frizzy. I thought it looked disgusting on a guy, although it would have looked OK on a girl.

"You'll get to know me," said Quasi. "I'm the smallest guy here, but the best. No-one rides me off and I can earn whatever I like." Quasi was under five feet tall with blue eyes and a wiry build.

Ian had a vast mass of dark curls almost waist length, but he made no reference to it. Although he was well built he moved fast and rode fast. The three of them introduced me to Mark when he came in. Mark had a smiling face with shoulder-length black hair and intense blue eyes. He was athletic looking, as were most of the other riders. What a strange looking bunch, I thought to myself. We chatted between sips of beer. Little was I to realise these people were to become lifelong friends.

A rider called Terry came down the stairs in a foul mood. He looked undernourished with his clothes hanging loose, as though he had recently lost weight. He was cursing and saying Mercury was a lousy company. I took exception to this insult, as I was proud of my new company.

"What's the matter with you then?" I asked.

"I've been told I'm not fast enough, so I have to return my bike and get another job. They don't seem to pay much anyway – look at that for a whole week's work! Lousy bunch, they can keep their f---ing rotten bike."

"I was also worried when I went up the stairs – it's my first week here too."

"Well they obviously kept you 'cause you're a female," he retorted.

That comment hurt like heck. I had never ridden faster or worked flat out without so much as a pause or tea break for a continuous week before. My sympathy vanished.

"Maybe you don't ride fast enough."

"Well I could certainly out-ride you. You females get away with anything – you probably made eyes at the boss. You can go to hell with the rest of them.".

"OK if you think you can ride, how about getting on your bike and proving it? I'll race you down the road and back, although I'm sure you'll be able to beat a pathetic little female."

"I don't need to prove anything," he said.

"C'mon now, you don't insult the lady like that and not take up her offer to prove yourself." This comment came from Quasi. I was delighted he had backed me up.

"Her bike's probably faster than mine," said Terry.

"Mark, lend that chap yours," said Quasi. "Mark's bike is brand new – just run in with 1,000 miles on it. Tizi's riding an old heap that's been round the clock and another 60,000 miles on top."

"Of course you can have my bike," said Mark. "Just don't drop it." He parked his bike next to mine. Suddenly there were thirty people all wanting to see the outcome.

I felt excited and found I was trembling all over. I could not lose the early signs of acceptance I had just received.

"You'd better win if you want to make it here," said Quasi. "Just ignore all the traffic and keep the throttle wide open. I mean it – all the way." He showed me how to hold the handlebar grip so it would stay wide open.

As we lined up, we were told to go down Askew Road to the roundabout and back. The finish would be abeam the entrance that they'd already marked with cones.

At the signal, it felt like UJ almost reared out of the starting stalls as we set off like a 'front runner favourite', gaining a stronger lead with every few yards.

With the roundabout approaching, the only thing I concentrated on was keeping the throttle open. I heard the grating of the exhausts and felt the right footrest against the road, as I scraped round the roundabout, still flat out, with sparks flying from the metal on the road. Terry had slowed. Unable to see he had slackened off, I still rode as though possessed, missing the oncoming stream of cars by half an inch as I sped through the middle of the road.

Terry had given up trying at the roundabout. When I got off UJ, Quasi patted me on the back and said: "Thanks for not letting us down – you're one of us now." That had to be the kindest comment I'd ever had. Now I felt I belonged somewhere at last. No longer the misfit trying to do something I was not up to.

Terry came up to me with his eyes lowered. He shook my hand and said: "OK, I take back what I said. I'll never ride like that, but if that's how you've got to ride round the streets, I don't think this is a job for me."

"Well thanks." I accepted his words and felt humbled. It would have been easier if he'd sworn at me, which I was expecting.

"Are you coming down the pub with us?" Mark asked.

"Sure. Come along, Terry, I'll drop you home after, if you like."

On arrival, I insisted on buying the first round.

"No, a lady can't buy a round, that's improper," said Ian.

"Then I can't come again, if that's how you feel. Besides, it's my celebration, now a confirmed Mercury Rider!"

That went down well and Quasi put in: "Let her buy a round. She's not a lady – she's one of us now."

I could have hugged him. What a feeling of acceptance! I still didn't care for beer, but at least it didn't show.

Some good news arrived, which was that my Kawasaki was repaired. Soon I was riding all day on the company bike, with the chance to get out and go further, visiting friends on Sundays riding my beautiful Kawasaki. Saturdays I usually opted to ride for Mercury as all collections and drop offs were paid at double the wages.

As the weeks went by, I still rode flat out with no breaks – determined to continue as I had started. Week by week I learned the intricacy and maze of London's system, shortcuts and one-way streets. I would be stopped for speeding, going the wrong way down one-way streets or going through red lights, two or three times a day by motorcycle police.

An accepted routine on spotting another rider being chased by a cop was for any other Mercury rider/s to instantly join the one being pursued, swapping position regularly. Then we would all pull up and totally deny the offence. Under an orange helmet, with everyone wearing Barbour suits riding orange and black bikes, no one could tell who was who.

On one memorable occasion, I was being chased by a bike cop and slipped through a side street to my intended drop where I hopped off to deliver the package. The bike cop approached as I was running towards my bike.

"Oy, I want a word with you, lad!" he shouted.

I walked up to him with my head down while undoing my helmet and then removed it. I had waist-length hair at that time which I scrunched under the helmet when riding. I shook my head and said very quietly.

"I'm sorry, sir, have I done something wrong?"

"Err, no. Well yes. Oh what the heck, they would never believe me back at the station if I said I couldn't keep up with you on this." He pointed to his Triumph 750cc.

"That's a fine-looking bike, sir and at least it's British, to be proud of. I still can't get my own 750 Kwaker round London like I can with this little baby."

I crossed my fingers. It had worked. We chatted very briefly about the joys of small versus larger bikes around town.

"I'll let you off this time, but I'll book you next time you jump a red light or go through London at 80 miles an hour, so go slowly and stay alive."

I would have heeded his advice, but unfortunately with the two-minute unscheduled delay, I had to go even faster to make up for stopping.

I considered myself lucky not to have lost my licence. My record for being stopped was 15 times in one day and no booking for any of the offences. Taking my helmet off and eating humble pie worked a treat. I was fortunate that there were only three female dispatch riders in London in those years.

Sammy, true to his word, looked after his riders. He also knew which riders owned larger bikes. When I had worked consistently well, Sam asked if I would like to use my own bike for long-distance drops.

"This is how it works," he said. "When we have a distant or foreign drop, we get one of the riders to pick up the 'special' while you go home and swap bikes. You RTB with your bike, swap your local deliveries for the long drop and call me empty from wherever. I pay all your fuel bills and any bike parts for your own bike. I'll also have my mechanics service your own bike for you on a regular basis if you choose to join in."

This was certainly an opportunity not to be missed. That same week saw me out to Birmingham, Leeds and France with more to follow. Naturally, the pay increased with these longer trips.

One Friday evening, I was chatting with the guys and we were joined by Richard, Duncan and Mole. Although I had spoken to Mole every day, I knew him the least. He was the Number One Controller on the bikes and vans. He had a wonderful calm voice and manner, which was so welcome at the end of a day and especially when there were problems. I had heard he was a terrific race rider from Richard, Duncan, Quasi and Sam but he always talked himself down as a rider, despite having won most of the races he entered.

Lynn, Mole's girlfriend, came in to join us and I was pleased to see she drank a beer. I had spoken to Lynn on the phone many times. She was the only staff on the phones (or radio) that had not previously been a rider. Although she was very small and slender with a quiet voice, she took no nonsense from irate customers on the other end of the telephone. Like Mole, her manner on the phone was calming and reassuring to the riders. Lynn fully supported Mole race riding and had always gone to watch.

"How do you start race riding?" I asked. Richard told me to apply to join BMSCC, The British Motorcycle Sports Competitions Club, or 'Bemsy' and to start with Production Racing as there was no cc limit if I started in the novice events.

This sounded fun. I could ride my own Kawasaki – surely no one could have a faster bike? It was the only three-cylinder 750 two-stroke on the market at that time. Even the largest available street bike, the 900 Kawasaki, was no match off the start for the 750 two-stroke.

"Hey, that would be fun!" I exclaimed excitedly.

"We could tune your bike up for you," said Richard.

"I'll take you up on that! When's the first race I can enter?"

"There's one next month at Snetterton," said Duncan: "I'm going up anyway with Mole. He's riding one of Sam's tuned-up specials. I could give you a lift."

Four weeks later, on my highly tuned machine, I was signed in at the office. I signed the disclaimer, in case of sustaining damage to bike or rider. The secretary, Barbara, was very excited on meeting me. "This is a special day," she said. "You are our first female racing member."

"Then I hope I win and don't let our side down by throwing my bike away!" I answered with a laugh. "I'm only hoping it will rain."

"You must be nuts – everyone else is praying hard that it won't rain."

"I've been told the novices slow down to two miles an hour when it rains but I've been riding flat out round the streets of London almost every day in the rain."

The clouds burst as Mole's race started.

"We didn't want this," Richard said.

"Surely Mole is better off with rain?"

"No, Mole's not as current as you. He has a fabulous record on the racetrack, but he isn't in practice and the rains are just starting so the track will be slippery not wet and washed, as they will be for your race. Hey, you'd better get ready. You're on next."

I wanted to watch Mole, but needed to be at the start, on the other side of the field. Watching Mole as I rode off, I saw him gently moving up from fifth to fourth, then to third position. He was riding well and creeping into second when some idiot lost control of his bike. Ignoring the wet surface, the rider sped up into the corner and slammed straight into Mole, causing him to slide off the track into the barrier. Poor Mole, I thought – what rotten luck, but I assumed he was unhurt.

Soon my race was under orders. I got away to a brilliant start. At the halfway stage I was pleased with my position. I just had time to think how good life was, as I opened the throttle round the bend at the top where, for the previous two laps a marshal had held out an oil flag, warning of oil on the track. The flag had gone, so I assumed the oil had gone and overtook the final bike on the inside.

CRASH!

The bike slid from under me for some 200 yards. I slid 100 yards in a similar direction down the track and partway across the grass. The bike and I both stopped short of the large crowd-protecting barriers. Winded, I paused a couple of seconds, then scrambled slowly to my feet. The marshal was already giving me a helping hand.

"Are you all right? Have you got a back-up crew?"

"Yes to both," I answered proudly, pointing to the bright orange-and-black Mercury van racing toward me.

"You OK?" asked Duncan on arrival. "We were so glad to see *you* get up."

I didn't like the way he emphasised 'you'.

"How's Mole?"

"Not so good – he's gone to hospital. We'll know more tomorrow."

It sounded bad. Suddenly the atmosphere had gone.

"That's so unfair, he was almost in front when that idiot went straight into him," I said bitterly.

Richard said it was lucky there was room for two broken bikes in the van.

Duncan agreed, saying the only reason they both fitted so well was they were both in bits and pieces.

"Sam will be disappointed," I said, "and there goes Brands Hatch in a fortnight."

"Don't you worry, we'll have your bike fixed in a day or two, eh Duncan?"

"Sure, it's only superficial. Who didn't want to throw her bike away?" teased Duncan.

"Shaddup. The oil flag had gone so I thought the oil was gone."

"Tizi, wake up! You thought the oil would evaporate? Or the marshals would risk life and limb going out on a 'live track' to clear it up while a race is on?"

"I didn't have time to think of that. It was raining awfully hard. I thought the rain might have cleared it."

"If you wash your greasy dishes with cold water and no soap, please don't invite me round for a meal."

Now I did feel dumb and mean all of a sudden. I had never offered a meal or even a drink to these guys who had done so much for me. The situation had to be rectified.

"How about a party at my place to make up for my stupidity? I promise to wash the dishes with hot water and soap before you come," I suggested and they leapt at the chance.

Back at the flat, I asked Anita if she would mind a party. She said it would be perfect timing as she had a friend, Pauline, who would like to move in with us. She had got us a larger flat round the corner: it would be at the same price and still council-supplied.

The house-warming party combined with celebrating my Kwakker's return to race standard, was a success, marred only by the fact that Mole was still in hospital and had not yet recovered consciousness. Although Lynn usually worked on the phones, Sam had told her to stay with Mole as he needed her more. Sam really did have a heart of gold.

Usually there were jokes and teasing if anyone had fallen off and taken too long in finishing. A sprained or broken wrist – caused by stupidly taking a damp corner too fast – was a pathetic excuse to pack up, so no sympathy could be expected or was given.

That week, there was no teasing or joking. We all were painfully aware of the absence of Mole's freckled face and ginger locks, as he knew how to get the best from all the riders. When it was busy, he would be short, clear but rapid on the radio. When he could tell a rider was tiring, he would throw in a silly comment or joke. He was an integral part of the operation. He was still in a coma. Brian had taken over Mole's control position. Brian earned more than most of the riders, yet never exceeded 30mph. He insisted that extensive London knowledge and shortcuts were more efficient than dashing about like a madman and overshooting most of the drops, needing a U-turn back down a one-way street. Sadly, he had been nicked on a Friday evening for being over the limit.

Toward the end of the week, the atmosphere was tense. Mole had passed the limit of time unconscious to be able to awake without extensive brain damage. Should he wake now, he was likely to be a vegetable on a life-support machine and last that way for years. None of us wanted that torturous state for Mole or Lynn, so when we finally received the news on the Friday morning that he had stopped breathing we were all saddened by the news, yet also relieved.

The following day at Brands Hatch, the mood was more subdued than at Snetterton.

Duncan broke the mood by telling me I had to go out and win.

"Ride for Mole, that's the least you can do. He would want that. He would have been riding today as favourite – last week's race was to get him back into practice."

I could have hugged Duncan; he was putting into words what everyone felt.

I tried as hard as I could but didn't even manage a place, finishing fifth of about 25 starters. I just couldn't get round the corners fast enough. I decided to sharpen up my race riding and cornering. Nothing like the present, so Monday morning I put an idea into practice. Every roundabout I came to, I rode round twice, trying to get UJ lower and faster each time. After a couple of weeks, my cornering had markedly improved.

During a trip to Staines, a large empty roundabout approached. I took it badly, so went thrice more round it, until I was satisfied with both speed and angle. Unfortunately, on the final exit, I misjudged the line and slid to the opposite side of the road. Despite the complete absence of traffic earlier, just as I slid over to the wrong side of the road, a truck approached. Too late to do anything, I desperately tried to lean further to the right, out of the truck's way, but was already at the maximum banking angle.

I awoke with a policeman offering to help me onto his bike, so I could sit while waiting for the ambulance. I had parted company from UJ while the poor bike was embedded in the truck, which had stopped as soon as the driver could, but he didn't have a chance to avoid me. The kindly policeman had put his Triumph on its main stand and helped me onto it.

"What happened?" I asked dumbly, and then memories came back in a hazy blur. "How is UJ?" I asked in alarm. This puzzled the policeman.

"You had a passenger with you?"

"No my bike's called UJ."

The PC walked over to UJ and returned with a piece of metal.

"I'm afraid the front of the bike smashed into the lorry's front step. You might want to keep this." He passed me the piece of metal.

It was one half of the number plate, which had snapped with UJ on one piece and D72M on the other. Cute, I thought, putting UJ into my pocket.

"The bike looks like a write off, but it's an old one," he added as if to reassure me. He couldn't recognise a thoroughbred, so I ignored the insult to UJ.

After being treated at the hospital for head injuries, I discharged myself. I took a bus back, feeling too guilty to call Mercury for a lift. When I arrived, Sam came down and asked how I was. He was so concerned I felt even more guilt-ridden. After telling him how and why it happened, I expected him to be furious and probably charge me for the repairs to UJ.

"I think that's perfectly commendable. You are so determined to win a race; anyone will lose a bike or two practising and you've owned up, whereas a lot of people wouldn't have. You can have a new bike right now and start tomorrow morning with it. I have two new bikes which both arrived today; they are both gold, awaiting a re-spray. You can take your pick of them. Go and see the boys – they'll look after you."

I couldn't believe it. I really wanted to hug and kiss him, but I was far too shy to do more than mutter a feeble thank you.

I went to the workshop to tell Richard and Duncan that I wanted UJ back, not a new bike.

"Tizi, that's not an option," said Richard. "Look at the wreck – the frame is bent and twisted. The forks, handlebars, headlight and speakers are wrecked. Even the number plate broke in two. Two of the walnuts from your salad lunch were broken in half in the back box. No one would believe you could have survived, had the policeman not told us you were sort of coherent when the ambulance took you away."

"But everything could be replaced, surely? His engine is the main part – you've done so much to the engine," I pleaded.

"OK, what about the frame? A new frame is a new bike – different serial number."

"Surely you can straighten the frame?" I asked. I had already placed the boys on a pedestal.

"Go and ask Sam, then, if you would really prefer having UJ rebuilt, to a brand new bike," replied Richard, seeing any other response would go round in circles.

Sam agreed to have the bike rebuilt. He knew I was fond of the bike and he told me it would be done over the Christmas period; I could ride the new bike until then.

A small price to have UJ back, I felt.

Sadly, on UJ's return to service, all the handling had gone. Cornering was difficult, and even the acceleration and speed had gone. I still rode hard but no longer wiped all the others off in the 'instant burns'. I decided that, bent bike or not, I would learn to ride it.

Pulling up at a red traffic light at the same time as another bike, a 500cc Honda with Pony Express panniers, I smiled automatically at a fellow rider. The rider smiled back and we both looked twice, neither of us expecting to see another female, as we both had our hair tucked under the helmets.

"Hi, I'm Tizi."

"Hi, I'm Fran, but I can't hear a word – pull over."

Ignoring the lights we moved ahead to the side of the road and chatted, about bikes, our companies and some of our recent trips – the usual conversation. Fran was very attractive with straight fair, almost blonde, hair and a pale complexion. Although she was thin with a fine-boned frame, she clearly had no problem handling a large cumbersome bike.

"Why don't you pop round when you've finished, for a chat and something to eat?" asked Fran. "We only live around the corner from your offices, in Holland Park Avenue – you'll see the bikes outside. Dick, my boyfriend, will be there if I'm not back; he also rides for Pony but he's working on his bike today."

"Sure," I replied.

Fran was home when I arrived from the office and she introduced me to Dick who had just put his Z1 Kawasaki 900 together after servicing it. Dick was six feet tall, thin with short dark hair. I thought it was strange to take a bike apart midweek, but he explained it was leaking oil at an uneconomical rate. However, he had found and cured the problem. He asked if I had my own bike and discovered I had a smaller version of his in the two-stroke model. He suggested I brought it round at the weekend and we try each other's bikes. The three of us chatted into the small hours, whereupon Fran suggested I sleep on the couch for the couple of remaining hours before starting work.

The following Sunday found me joining Fran for a ride-out with Dick and their friend Mike. Mike rode for Swift Express and had a Ducati 860, an ugly red-and-black monster. Mike had a strange-shaped face, almost like his Ducati. We all swapped bikes. I found Fran's Honda the most difficult to get round a corner but the ugly Ducati handled like a supple ballet dancer – fast, with terrific acceleration and unbeatable round corners. Dick's Z1 was my favourite of the others, even though the handling was not as good as the Ducati. It was so quiet that I figured it would be useful round town – not attracting the police, as with my 'street-legal' racing two-stroke demon, which I loved as much for the noise as anything.

The following Friday evening, again in the pub, I was sad to hear that Quasi was returning to Canada, Spock was leaving to start up as a motorcycle engineer in a large bike shop in Chelsea, and Richard and Duncan both had job offers in Australia.

Richard, Duncan and Sam had introduced a 'Golden Pannier Award' scheme. There was one set of Mercury panniers in gold and black instead of orange and black, awarded at the end of each week to the rider who had fallen off the least. Quasi was a regular winner. I never won them. Now the backbone of the company was to be parted.

Chapter 3

THE YELLOW PERIL

That weekend, as was now becoming a habit, I chatted with Fran, Richard and Mike about the demise of the great Mercury team.

"Well the timing could not be better," said Richard. "The three of us have been approached by someone who wants to set up the biggest despatch riding company in London. Bigger than Pony Express and even bigger than Mercury."

"What's that got to do with the price of eggs?"

"Dave is the man behind the idea. He's the number one controller at Pony, so he knows all the details, the running and profit-making of the business. He wants to start with the top riders from each company, in fact just five riders with their own bikes, to begin with. No one else joining until the business expands, so there will always be enough work for everyone. The three of us have agreed and another guy called Garlick Gertie is joining and he wanted us to ask you to join the five-man team. There's a fabulous deal on offer."

"What's the fabulous deal?" I asked.

He said it was agreed that the first five would always be offered any of the long trips and always prioritised for work over other newcomers if there were a quiet patch.

Richard was to be paid to service the bikes for people that didn't want to do their own and repairs/write-offs would be rectified at company expense, as would fuel.

"Wow, that would mean I could be paid to ride my own bike, and it wouldn't matter how many times I fell off it!" I said without thinking.

"They'd stand it for a few weeks until they got your fuel bills – then they'd expect you to get a sensible four-stroke."

Already I was envisaging a Norton Commando with handling over and above any other bike, fuel consumption better than some cars and a lovely British sound to the engine.

"So I take it you could be tempted? The company is to be called Delta Dispatch, after the Delta wing aeroplane," Fran said.

"Let me chat to a few people and think it over."

There really was no other option. My racing would cease without the backup of Richard and Duncan, as they were both leaving Mercury. I asked Quasi for his opinion, and told him I may consider a more fuel-sensible Norton, should I take the position with Delta. He told me to go for it and suggested he accompany me to Coburn and Hughes, to look at a few Nortons.

Given a fair part exchange on my golden delight, I found myself riding home on a new Norton Commando 850, with Quasi on his Norton Dominator. The two Nortons sounded good together.

The following morning Fran heard the Norton arrive at Delta's new office block. "That was rapid, when did you get that beast?" he asked as she admired my new red bike.

"Yesterday."

"So what's wrong with a second-hand Norton?"

"Quasi explained that Nortons are the best, but only if you get them from the beginning, run them in properly and change the oil every 1,000 miles. A second-hand Norton will probably give more loss of time, breakdowns and trouble than any other bike. I'm about to put it to the test. Yellow Peril here is getting the best treatment he can."

"But Tizi, the bike is red. Haven't you noticed?"

"A Norton has to be yellow. The shop is spraying it this weekend for me – included in the price."

The first week with Delta, Dave was true to his word: no multi pick-ups before dropping any of the items on board. For once the 'you are going straight there, aren't you?' question could be answered honestly. Delta subsidised our pay at the end of the week.

Since starting with Delta, I had often stopped over with Fran and Richard, as it was closer to Delta's office. Fran suggested I move in with them and help toward their rent. This seemed sensible as I knew Anita had been hinting that she wanted to move flats again, but the area would not be so central for Delta. At first I thought of asking my mother if she would look after Finn, as Fran's had no grass anywhere nearby for a dog to relieve himself. However, Anita was horrified at the thought of Finn moving out as she and Finn had become very close. He enjoyed the runs and Anita appreciated his company while running. My mother didn't approve of me despatch riding as a job, but seemed to agree that I was meeting a better class of people than the racing lads. Mind you, I didn't mention any of the bike crashes to her.

"Life's good," I announced. "Anyone for a beer?"

"I've done better than that." Fran nipped out to the kitchen, returning with a bottle of fizz. "To celebrate our first week with Delta!"

The following day, Saturday, I took my Norton back to the bike shop as agreed and later collected my proper Yellow Peril, who looked terrific. Now resplendent as a racing model with clip-ons, rear sets and a small handlebar fairing – a plastic cover for the handlebars – and a little backrest in place of the second seat space, Peril was now a single seat version.

The mechanic advised me of the changes.

"This machine belongs to your husband, does it? It looks as though it's had a hard life in its first week."

"No, it's mine." The usual response was getting more boring than embarrassing.

Strangely enough, customised, the bike was a pig to handle. Slow speeds, stopping, trying to do a U-turn and parking was hard work with all the weight seeming further forward. At high speeds and long-distance riding it came into its own. Lying against a well-padded tank bag was certainly more comfortable than sitting in an armchair.

As the months passed, Dave and Delta were true to their word. More riders were employed and we still got the better trips. We did not say where we went and the other riders were not told, so there was no friction or disharmony among the newcomers and us.

At a set of red lights, a fellow Norton rider shouted 'hello' and indicated I should pull over for a brief chat, which I did. Paul was very friendly without being patronising. He encouraged me to join a British Bike Owners Club, the '69' club held weekly in the centre of London. After attending a few times, I was disappointed to see very few British bikes, the vast percentage being Japanese, but I joined, obtained their badge and attached it to my leather jacket with misguided pride.

Returning late at night from a long drop, a different Norton rider sharing the same red traffic light pointed at my new badge, and then at his badge, the 'Jailhouse Rockers' then beckoned me to follow him. Having finished work, I figured nothing ventured, nothing gained, so I followed him to the eastern edge of London, almost to where the A12 turns into a dual carriageway. The rider kept looking over his shoulder to check I followed.

He rode fast, and then turned into a small, secluded driveway, almost hidden by a narrow entrance flanked by large trees on either side. He dismounted, came toward me and introduced himself as Eddie and then told me to come and join a real club. Eddie was small and compact, with no spare flesh and gave the impression he was ready to explode with enthusiasm, even while he was talking.

"I saw that beautifully customised Norton; was staggered to see a female riding it, but couldn't take it when I saw your new 69 badge. That is one helluva pathetic club. I bet they told you it was full of British bikes? There's probably 40 or 50 members and a total of three British bikes. Besides, they don't do anything except drink tea – if you please. Come and see a *real* club. No one is allowed to enter here unless their bike is British. C'mon, meet the gang. They're a great bunch and everyone here can really ride a bike properly, not like those pansy Jap-crap riders."

How could I admit I'd only moved up from the 'Jap-crap' he was referring to, a week ago?

Wow, what a club it was! The 69 club had been a run-down rented room with plastic chairs and a tea urn with biscuits available. All the bikes were parked around the corner out of sight.

The Jailhouse had a vast parking area with a spiral staircase leading up to the clubroom. There was a pinball machine in one corner and a jukebox in another, with comfortable upholstered chairs and sofas. From the front window, the bikes were all visible below. There was a fully stocked bar, but I never noticed a kettle.

Eddie introduced me to the dozen or so people there, chatting, drinking beer or playing pinball. The jukebox played rock and roll, my favourite at the time.

"What you drinking?"

"Love a beer," I felt it necessary to answer, as everyone had a can in his or her hand.

"Have the first on the house," said a tiny, wizened, dark-skinned man who could have been any age between 50 and 100. "I'm Jack – I started this club."

Apparently, no one could ride him off: when he rode, he seemed part motorcycle. He could repair a bike puncture in less than two minutes. From three half wrecks, he had put together his own Norton which no one could beat. He claimed he was a true Romany and spoke the language that was understood by Romanies the world over.

A month after I had joined the Jailhouse, two riders came in on Hondas. When they tried to leave, they found their tyres had been slashed to ribbons and a note 'Jap Crap Not Welcome Here'. I thought that was unkind, unfair and probably illegal, but I was too pathetic to say anything. Besides I was beginning to enjoy my visits so much I didn't want to be thrown out.

After a few short weeks and quite a number of visits, I was feeling comfortable with the crowd. A stranger on a BMW came in and asked for a cup of tea. He was asked what bike he had and rather unwisely stated 'an unbeatable BMW that was leading the world in reliability for bikes'.

It was certainly the wrong place to pass that remark about anything not British. So he was forced to prove the bike was as fast and good as an outdated British one.

The BMW owner, Carl, agreed to prove his bike was the best, with a race against something British. I thought Jack was going to ride him off and looked forward to seeing the finish. I had been shown their winding course in the east end of London, outside the Jailhouse. I had even ridden it on my second visit. It was twists and turns and roundabouts without as much as fifty yards of straight road.

"Well, Carl, we'll give you an advantage – in fact a big one. We'll let you prove your bike against our new little girl, riding her new bike," said Jack. "She's one of us and has a Norton. We'd all like to see how far in front you come back. Of course, assuming you do beat her. You accept our offer, then your beers are on us all evening. Of course, if she were to beat you, it'd be the reverse, but it's only a girl, so it's really a case of how many lengths you win by."

I wanted to curl up and die. A race on the track is one thing and at Mercury it was another but not here in front of all these real tough guys, most of whom had served jail sentences, hence the club's name. I found myself shaking, this time with fear not excitement.

Carl had no option; he looked keen to start the race. Jack came out with me to my bike.

"Don't get worried, my mate," Jack said. "Those German bikes don't take the bends like a Norton. There's no stretches to open up, so you'll have no problem. I've seen you ride, just relax and enjoy it, but stay in front."

We got away neck and neck. The Norton had not got the acceleration of a 1000cc BMW, but there were a series of bends with nowhere to open the throttles, apart from round them. I shouldn't have worried. The Yellow Peril took control and nipped round the bends, surging ahead at the first hairpin. Then he leapt into the lead throughout all the corners. Three times, I'd gone past my own limit in angles – yet the Peril stayed the right side up. Three times, I'd thrown him down as Carl crept up, yet Peril wouldn't fall over. The race finished after the last bend – no straight for a fast foreign bike to overtake with a turn of speed.

The cheering was fantastic. My relief was tremendous. I was shaking uncontrollably. I needed that beer.

That had been my 'acceptance'. The 'initiation' earlier had been on my first visit, when I had gone outside to ride home. A bunch of the guys had come out to watch me get on. My poor Norton was covered in little thin almost transparent balloons. Some were blown up and tied to the bike; some were not blown up but had been pulled over the handlebar grips.

I looked at them puzzled and sighed aloud.

I took my little flick knife out of my pocket and cut the balloons off the grips, together with the ones tied to the bike. I passed the bunch to Andy, as he was the closest and asked if he wanted to chuck them for me.

"Hey those balloons, as you call them, were expensive!" someone shouted as I rode off.

There were no more practical jokes.

The Jailhouse became a very special place after a few months. I could relax with great music, great company – genuine bikers all united in their belief that British was best. I was no longer treated as a stranger or under trial. Some of the guys were married but no one brought their wives down, yet they accepted and welcomed me as if I was one of their gang.

A few of the Jailhouse bunch were discussing taking the bikes to Calais for a 10-day break.

"What's the deal?" I asked.

"Well Tony can get some real cheap ferry tickets," said Eddie. "We can take the bikes, just cruise around Calais, have a week-long party, roughing it in tents and sleeping bags. Just have a great break at a low cost. We're going on Saturday – about half a dozen of us. You in?"

"Well, sort of count me in. I'll see how much I earn – if it's a good week I'll come but if I get problems with the bike or anything, then not. Can I let you know Thursday?" Eddie's wife was coming, apparently, so it had to be fine.

My best week's work despatch riding to date netted a record of £100, so it was a 'yes' to Calais.

Chapter 4

THE WALL OF DEATH

With a packed sleeping bag, a small borrowed tent, minimum tools and spares for the Norton, I was handed my free ferry ticket.

I looked at mine: it said Dover – Ostend – Dover.

"Thought we were going to Calais?" I asked no one in particular.

"Well it's a foreign place the other side of the channel, none of us 'ave bin before and the tickets are free. You grumbling already?" quipped Paul.

"No it's fine. So when we going?"

"Now!" came the chorus and there was a sudden mad dash for the bikes. Jack was staying behind to keep the Club open.

When the ferry docked at Ostend, we were all in a mad rush to get somewhere – but no one knew where. The idea was to ride in the general direction of Germany until we were tired, then pitch the tents and find a local bar.

First off the ferry was Eddie.

"Follow me!" he shouted, then tore down the left side of the road despite all the notices that warned drivers to keep right. Just missing an oncoming car, he wanted to turn round and chase the driver for nearly killing him. Dragging him back, we explained the signs were for us too, even though we were riding bikes not driving cars. He thought only cars went on the wrong side.

We made good progress into Germany until we found a sign pointing to a camp-site, where we pitched the tents and found a bar for entertainment. On the way back to the tents later, Peril started coughing and dying. I slowed down and then the engine expired while I wondered if I would find the camp-site later. I'd been watching the bikes, not really paying attention to where we were going. I examined the bike for ages and couldn't see what was wrong, but now he'd stopped, Peril refused to start, even after over 100 energetic kicks.

"What's up?" Eddie had returned for me, bless him. He took a quick look at Peril and five minutes later found the problem to be the zener diode, which is a voltage regulator. He couldn't fix it – I would have to get another from a bike shop the following day. We had no tow-rope, but by sitting astride Peril and holding the back of Eddie's Norton, he towed me back to camp.

The following day, after having located a bike shop and the necessary spare part, Peril was fixed and we decided to tour Hamburg.

The boys all wanted to see the Red Light district. I wanted to look at bike shops but they insisted we all stuck together, so I joined them. Suddenly Andy said: "This is where we can go shopping."

"What they selling?" I asked.

"Women, you idiot," Tony answered. "Hey, you girls had better stay outside."

"Bloomin' cheek," I said. "They won't even notice I'm a female. I gotta take a look in this 'shop' as you call it. You can't sell women even in Germany – slavery went out long ago."

So I followed the lads into the strangest place I could have imagined. There were many very attractive women in nightdresses, some almost teenage and heavily made up. I vaguely wondered why women weren't allowed in. Then I saw some of the women go up to the guys and put an arm round them. It was hot inside so I decided to remove my helmet. Just as I removed it, a woman put her arm round me.

"Oy, d'you mind, I don't want a slave," I said quite loudly.

There was a complete silence and two large men came up to me and forced me out of the building, accompanied by screams from most of the girls.

"Well would you believe it," I told Jane, Eddie's wife. "There's a room full of young women in nightdresses putting their arms around total strangers and they all screamed at a female in their presence. Must be drugs they're selling."

"No, Tizi, that's a brothel – the guys only want to window shop," explained Jane.

"But your husband's in there – don't you mind?" I asked incredulously.

"No, we discussed that earlier – he'd have been teased mercilessly if he hadn't gone in." What a wonderfully understanding wife she was. My respect for her went right up.

When the lads finally came out laughing and joking, we walked back to our bikes. Andy and Tony called out: "Hang on a tick, we're just going to be a couple of minutes." They had seen two women standing separately, some 20 yards away and headed in their direction.

Eventually, Andy returned looking fairly luckless, followed by Tony who was grinning from ear to ear. He bragged he had bargained 'his lady' from 50 marks down to 10, but hadn't parted with any cash.

I thought it was wicked playing with people's emotions and livelihoods as a joke. Eddie tried to explain to me there were no emotions involved, it was purely business on the part of the women. I was relieved there was no Red Light district in England ... or at least I had no idea that there was.

The following day, Mick suggested going to the fairground. We all agreed and parked the bikes outside the Dom, which was the large fairground in central Hamburg.

The rides and attractions were all very expensive, so apart from nibbling at the food stalls, I was reluctant to part with my fuel and 'emergency breakdown' cash that may be needed for more diodes or whatever took Peril's fancy.

"Hey there's something you have got to see," shouted Eddie, excitedly. "They've got a Wall of Death with the old Indian Scout motorbikes. It's expensive – four Marks to go in – but worth every pfennig-fing."

"OK, I'll go take a look. Where do I see you guys later?"

"Anywhere around, or we'll come back to the Wall."

I hurried over excitedly. I could already hear the noise of an Indian Scout being ridden. A small well-dressed German knelt on the bike, swaying it from side to side while waving with both hands at the crowd.

Flames emitted from the exhausts of the Indian. It was the loudest bike I had ever heard. The silencers had been removed, hence the noise and flames, but it looked and sounded dramatic.

Most of the crowd had paid and gone up the tall narrow staircase to the top of the six-metre high structure.

A man was speaking into the microphone. Not knowing any German, I was more interested in watching the smaller guy, whose named I found out was Hase, with his antics on the rolling road. The rolling road consisted of two large rollers, on a platform, fore and aft, which supported the two wheels of the bike. As the bike's wheels gathered momentum, the rollers travelled faster. The bike increased speed without going anywhere.

I thought that although what he was doing looked impressive from the sound and lighting effects, it was nothing difficult as such and I really wanted to try it. I also thought that trying to ride around the Wall would be more fun than watching.

Hase stopped his Indian and got off, ready to start the show; he saw me watching and beckoned, suggesting by gestures that I paid to watch the show. He was small and wiry, dark-skinned with a handsome face. I pointed at myself and at the Wall and tried to indicate I wanted to ride. At first he thought I wanted to watch from inside but after a crazy amount of sign language, he understood and called Klaus over. Klaus was a large stocky, short guy with fair hair and a massive beer belly.

After a short discussion, Klaus escorted me down the steep ramp to the tiny area at the bottom of the Wall. The planking of three feet was a sharp rise to where it joined the vertical sides. I had expected a gentle slope to start with, like a beginner's slope, then a sharp join to the Wall proper. There were two 600cc Indian Scouts and a 24-year-old 500cc BMW, all painted bright red-and-white – fairground colours.

Hase was busy talking to the crowd, none of which I understood, then he pointed to me and the Wall; he must have been telling the crowd I was riding. This had suddenly become rather exciting. I couldn't wait for them to begin; yet the ramp was still down and no signs of it being taken up to complete the Wall. Then I saw the reason for the delay. Klaus arrived puffing, pushing a little Zundapp 250cc bike. As soon as he was down the ramp, it was swung closed with an alarming bang – all stage effects, I later discovered.

Hase took the Zundapp and Klaus got onto the BMW, also with the exhaust pipes removed, and started smoothly riding up the planking, onto the Wall and round fairly fast, with incredible noise. While Klaus started the bike, Hase had offered the Zundapp for me to sit on. So I perched on the bike while watching Klaus on the BMW.

Klaus came down and then Hase rode up the Wall on an Indian he had already started-up when Klaus had begun his ride. Hase rode an excellent, dashing, fast show, sometimes riding from top to bottom of the six-metre Wall in a mad dash, then slowing down and riding round the centre, removing his hands from the bars, and changing from sitting on the bike to kneeling on the saddle. It looked impressive. I thought there was probably a knack to riding on the Wall, although the largest problem I could foresee was traversing from the floor to the planking and from the planking back to the floor.

Hase finished his ride, made a smooth transition to the floor, propped the bike up against the pole in the centre then started what I later learned was a long 'insurance speech'. He apparently told the spectators that they were performing the most dangerous act in the world and of course, they could not obtain any kind of insurance for their wives and children. He urged the audience to show their appreciation by throwing any spare change down on the floor. He finished, then picked up a large white box with a red cross painted on it and shook it.

This resulted in a large number of coins and notes pelting or fluttering down. Hase and Klaus looked appealingly at the audience, then they both mounted an Indian each and rode the two bikes round and round, missing each other by inches, as they criss-crossed up and down, overtaking each other. The whole Wall shook and moved about considerably. I often wondered how safe the construction really was, as it was apparently erected every three or four days. However, when performing at the Dom in Hamburg, the individual fairground acts stayed for a full month.

Hase and Klaus finished to a tremendous applause, and then Hase made another short speech and pointed again at the Zundapp and me. I put my foot on the kick-start lever and looked at Hase questioningly. He nodded, so I fired up the bike and took it to the edge of the planking.

The total lack of communication was now a slight problem. I would have given a fortune for someone to tell me how to get up onto the planking in my own language. Hase was indicating to start on the planking, not take a run as I intended, drop the bike as if to lay it down, open the throttle, then ride.

It sounded so simple.

I tried, but lost it as the bike fell over. Luckily I was the other side of the Wall to both Hase and Klaus, or I would probably not have been given another try. Intent on mastering this new challenge, I kept the throttle open while I picked up the bike. I then got back on and tried again. Once more, the bike fell over before I could get on the planking.

As I fell down, my only concern was to keep the clutch in and throttle open, so the engine wouldn't quit. It worked; I rapidly remounted and tried again. This time Hase reached me before I released the clutch and tried by hand signals to show me how to conquer it. I thought I'd understood, so attempted again but the with same effect. Klaus made a sign of cutting his throat, telling me to quit. I put one finger up to show I wanted one more try. Hase called to the crowd. Even I knew they wanted me to try again, so again Hase went through hand signals of how to get up. I managed to ride round the planking and felt terrific, then fell off as I converted from the planking to the Wall.

This time Hase could see I was getting damaged. There was blood everywhere, although mainly on my hands as I had not worn gloves, having not expected the luxury of being allowed to try. He pointed at my blood to the crowd who groaned in sympathy and some people threw more money down on the floor, all shouting 'fur die machen' (for the girl).

At the same time he closed the throttle and said firmly, "nicht mehr" (no more).

After the crowd had gone, we were allowed out to the surface of the container. A helper had to undo the heavily bolted door from the outside, as the exterior of the ramp was an integral part of the Wall.

Hase and Klaus both shook my hand and said a few words that I understood very little of. When I climbed down to the ground, my group were all waiting for me. I had forgotten completely the arrangement was to meet up back at the Wall if we didn't run into each other.

"Failed miserably," I said to Eddie. "I couldn't get past the planking. It's so steep."

We returned to the camp-site and I spent the rest of the evening and night thinking about the transition from floor to planking. It had looked so easy. Hase had made it seem so simple as he had tried to explain, wordlessly, using gestures.

The following day the rest of the group were planning on going to a craft exhibition.

"Are you coming?" Jane asked.

"No, I'll just take a cruise round town, window shopping at bike shops or something." I replied. My plan was actually to return to the fairground with my new 'calculated theory' of getting from the floor to the planking to the Wall without falling off … and perhaps I might be offered a job.

I returned to the fairground and made my way to the Wall. Hase spotted me and beckoned for me to join him on the platform. Having been so pathetic the previous day, I hadn't really expected a welcome or even any form of recognition.

When the show was due to start Hase beckoned me down the ramp. I followed and saw 'my' little Zundapp was still lying on the floor where it had been left. Hase picked it up and offered it to me as a seat. He then took my hands and inspected them for damage. I made a dismissive gesture to which he gave a smile as if acknowledging it was past tense – forgotten. Good, no china doll treatment here, I thought and vowed not to fall off this time.

With the breathtaking rides from Hase and Klaus, I paid special attention to how they mounted the planking and the Wall – but they both made it look so easy. I thought perhaps that I could just get on with it, without a fuss.

At Hase's nod, I kicked the Zundapp to life then attacked the Wall with a determination I had not felt before. The planking negotiated, the transit to the Wall had me giddy with delight. Nearly halfway up the Wall, I decided to slow down a little, so closed the throttle and promptly found myself in a heap on the floor, under the bike.

I was furious with myself; even the poor Zundapp had stalled, in disgust with me, no doubt. I got up and tried to restart it but Hase came up and stopped me. The show was over, he told me with hand signals. I misunderstood that he had no wish for me to try again, which was justifiable as the poor Zundapp was suffering more than my flesh, which suffered quite a few more cuts from the last arrival on the floor.

Not missing a chance, Hase held my bleeding hands to the crowd and made more pleading sounds. It was probably about how dangerous the sport was to attract more 'red cross cash' to be thrown down; and the crowd responded.

When the crowd had filed out and the ramp was raised, I thought I might as well go. I had failed. Walking down the stairs with a heavy heart, I turned around to wave goodbye. Hase saw me going and called for me to return. I walked toward him, as he spoke to Klaus, while watching me return. Klaus disappeared rapidly to the neighbouring caravan, returning with a young lady called Monique. She spoke fluent English.

Monique asked if I would stay with Klaus, Hase and his wife Sonja, and take a full-time job riding the Wall of Death.

"I could think of nothing better, but I failed so badly; why are you interested in offering me a job?" I asked in barely controllable excitement.

Monique spoke a few sentences in German to Hase and Klaus. She told me that many people want to try riding the Wall. No one succeeded after only a few attempts; the first time someone fell off they didn't usually want to get back on.

"And they told me they had to peel you off the bike when your body was bleeding everywhere," said Monique, sounding horrified. She was a beautiful, dainty woman, heavily made up and exquisitely dressed, I could no more see her trying a motorcycle on the road than building a house herself, brick by brick; but certainly not riding the Wall. I guessed she was bracketing me with one of her set of immaculate friends, rather than a type of girl more used to the outdoors.

I asked Monique if she lived with the fairground, which was a dumb question. Of course she did not, but I could take advantage while she was there and ask anything I needed to know in the next busy period of 'settling in'. Hase and Klaus would like me to move in that evening or the next morning. She would show me the caravan I would share with Veronica. When I could ride the Zundapp, I could move on to the BMW then lastly, onto the Indians. The Indians were the last available in Germany so they couldn't risk breaking them.

The fairground attractions were all independent from each other. They put bids in the previous year for the 'slots' at venues. Sometimes there would be two or three days' travel between shows with up to a week in the same place, and then on to the next venue. Hamburg was the exception when everyone congregated at the Dom for a solid month. It was a very expensive venue, but it paid the highest.

I enquired what happened in the winter. Apparently, after the arrangements for the following season were taken care of, everyone visited friends, drank coffee and relaxed after the long summer. There was plenty of spare money from the summer to last the winter; I was told I would not be laid off.

"Everything you need will be supplied – money, food clothes, and we will maintain your Norton. But ..."

"What's the 'but'?" I asked, slightly worried.

"You must learn to speak German. No one apart from me speaks English and they have no intention of trying. Or you could learn Zigeuner. That is the true gypsy language which is understood throughout the world and we are all gypsies here," she added with such pride, I couldn't help admiring her.

"You are Zigeuner, but you don't work on the fairground?"

"Being Zigeuner does not mean you are committed to life only on a fairground. I have my own work in town." I assumed her to mean Hamburg. "Zigeuner may not marry commoners – it is not allowed," she added.

It sounded as if she were trying to warn me. I vaguely wondered in which direction the warning lay.

Life seemed perfect. Now with a bilingual interpreter, I could learn with clear instructions how to master the Wall.

I asked Monique to let the others know I would go back now to the camp-site and ask my friends to return various bits of radio equipment to Delta. I would return in the morning to move into my new Home Sweet Home and meet Veronica.

"Hey Titsy, it is only a small caravan you will share with Veronica, it is not grand like the others." She pointed to the beautifully painted and immaculately maintained travelling 'gypsy homes on wheels'.

The Germans pronounce the 'z' with a 't' sound in front of the letter, which meant my name sounded horrid if I wrote it down. By pronouncing rather than spelling it, the problem was solved.

Arriving back at the campsite, I told the group I would not be returning with them as I had been offered a job. "OK, where have you been? We all reckoned you'd returned to the Wall," said Eddie.

I told them what had happened. I had been offered a job for life and it was the best thing that had ever happened to me – certainly the most exciting.

"Well, this calls for one heck of a celebration – although Jack will be sorry to lose you from the Jailhouse," said Mick. "How about doing us a grand cook-up, Jane, if we get the ingredients?"

Jane agreed, so Andy and Mick jumped on their bikes to go shopping. We were down to just a few potatoes and a couple of tins of sardines. I offered to lend Jane a hand, but she insisted I chatted with the rest of the group, as it was my last day with civilised company I would be able to understand. Eddie pointed out I might as well start counting my days left as he had heard the average lifespan of a Wall rider was three years.

The next morning was touching. The group was sorry to leave me behind. Eddie told me I'd be missed at the Club – all the Rockers had pulled their socks up, curbed their language and ridden much faster than before I had arrived, to impress me.

I was overwhelmed. I had been so happy to be accepted there and although I had noticed the language was pleasant, I had not realised it was for my benefit. So with a tinge of sadness, I rode to my new home, the fairground.

Hase invited me into his caravan and introduced me to his wife, Sonja and son, Carl. Sonja had bright red dyed hair, which she tied in a bun. Her face was heavily made up and she wore a bright red dress with a white checked apron tied around her waist. She had pale skin with fine bones and a slim frame. She looked like a gypsy doll you would expect to see in a children's book. The caravan was beautifully decorated and full of highly polished brass objects and trinkets. Deep thick pile carpets and even thicker rugs covered every room. It was similar to a painted barge, but everything was painted in the red and white of the Wall colours. All that was missing was a horse to pull the home.

I was also introduced to Klaus' wife, Claudia and to their two enormous Great Danes Zoller and Beretta, who must have been twins. I never could tell them apart. Claudia was round and cheerful with no make-up. She looked like a farmer's wife in her simple pale blue dress with a checked white apron.

There was a lovely Alsatian watchdog, Butcher, whom I was warned not to touch as he bit everyone. Then I was introduced to Veronica and shown my new home. It was a very small caravan, similar to those seen towed behind small cars every day in England on bank holidays, but it was my new home and I was happy and excited with a new life beginning. Veronica was about eighteen years old long blonde hair and beautiful finely chiselled face.

For the first few days, I struggled hard with no German vocabulary. Every time I needed a word I asked with signs and then wrote it down in my booklet which I kept in my pocket. Throughout the day and in the evenings, I learned each word. Veronica helped with my grammar, explaining the order to put the new words in each sentence.

My training commenced the following day. I was hoping Monique would be there to explain what I was trying to achieve. But I never saw her after the initial meeting. During the morning, I was told to go for a walk round the fairground with Veronica and four-year-old Carl. All the rides were free, unless there was a queue and it was busy, in which case we went to another attraction and returned later. Veronica was an *au pair* for Carl, so she took him on the baby rides or asked me to hold him while she tried some of the others.

Carl was more gutless than the average child, probably from being spoilt beyond belief. He had blue eyes, short fair hair and was somewhat tubby. He was too scared to go on any of the rides bar the gentle roundabouts, even if Veronica or I sat with him.

Although we had been told to return at 4pm, we came back a couple of hours earlier as I was hoping to have a practice before the show opened. The Wall did not come alive until 4pm during the week or 1pm. at weekends. I was surprised they did not run shows all day as the seats were always packed before they started.

The first day, Sonja called me into the main caravan for something to eat. Although all the rides were free to fairground operators, the food was not. Hamburgers, hot dogs, chips and drinks were paid for, as the ingredients cost substantially more than petrol or electricity, which was not increased for extra people on the various rides.

Sonja gave Veronica and I a generous plate of assorted sandwiches, which we ate back in the caravan. I'd noticed Sonja, Hase and Klaus were all scruffily dressed and I was relieved, having no smart clothes with me. At about 3.30pm the Wall was suddenly deserted; at 4pm Sonja arrived looking as though she had walked out of the hairdressers and a fashion show; impeccably dressed and highly made-up, wearing her red dress and apron. She was on duty at the box to take the money; I later found that she trusted no one else.

Hase and Klaus looked striking in smart, matching, maroon breeches and white shirts. Even the helpers, Oouver, Peter and Hans had smartened up from their working overalls. I went guiltily over to Sonja to try to explain I had nothing smarter than the clothes I wore. She pointed out to Hase, who shrugged as if it was unimportant. The warm-up was to take place on the rolling road. Hase got on the Indian Scout, parked on the rolling road, then changed his mind, called me and beckoned to the Indian, which he had left running. He indicated to do anything I could on the bike. He then took the microphone and started his regular 'pitch'.

Riding the Indian was novel as I had not tried a 'side valve' bike before nor a foot-operated clutch on a motorbike. It sounded terrific, with flames shooting out of the exhaust pipes, which were cut off halfway for a louder effect.

The rolling road was interesting with no feeling of speed wherever the throttle was positioned, as there was no forward movement.

I took my hands off and waved to the crowd then climbed onto the seat, kneeling as I had seen Hase do on the previous occasion. Then I sat on the bike side-saddle, which I felt most comfortable with, weaving the bike around while waving to the crowds. Hase looked apprehensive, so I gave him a wave of reassurance. He smiled and seemed happy enough so I thought I might as well stand up on the saddle.

Not such a good idea. As I lost my balance and fell off, the bike leapt off the 'road', falling over, but was retained by a giant safety chain, which prevented the bike hitting the crowd should something go wrong. The bike stalled on reaching the ground. I got up and headed for the bike, worrying that I was reducing the number of Indians in Germany to two. How would they entrust me with the Indians on the Wall?

Klaus was with the bike before I could get up. For a large man, he could really shift. With one hand he picked it up, looked it over and gave me a thumbs-up sign..

We went down the ramp as before and I attempted the Wall again with 'my' little Zundapp. A little better than earlier, but again I fell off when I tried to negotiate the floor from the planking, coming down. But at least I felt happy with getting up there.

The following days were similar with my place settled on the rolling road, although it was suggested I waved to the crowds while kneeling, sitting side-saddle but not to stand. I did not fall off the road again.

However, a few days later, the rolling road got stuck and the bike leapt off. It felt as if I was going to ride straight into the large crowd. As the front wheel went over the four feet high platform, the bike safety chain pulled the bike up sharply.

This time, I stayed put. It felt more like a horse stopping dead from a fast canter at a fence. Klaus apologised and called Peter over to grease the road to prevent a repeat performance.

The Wall itself also had a strong heavy-duty wire rope lying inside the top of the wall about 18 inches from the Wall itself as a crowd safety feature. The sides were bare wood with a large, thick, red line painted about a foot from the base of the upper surface, with white paint from the red line to the top. Above the red line were heavy metal brackets holding the wire.

Should either wheel go over the red line, it would collide with the brackets or the wire and the bike would be forced from the Wall to the ground. The option was the prospect of the bike jumping over the wall, flying off the top, being brought up short by the soft canvas of the tent … or not, as the case may be. Comfortable enough for the rider and bike, but possible death to any spectator that may be watching. The red line was for the riders' safety and the wire for the crowd's safety.

Chapter 5

TURNING TWENTY-ONE

Before the Wall of Death left Hamburg, I made great friends with Butcher with whom I had no language barrier. He was not at all vicious, just misunderstood – chained up all day and night and ignored by everyone, so he naturally started barking for attention and biting anyone in sight when totally ignored. I felt a kindred spirit with Butcher. We were both out of our usual environment, but everyone was so good to me, whereas no one was good to him. I told him I would be his friend. He had understood the first time we met.

I took him for long walks every day starting with the evening after my first show. I was not allowed to take him with Veronica and Carl, in case he bit Carl. After the third walk, Butcher no longer needed a lead. He was as attached to me as I became to him.

My birthday fell during the second week at the Dom. I had mentioned it to Veronica one evening, but told no one else. On the 27th August, the day before my 21st birthday, the day was normal enough. After we had finished the last show, I was about to take a long walk with Butcher when Peter came up to me and asked, with signs, if I would like to come for a drink with Hans and Oouver. I agreed if Butcher could come, which was accepted. I asked Veronica if she would join us. She said no as the talk would be about bikes and she did not like them.

The evening started in one pub, then another and then another. Each time we went to a pub, Peter would go to the jukebox and put on a few records or just look through the list of records, get a round of beers and we would move to another pub.

At the third pub, we stayed for three rounds then, just before midnight Peter went up to the jukebox. As the clock struck midnight, the jukebox was churning out 'Happy Birthday' in German, which I thought was so good of the guys; I was deeply touched and still wonder how they knew. It was a wonderful start to my new life.

When we arrived back, Sonja gave me a delightful present – a German/ English Dictionary.

After a month at the Dom the travelling started. The next stop was Kaltenkirchen, which was a two-day journey from Hamburg. The length of journey was really for the travelling time together of the circus team and backup, as it was known. Stopping periodically to check the safety of the equipment or retying bits that tried to fall off, the journey took much more time than it would have by either bike or car.

After packing up the Wall from the time spent at the Dom, Peter and Oouver were looking at my Norton, Hase asked me whether I wanted to ride behind the truck on my bike or ride with them inside, with the Norton packed on the truck. The journey might take a few days and I would have no transport with my bike packed, but I would perhaps be more comfortable riding inside.

I chose to join the others. It was the only time for long chats, as I discovered later. I had really settled into this gypsy way of life.

The best part was the enormous honour bestowed on me from the gypsies. They treated me as one of their family and yet I was not a gypsy. They really did not integrate with the 'commoners', yet they welcomed me into their fold.

At first I thought there may be friction between me and Veronica, as they treated her like dirt, gave her very little money and expected her to work all hours of the day cleaning their caravans. She was a full-time Nanny to Carl but was never allowed to join them for meals. She had sandwiches for lunch and a bowl of stew for her evening meal. I joined her for the first couple of days, but after that I was invited into Sonja's caravan for lunch and supper.

I was not allowed to wash up or do any menial tasks as Sonja explained I was 'nur fur die Wand' (only for the Wall). Veronica washed up after their meals.

She had been told to help me learn German as soon as possible, which she did a good job of, although she told me she was embarrassed to pick me up on words and grammar as she told me in German that "it didn't seem right."

She later confided in me that she was in love with a man called Johann, who ran the Hopser (the Hopser spun round on itself while it went round, up and down). She and Johann could only meet in the late evenings after the fairground slept, as Johann was a true Zigeuner and she was a commoner, like me, so they were not allowed to become partners. Their love was just like Romeo and Juliet. Veronica even had the name Johann self-tattooed onto her arm.

When we travelled to a different venue, sometimes people had not seen the Wall before. There could be large crowds waiting to pay their money and watch the show. On other occasions when there were only a few people in the gallery, the speeches would go on for sometimes over an hour and my rolling road rides would stretch out for longer, before the show started.

Often Hase would run up at intervals to check how full the gallery was. However, if there were no more people coming and they had spun the start speeches out for as long as they could, they would always put on a show.

Kaltenkirchen was a memorable place for me. Although I still fell off every time I transited from the Wall to the floor, I was offered the BMW to try on my first ride at the new site. Admittedly I had hoped for some instruction, but even with the German I was rapidly picking up, it was still difficult to learn a 'knack' to something new with a foreign language.

I looked with awe at the 500cc BM, twice the size of my little trusty Zundapp who had taken so much battering that I had grown rather fond of it.

I was worried about how the BM would take to being dropped every ride. Klaus assured me it was tougher than the little Zundapp. It had large crash bars to protect my legs from being squashed, plus protection for the bike. I was, inwardly, a trifle concerned about my damaged left leg and the weight of the BM on it.

I had not admitted to anyone about my leg, since they probably would not have wanted any responsibility should anything have happened – like losing it, which was always a possibility. By pushing my left leg forward prior to landing on the floor, I had managed to avoid losing it, so far. I was not so sure of the BM. Part of the landing transition problem was probably due to my 'over protection' of my left leg. The Wall was always ridden anticlockwise, as also are the British ones.

Klaus was still waiting for me to mount the BM. When I hesitated, Hase told me to get on with it. So I did.

Klaus had already started it and I threw the bike at the Wall, staying upright, round the middle – I still couldn't (or wouldn't) take my hands off like Hase did. But I rode down to the planking. I rode several times round the planking as I knew I would fall off, so I kept going round the planking until Klaus shouted to get down. As I tried to get down, I fell off.

Nothing hurt. No blood either as I now wore gloves! The cylinder heads that I thought were so unsightly had stopped the bike squashing my leg. I got up beaming all over.

Hase had hoped I would be content riding the Indians on the Rolling Road, but I still wanted to try them on the Wall.

With my position firmly fixed on the Rolling Road and mainly on the Zundapp, life continued happily living with the gypsies. After five days at

Kaltenkirchen we moved on to other places. As my spoken German improved, I was able to chat to people who came up asking questions about the Wall, which happened at every show.

After the last show, wherever we had stopped, we would all immediately dismantle the Wall. Starting around 10pm., it was usually packed onto the truck by 6am or 7am. At first, when I felt tired halfway through the night, Klaus saw me slow down and asked if I was tired. I agreed I was. He gave me two little white tablets and told me to swallow them and I would not feel tired. They gave me instant energy and from then on, I had two tablets every time we finished the last show. I never discovered what they were. Klaus always gave two to Peter and Hans but I never saw Oouver take any, yet he seemed to have no problem staying awake the whole night.

When the Wall was packed and our site thoroughly cleaned and swept, we set off in the procession. The large platform truck with the Wall was driven by Hase and hitched behind this was his large caravan. Klaus followed driving his large caravan with my small one towed behind.

Either Peter or Hans drove the remaining back-up truck, with their smaller caravan hitched behind. The average pace was less than thirty miles an hour. There were always many stops before finally halting for the night when a cafe was found that had parking room for the 'train'.

On arrival at the new venue, a search began for the exact pitch before unloading commenced, then the marking out and setting-up of the Wall itself, which took three long days. Everything had to be measured, screwed together, checked, tightened and levelled at every stage, with safety being paramount. There were about twenty spirit levels in constant use at every separate stage of the construction. Looking at the solid finished product and knowing what it had to withstand, I thought it must have taken months to put up, when I had first seen it at the Dom. In fact, I had assumed everything stayed at the Dom all summer as the fairground was so vast it looked like the individual entertainments were integral.

On the way to Rendsburg, the large truck broke down. Hase tried to repair it, but the part required was not to hand. It was finally agreed to drive the remainder of the train to Rendsburg, unload everything and to leave me to look after the trucks and caravans – with Butcher to look after me. Klaus told me to sleep until they returned. They left me with a vast pile of sandwiches to last until they all returned. I took a short nap and then took Butcher for a walk, keeping the trucks visible.

I had no idea how long everyone would be, but looking at the large pile of sandwiches, decided it could be several weeks, which was good news giving me time to get closer to Butcher.

When evening came, I looked everywhere for dog food. There was nothing at all, so I figured the sandwiches must be for both of us. We ate and slept in the caravan, with much the same actions the following day. I had no idea where the nearest village or town was. I did not have my Norton, as it was packed on the truck and inaccessible until the whole lot was unloaded.

It was a few days before anyone arrived, by which time Butcher and I had finished the sandwiches. During construction of the Wall, someone asked for a sandwich. I explained I had finished them with Butcher. I thought I was going to be killed when I was met with their reaction. A dog had shared their precious meat sandwiches! I mentioned delicately there was nothing for Butcher. They said he would not have died in three days without food, but what a waste of the sandwiches, which were to last everyone during the erection of the Wall. I was then told it was unhealthy to make friends with the vicious guard dog and why did I not take a boyfriend at each venue? After all, they were there for the taking. I told them I did not care for temporary friendships and Butcher would always be here. They explained that was not the way of the circus folk and how could I talk to a dog? I carefully did not point out that Butcher and I had no language barrier.

That was the first time I understood why the English are called a nation of animal lovers – despite the horrific cruelty that some poor 'pets' in England suffer. I decided I would have to stay with the gypsies, if only for the sake of Butcher. My own dog in England, Finn, had my flatmate Anita to look after him while I was away. But Butcher had no one.

After a few more venues, while packing for another move, I realised my passport would soon need renewing. The season was coming to a close in a few weeks, so it seemed sensible to wait for the season to finish and then return to England to renew my passport. With no fixed address, although I could write home, I could not receive any letters, or news – and I missed my letters.

At the end of the season, I packed a few clothes on my Norton and prepared to return to England. Sonja asked if I had any petrol money to get home. Since Klaus had filled the Norton, I hadn't thought about spare cash but one tank wouldn't get me home. Sonja gave me 50 Marks, which was plenty to get me back. I had not been given a wage while working on the Wall, but I was treated like a family member. If I wanted anything, all I had to do was tell them the price and I was given anything I asked for. They looked after the Norton, and food was supplied. If I wanted to go round the fairground and eat anything, I was given some cash and always given enough to be able to go to a pub with the guys. If I wanted any clothes, I told them what I had seen and the price and nothing was refused, yet I never had any 'spare cash' as such.

When I wanted to go out with Veronica, I would be given whatever I asked for, for the both of us, yet Veronica was given a small wage and no tips or extras. It was almost as if I was meant to feel like a family member and Veronica a servant. I felt awkward, yet Veronica seemed happy with her life. She told me she was so lucky as she was in love.

I often thought that, with her love for Johann, she would never leave the fairground, but Johann and his Hopser rarely joined up with the fairground after Hamburg. There were so many venues to apply for on the different dates, it was not often that the same entertainments would be at the same venues. I felt I was luckier to have a trustworthy friend like Butcher than a human I would see maybe twice a year.

Sonja had suggested I dye my hair 'to be more obvious to the crowds that I was a female' and to wear some make-up – all the fairground girls had rather striking dyed hair and plenty of make-up, whereas I'd never worn it. Eventually I gave in and she dyed my hair blonde. I stayed blonde the whole time I rode with the gypsies but would not wear make-up, mainly due to the shortage of space and especially the lack of any running water at the caravan to clean off the paint.

A temporary farewell was said to all my new friends, particularly Butcher, who sensed something was happening and whined sadly and quietly. Thankfully, Veronica promised to look after him while I was away; even so, I was determined to hurry back.

The ride from Regensburg, the last stop, was uneventful while my Norton purred gently down the autobahn at 125mph. It seemed so strange to be riding forward; I found I was permanently bending to the left, to get up to a Wall that was not there. I had only ridden an Indian once off the Rolling Road, around an empty fairground before the bike was packed on the truck. Being very low, there was a false sense of speed on the Indian but I had no idea of the actual speed, as there was no speedometer. However, even flat out, it did not feel fast.

Having no windscreen, the Norton wasn't equipped for high-speed riding at the latter end of the year; so I decided to leave the autobahn and take the main roads. I still had the map, which I had come out with, but decided to go through the villages and see some of the places rather than just rush back in one day. I only needed to renew my passport, see Finn, my family and some friends and then return. By driving throughout the day and night, I should reach a ferry just as they started operation, although I had no idea of the timetables.

In hindsight, I should have stayed on the autobahn. Along a narrow lane through a sleepy village, by now very dark with a gentle drizzle, the Norton hiccupped and quietly died. "Hey Peril, you can't do this to me," I cried in vain. The engine had sounded fine earlier with no knocks or warning splutters. There was enough fuel, oil and a fresh plug to ensure a trouble-free trip. It didn't sound like a filter was clogged so I did not check it unnecessarily, but there was an ominous smell of burning. I tried bump starting, which warmed me up if nothing else, but had no effect on Peril.

Being around nine o'clock at night, there was no shop open to ask advice, help or directions to a garage and it was too early to sleep outside without a blanket, or shelter in the drizzle – which had now turned to rain. At least with the rain, Peril was unlikely to catch fire and the burning smell had gone.

Strange, I thought, how all my bikes have broken down only when it is raining, dark and/or cold. I could never recall a breakdown where one could sit in the sun while taking an engine apart or even awaiting a breakdown service in England. Even punctures seemed to join in this strange behaviour.

After knocking at a few doors, I found someone who knew where there was a bike shop 'just round the corner', which turned out to be seven kilometres away. Armed with drawn directions, I set off – pushing Peril. I found myself wishing I had not had the bike customised. Pushing a mile with ordinary handlebars would have been hard but with the low bars and my close-fitting leather jacket, I soon found I was glad of the cold weather and of the rain.

After each half mile I stopped and lay down for a little while, then pushed a bit further. When I finally made the garage, I parked the bike outside and slept soundly until awoken by the arrival of two large German guys who jointly owned the shop. They asked what I was doing there. I explained and asked if they could help as I was trying to return to England.

To my delight, one agreed to have a look straightaway. He told me he would have to rewire the entire electrical system, as the wiring had come adrift. It had been pressing against the engine and completely burnt out. I had no option, so told him to go ahead.

Soon Peril was fixed and running sweetly. I asked how much and was told it was 50 Marks. I explained I only had the 50 Marks for fuel to get home, so could he accept a cheque? He agreed until he saw an English chequebook.

"No, it is no use in this country, I need cash or a German cheque," he insisted.

"Well I suppose I could leave the bike here, hitch home and try to pick it up when I return, though I doubt I'd find this place again. Could I send you a Money Order or Travellers Cheque when I get to England?"

"No. How do we know we can trust you?" Which was a fair question.

I stood up straight, looked him in the eyes and said, "Because I am English. My word is my honour and I give you my word, I will send you the money as soon as I arrive in England."

He looked at his partner, who had also been listening. They both nodded.

"Then of course, that is what you shall do," he replied and wrote out his address on the back of a card. He then suggested I had a cup of coffee or tea before I left as I still had a long way to go. After the tea, with good feelings all round, I set off trouble-free to complete the trip home, very proud to be British.

The first thing I did on reaching London was to send a Money Order to the garage, because I owed it, but also to maintain their trust in the British.

After renewing my passport in London, I visited my old flatmate Anita to see Finn, as I thought she still had him. On reaching Anita, I found she had returned Finn to my mother, as she had changed jobs and exercising him was difficult. Complete with renewed passport I rode home to a wonderful welcome from my mother and Finn.

One of the most understanding mothers I have ever come across. Although I had left home at sixteen, there was always a room kept for me, should I drop in for a visit, or to return for a while when a job had unexpectedly closed. She had only ever asked if I could send her a postcard once a month, when I was away, so she could at least know I was alive, and possibly in which country.

As I intended to stay for about a week, my sister Toto came over to say hi. Toto worked in a bank, NatWest and had worked her way up to become assistant manager. Unlike me, Toto was sensible and cautious and likely to reach an old age – many people had bets on whether I would reach forty, or possibly only thirty with the risks I often took in life.

After a lovely homecoming, I remembered the Norton's clutch had been slipping a little on the return trip so I decided to rectify the problem before returning to Germany. However, my mechanical handiwork still left a lot to be desired.

British bikes were considerably easier to work on than the new complex Japanese bikes, which were being produced in vast numbers, so I happily reset the ignition timing. Finally, after my efforts, the bike seemed to be going well. I rode to London to say hello to more friends, stopped at a petrol station on the way back and kicked the bike to start, but there was no sign of life. A few more kicks until I gave a harder kick than usual and Peril kicked back viciously, throwing me over the handlebars.

I discovered – painfully – I had set the ignition too far advanced. This was an awkward situation, being 30 miles from home with a fast-swelling ankle and a bike refusing to start. I limped over to a large rider who I saw was filling his own motorbike. I explained what had happened and asked for his help. He gave a hefty kick to which Peril responded immediately, so the journey was made home with a great deal of care not to stall en route, or I would have been stuck. The gear-changing was traumatic, not being able to move my right foot without pain. I had to bend down and use my hand for each gear change.

When I arrived home I parked outside, unable to get off unassisted. Luckily my mother came out as she wondered why I had kept the bike running for so long and then she helped me hobble inside.

Chapter 6

TURNING TRAITOR

The following morning, my mother insisted on taking me to the Outpatients at the local hospital, where x-rays showed a bad break.

So much for a rapid turnaround to get back to my gypsy family. I wrote to them explaining there would be the delay and asking for an address in six weeks' time, when I would be out of my 'heavy shoe' and able to return. My written German was abysmal but since my flatmate Anita was half German, she kindly translated it for me.

As there was no advantage in staying still, I decided to continue despatch riding until I was out of plaster. I rang Dave at Delta asking whether they would like me to return for a few weeks. He agreed and the following morning, I found a volunteer to kick Peril into life. I then rode to a local dealer and part-exchanged Peril for a new Kawasaki Z1 900cc. It was Japanese, but it had an electric start, so I could still ride without the worry of a painful kick-start.

The bike was quiet compared to any Norton. It seemed to be reliable, but the handling was terrible in comparison. Perhaps the 6mph extra speed and slightly better acceleration should have made for a faster bike, but that was only the case on motorways. I had discovered why there were so few British bikes on motorways. They took the challenging and winding A or B roads whereas the Japanese bikes with the poorer handling went fast in a straight line, on motorways.

After the first week riding the Kawasaki, I removed my crutches from the bike and hobbled into the Jailhouse Club to a warm welcome. Eddie asked how I started the Norton with my foot in a cast. I admitted the terrible truth that I had swapped the Norton, temporarily, for a Z1 until I was out of plaster. I had not planned the Z1 to be temporary when I bought it, but I already missed the handling of the Norton. Jack asked me to park the bit of 'Jap Crap' round the back when I visited or it would look as if everyone on a Japanese machine would be welcome.

"Jack, I haven't turned traitor, but there is no British bike available with an electric start. There was no option."

"That's OK, Tizi. You'll always be welcome and there's going to be a Norton Commando out soon with a button, I've heard."

Work at Delta became very busy and initially I had to convince Dave I would really be no slower delivering 'in plaster' as the crutches gave no drag when strapped to the side of the bike.

When the plaster was removed, Dave asked if I would stay the winter. I was aware despatch riders were hard to find in winter. It's not everyone's idea of fun to get on a motorbike at 8am on a freezing morning, to ride non-stop and possibly still be on the bike at 8 o'clock that night. The logic of the situation was that the gypsies would be wintering in the big house, meeting friends, chatting and drinking coffee, so I decided to stay in England. Butcher had Veronica looking after him and Finn missed me when I was away.

I had made a drastic mistake in buying the Z1 and advertised it for sale after just two months, as I missed the handling of a Norton. With 4,000 miles on the clock – accepted mileage on despatch rider bikes – I would make a heavy loss on the purchase price. Everyone told me to accept my mistake and ride it for the winter, under warranty, and sell in spring when prices usually went up.

Although I'd only owned the Z1 for a short time, I did have some adventures on it. Shortly after I bought it, my paternal grandmother died and left me £40, a large amount in those days, and I decided to use the money to ride my bike to Vienna to see the fabulous Lippizaner stallions that I'd so admired at a Horse of the Year Show I'd been to. They were worth the trip. After seeing the performance, I decided to stop and pitch my tent on a hill in the woods, but the following morning I awoke to deep snow and a bike that was frozen solid. I had to freewheel down the hill until it defrosted and agreed to start.

I'd seen another Z1 while in Vienna: there were not many around as it was the fastest bike available at the time. I gave chase and spoke to the rider at the next set of red lights. Gerhardt was amazed to see there was a woman on the bike and we started chatting, eventually going to a party together that night. I slept on his couch and the next day he said he was riding to a party a thousand kilometres away (600 miles) in north Germany and would I like to join him? It sounded fun, so I agreed. On the way, we played silly fools by riding abreast and holding hands on the autobahns at 125 miles an hour. I'd had a throttle friction put on the Z1 which meant the bike would stay at the same speed without having to hold the throttle: just another silly thing to do. I had a sleeping bag on my petrol tank so could literally lie down on the sleeping bag without having to hold the throttle. I was totally relaxed and wide-awake by the time we got to the party, whereas poor Gerhardt was almost too tired to dance.

*

Anita Costello had returned to Canada and Pauline had taken over the flat when she had been offered a pay rise on changing jobs. She now shared the flat with her brother and a friend of his. I could see I would have been in the way, so I accepted a share in a house in Hounslow with Quasi (back from Canada to work in finance in London), Ian and Alex from the Mercury days and with Olli, Quasi's girlfriend. Of course, Finn was welcome. No-one was a despatch rider any longer but everyone still had a bike, with Olli riding pillion to Quasi. Olli was a lovely person, very slim and petite and she had an olive complexion, with a lovely delicate manner. She looked so fragile anyone would take an instant desire to protect her, yet she was tougher than any female I had met. She took no nonsense from any of the lads. She cooked very well and insisted on laid tables and manners during meal-times. I struck up a permanent friendship with Olli almost on sight.

As winter tried to melt into spring a letter came from my gypsy family. Hase said the fairground season started soon and they needed me on the Wall. He also wrote that Veronica had run off with all their cash, (over 4,000 Marks), so I would have the caravan to myself. I was sorry to learn that latest piece of news, as we had got on well together, but the gypsies had treated her like a slave with no feelings of friendship and certainly no respect. I vaguely wondered about Carl but was far more worried about Butcher.

When the letter from Hase arrived I re-advertised the Z1. A reply came from a 'John Green', calling from a phone box, who said the bike sounded perfect, so he would hitch from Norwich to make a cash purchase.

John arrived without a helmet so I lent him one and offered him the pillion. He had told me his last bike was a Triumph Bonneville, but he wanted something faster for regular long journeys on motorways. As he claimed he had only ridden British bikes, I naturally liked him and trusted him automatically.

I took the bike down the quiet back road on the outskirts of Chelmsford with John pillion and then wound it up to 200kph. I could see John peering at the speedo but believe he hadn't noticed it was reading in kilometres. He tapped me on the shoulder and asked me to stop. He looked terrified and asked if he could take the bike slowly to the roundabout and back, by himself. We had barely covered five miles. Feeling sorry for him, I let him get on my bike (with my helmet) and never saw him again. I had been duped.

After dealing with the police and with my insurance company, and armed with a bridging loan from my unfailingly helpful bank, money was secured for another Norton.

Yet again I packed up, this time on my new Yellow Peril, customised from the showroom. I returned to my 'gypsy life' at the village of Gutersloh, situated in the north Rhine near Cologne, where the fairground was busy setting up for the first show of the season.

I had expected the extra space in the caravan but discovered my old one had been discarded and I had a partitioned-off portion of Klaus and Claudia's rather larger wagon. This one was higher from the ground and constructed of thicker wood, so it was correspondingly warmer. Moreover, I had a power point and a coffee maker. Although a coffee maker is a somewhat cumbersome and slow way of making tea, it was at least possible now and there was an unexpected luxury – a supply of hot water – albeit only a coffee-pot-size at a time!

The only sadness to greet me was the terribly thin and poorly state of Butcher. He was so delighted to see me, I immediately felt it had been the right decision to return. Hase and Sonja both told me Butcher had missed me. In the following weeks he soon put on weight and regained his bounce for life.

The routine had not changed, yet I still felt the same excitement for every show – it seemed as if life was a play, a feeling of being on a permanent stage. Sometimes we would be in a small village for a couple of days, or in a town for over a week.

Lippstadt was to be a long stay of three weeks. At the end of the last show during the second week, a British soldier called Olly came to ask me questions about riding on the Wall. We chatted a while then I excused myself as I was going to take Butcher for a walk; he asked if he could join us. Butcher seemed to have no objection. Olly's fair thinning hair was cut short, Army style, and he wore blue trousers with a clean starched pale blue shirt. Olly told me he had a small 175cc Harley Davidson trail bike and asked if he could try it around the Wall.

With Hase's permission, the following day Olly came with his Harley and handed it over to me. I was surprised, as I had thought he wanted to ride – but he said he would not dream of it; he just wanted to see his bike being ridden on the Wall.

Since I still fell off at the end of most of my rides, I was obviously worried that I would hurt this rather smart-looking Harley.

"And if I break it?" I asked Hase.

"Well, if you break it, we will either repair it or pay for the damage and if you find it easier to ride than the Zundapp or the BM, we will buy it for you."

I was delighted. Olly liked the idea, since he wanted to swap the Harley for a larger road bike for touring Germany in his free time.

Hase, Klaus and Olly followed me down the ramp as I rode the Harley round the small flooring space at the bottom of the Wall to get used to it. It would have been smarter to ride it down the road before trying it on the Wall, but I figured a bike was a bike and this one was light.

I rode it smoothly up the planking onto the wall, noticing straight away how light and responsive it was. It was low geared and eager to go; I could not resist the urge to wind open the throttle. That was the biggest mistake I could have made.

The bike almost flew straight to the top of the Wall. I don't even remember seeing the red line, or hitting the safety wire, after which the bike was catapulted from the wire to the flooring, six metres below, landing on top of me.

I remember awakening in a haze, wondering where I was and what I was doing in crisp white sheets.

The first person I saw, out of the one eye that could focus, was Olly. I then awoke with a start, remembering everything up to the middle of the ride. I thought perhaps I had come off trying to take the floor from the planking and had damaged the bike, otherwise why would Olly be there?

"Is your bike broken?" I asked him.

"No, it's fine. How are you? You've been right out for a few hours."

"Well that's an improvement on the last time!" He looked puzzled.

"I offered to be with you when you woke – your people at the fairground were busy preparing for the next show."

I tried to pull a bandage from my head and a German nurse rushed over and told me not to touch it. Since my right eye was covered with a patch I was worried what had happened to it. I asked her if the eye was still there and whether I be able to see with it again.

"Perhaps, later," she said.

Since apparently there were several stitches around the eye, it would stay 'perhaps' until the stitches were removed in ten days' time. But, until then, the bandages were to be left alone.

Sight is a necessity not a luxury; the prospect of losing half of it bothered me.

Naturally, I didn't want to show these concerns to a stranger, so I chatted to Olly as if nothing was wrong, although I felt desperately self-conscious, dressed only in a flimsy hospital gown. Olly volunteered to get me anything I needed from the caravan and he returned with clothes, a nightgown and washing things.

"Did you come on your bike?" I asked.

"Well no, it is a little hurt. In fact, I think it's a write-off. It had quite a fall from the top of the Wall, when you hit the piece of wire. But your people did agree they would take care of it if it was damaged, so you needn't worry about that."

Olly came to visit every day, which I thought was sweet of him. I had given him a note for Hase and Sonja, asking where they would be when I was discharged. Lippstadt would be closed at the end of the ten days. I also asked if they would reimburse Olly for the current value of the bike.

On the next visit, Olly had a letter for me. I found to my dismay they had backtracked on their word of taking care of the bike. It read:

'My dear Tizi, we are so pleased to hear you are recovering. You frightened us all when you had the fall. Our next address is at the bottom of the page. Please hurry back to us as soon as you can. We need you for the shows very badly.

We will have nothing to do with that motorbike. It is guilty. You would not be hurt if you had not ridden that bike. None of our bikes have hurt you. We will not repair it and we want nothing to do with it. But we need you badly and look forward to seeing you very soon.

With best wishes,

I could not believe it. Only now did I realise what my poor mother had tried to warn me about settling down with people from a different background who have different values. I had been brought up to keep my word and pay my debts.

"You really should stop working for them if they are not going to treat you properly," said Olly. He voiced my inner thoughts.

Having been hospitalised for seven days, I needed to get out in the fresh air. I asked if I could go outside, or even back to my caravan and was told 'no', so I discharged myself, took my handful of belongings and wondered where to go from there. I figured that I could remove the stitches from my eye myself after another three days – which I did, using nail clippers.

Added to the problems, my new Yellow Peril had broken down while we were at Lippstadt and he needed parts the gypsies didn't have. Klaus had kindly taken Peril by truck to a bike shop, where they had agreed to repair him and then he had returned to the fairground … which had now moved on. The bike was only six miles from the hospital, so I figured I could walk that distance fairly easily. I only had two carrier bags that were not heavy.

I found after three or four miles I was getting dizzy and disorientated. I kept going as the bike was my only means of transport, but soon passed out. A car stopped and a kind lady bent down to ask what had happened. She had a quick word with her husband and they helped me into their car and drove me to the bike shop. They tried on the way to dissuade me from riding but I had other worries, such as how to pay for the repairs and some fuel to go anywhere.

On arrival, Peril was ready, looking handsome and smart. Luckily the manager had insisted on cash up front for the repairs from the gypsies before he would work on the bike. A new piston had been needed. So the bike was not only ready and available, but also full of fuel.

Chapter 7

WHEREVER I HANG MY HAT

During the two weeks riding at Lippstadt, I had dropped into the local – Corkykeller – for an occasional beer and had made a good friend called Avril, who was Jamaican-born but had settled in England, then moved out to Germany. She now worked at Corky's, which was run by Corky himself and his wife Christian.

"Tizi, where've you been?" asked Avril. "You look terrible." Avril was the most beautiful girl I had ever met. She had a flawless complexion, which needed no make-up, and moved gracefully. That day she was wearing a floor-length white linen dress with short sleeves that showed off her lovely bronze colour. I explained what had happened.

"Well you obviously can't go back to them now, so what are you going to do?"

"I don't want to return to England just yet – I'd rather get a bit more fixed up. My mother doesn't even know I'm riding the Wall; only that I've joined a band of travelling gypsies and am having an absolute ball riding their exotic bikes. Right now, though, I need a job – I don't have any money. They want me to return, but they broke their word."

"Of course they want you to return until they can find another sucker, who will try to kill themselves. Let me go and talk to Christian."

Christian greeted me like an old friend. I had spoken to her only twice before as she rarely came downstairs. Christian was small and slender, with a very pale complexion and a permanent frown. She wore wide-rimmed glasses, which dwarfed her face., and her light brown hair was in a bun.

"Avril tells me you want to work; well you don't look fit enough to work but you can certainly stay here until you are able to. Come, I'll show you where the food is kept and where your bed is. You don't need to pay me anything, but when you feel you can work, just let me know as Corky could do with some extra help in the bar."

Relief flooded through me; I seemed to be blessed with luck throughout my life.

Christian showed me the food – a large saucepan of soup or stew to which fresh meat and vegetables were added daily. She also showed me my bed, sharing a room with Iona whom I had met previously and liked.

"Where are your suitcases?"

"Err, I have my belongings downstairs in two carrier bags." I felt a trifle ashamed that I had fallen into gypsy ways already.

There was something strange, almost fairy-tale about my life at the moment. I had no idea what everyone here did to earn the vast sums of money they wanted. I went down to ask Avril what she did. I had never seen her pull pints, but assumed she happened to be off duty when I came in.

She said, "I get paid to take my clothes off" as if it was the most natural thing in the world.

"You're not telling me I've just walked into a brothel, are you?" I was suddenly terrified out of my wits.

"How could you think that of me?" Avril was shocked but then explained that she danced to music while she stripped. When the dance was finished, she would put her clothes back on and then get paid to talk to the clients. But only to talk, she had stressed. There was one other girl, Katrina, who also danced, plus Iona and Donna, who I had met before who worked as hostesses; they only talked, but did not dance, so they earned considerably less. It all took place in the upstairs lounge. The clients preferred to talk to the girls that danced, so the dancers could earn more money. Their salaries were all adjusted to how much the client spent on the overpriced drinks, which were inflated by over 100 or 150 times their value. The 'champagne' was actually only cheap German Sekt with the bar's own label on it.

She warned me against accepting a pils or a glass of wine if a customer offered me a drink. I would get drunk quickly, as almost every customer would buy one for me when they ordered one.

"It is German custom here," she said.

"OK so what must I drink?" I asked, wondering what she had in mind.

"Ask Paula when she starts her shift." She finished with a twinkle in her eyes. "It's time I changed for work."

I went up to bed as Avril started work. After a deep hot bath and an early night I awoke refreshed and started the day with a bowl of stew. It seemed a strange breakfast, then I realised the girls got up around lunchtime as they worked through the evening and early hours and this would be their lunch.

I wandered down to the bar later and asked Corky if I could watch him for half an hour and perhaps pull a pils or beer to get into the swing of things.

I found pouring a pils in Germany was on a par with making tea in Japan. It must take seven minutes to pour or the pils would be returned, as the 'head' would not stand above the glass by at least two inches. Three pulls, with three waiting periods and the final top up.

I also found that when a customer sat at a table with a beer mat, the barmaid was expected to walk across to take the order. She returned with the drink and a pocket full of change if the customer should wish to 'settle up'. When they were expecting to order further drinks, either a P for a pils or a line for a beer would be marked on the beermat. Then the beermat would be reckoned after the last drink was finished.

Less than half the customers would take a table and the rest would come to the bar. There was no service charge for sitting at a table and being waited upon. However, the table customers nearly always left a tip, whereas the bar customer' usually bought a drink for the barmaid with every drink or round ordered.

The following day I met Paula, who worked on the 8am to 3pm shift. She was a conscientious worker and cleaned the bar table every spare second. She told me how to double my earnings. She said to ask for a brandy/cola when offered a drink, then to fill the glass mostly with cola and hit the brandy optic to give it the right smell.

"Then you put 20 Pfennigs in the till for the cola and two Marks in your tip box, which will add up as the customers get to know you."

From the first day I fitted into the routine and Corky soon asked me if I would like the spare shift, of 3pm. to 10pm.

I agreed to start the following day; it would also brush up my spoken German. My right eye was beginning to focus and was probably better than only having sight from the left. I was aware that the more I tried to use it, the quicker it would return to fully functioning.

The pub opened 24 hours a day, with Corky taking the worst shift from 10pm. through till 10am. Although he could take a nap during the early hours, he had to clean out the toilets, wash the floors, clean the tables and replace the beer mats.

At the end of my first week I called the solicitor I'd used after my previous accident, for a loan to repay Olly for his bike. The accident had been several years ago and I was expecting some form of insurance payout. To my delight, I was told the claim had just been settled. He agreed to send a cheque immediately for Olly.

When it arrived, I rode Peril to the army camp with the cheque, so he could now replace his bike.

When the insurance money was settled into my bank account, I decided to get a car. I didn't care for cars at all and had only got my driving licence to be able to take Finn around London legally.

I decided on a Marcos. It was the only car that impressed me. My cousin Richard Falconer had two Marcos cars: I had rented a room from him, in Chiswick, for a few weeks while between flats when I worked for Mercury. Seeing the two gleaming Marcos cars on a daily basis, I had become hooked on the idea that if I ever bought a car, it would be a Marcos or a Porsche ... but the insurance claim didn't run to a Porsche.

On my next day off I called Richard and told him I wanted to buy a Marcos. Could he find me one, as I was in Germany?

Two days later Richard found a three-litre, red Marcos with a Volvo engine and steel chassis.

"It's a good one," he said on the phone. "I am sorry it is red because I know you said you didn't want red. Do you want me to buy it for you?"

I agreed, asked Corky for two days off and took a few trains and a bus to reach Richard's house in Chiswick. An attractive sight greeted me: my new red Marcos flanked by Richard's white one in front and the black one behind.

I swapped a cheque for the various documents, as Richard made me a reviving cup of tea, and then set wheels for my return to Lippstadt.

The return drive was almost completely uneventful, except whilst trying out the top speed on an autobahn barely an hour from my destination, I inadvertently touched the brakes too firmly on the ice-covered roads which ended up in a 360-degree turn. Luckily the Marcos came into contact with nothing else and there was no other vehicle on the road. I continued the journey somewhat chastised, at a very leisurely pace.

Work resumed at Corky's and in my time off I had fun trying the Marcos. Avril would not accompany me for a ride, although I couldn't blame her, but there were a few people ready to risk my terrible driving who came on trips.

Then Avril met an English soldier called Graham from the Lippstadt barracks and romance followed, resulting in her wishing to follow Graham to England when his two-year German posting expired. The life and soul of the pub seemed to leave when Avril departed. A large number of customers no longer visited the bar, so the business was quieter all round.

Avril's letter from England arrived a few weeks later and enclosed an invitation to her wedding to Graham. I knew this was something not to be missed, and since my health was steadily improving, I decided to return to England. I could now partially see out of my right eye and use my right hand again.

I was sad as I packed. After returning to Germany with the Marcos, Peril had broken down again. I could not find the fault. Rather than get a train from

England later, sort out the problem and ride back, it would be simpler to put Peril on a train or truck to England, where I would get him fixed at home or a local garage.

I drove home to a lovely reception from Finn, my mother and John Cramphorn.

My mother had met John during Pony Club meetings, where she lent a hand wherever she could. They saw more of each other as time went by, my mother widowed and John divorced. Although it was some years before they married, I looked upon John as a stepfather fairly early on.

Over dinner, my mother asked what my plans were and suggested I should take some form of training, which could lead to a job that would lead to a career, rather than to continue riding bikes for a living. I was 22 and still young and impressionable: the world was my oyster waiting to open. However, I could see sense in what she said and agreed to think it over.

A couple of days later, while visiting my friend Steve Trimnell and his wife Laura, I mentioned I was trying to decide what to do in life. Steve suggested I learn to fly an aeroplane.

I thought flying was only for men and that it was a dumb idea.

"There's a flying club at Stapleford," said Steve. "Just down the road from here. It probably isn't expensive to take a trial lesson. Why don't we go there to see the aeroplanes?"

"Now?"

"Why not?"

We arrived at Stapleford Flying Club and Steve pointed out the tiny Cherokee aeroplanes – training aircraft. They looked like toys: I'd had no idea that you could fly these things that were smaller than a car with wings.

At the Clubhouse, we asked about prices of trial flights. It was £5 each, so Steve and I promptly booked a trial lesson each for the following week. I tried persuading Laura to book a lesson too, but she was staying firmly on the ground. Steve told me I could ride in the back of his flight. He would sit behind me on mine so we would both get double value.

As soon as we were airborne, I realised that this was where I belonged. It was like being a bird, flying wherever you wanted to go, whenever you wanted. It seemed as simple as driving a car and I felt I must get a flying licence. On enquiring about the cost, it was about £1,000. As I'd paid £1,700 for the Marcus, it seemed obvious to sell the Marcus, get a licence and then fly for a living. Further enquiries showed that I could get an instructor rating immediately after my licence, which meant I could get paid for flying. It might not be much, but I had never worried about living more than a simple lifestyle.

Chapter 8

STUNT RIDING

While staying with my mother and John, I read through some motorcycle papers and saw an advertisement for a stunt rider to join The Gerry Gooch Motorcycle Display Team. It looked fun, so I applied.

As I was determined to become a pilot and eventually fly for a living, it made sense to earn some cash: I could do this immediately by riding motorcycles. My stepfather John didn't approve of my despatch riding – he'd done some in the army when he was much younger; and my mother's only recollection of riding a motorbike was when she was riding on the back of my father's bike before they were married: they hit a tree and she got concussion, so she was not a fan of motorbikes.

I rang Gerry Gooch and was interviewed over the phone, ending with a time and date for a trial ride on one of his display bikes, which were BSA 500cc singles.

In a paddock just outside Egham in Surrey, were two yellow BSAs with odd-looking metal structures attached to them and a ramp in the centre of the field. I introduced myself to Gerry, who was a generation older than the rest of the team and was well built with no spare flesh. He wore checked trousers which reminded me of Rupert Bear.

"Oh-oh-oh, hello," he stammered. "I wondered fr-fr-fr-from your voice if you were female. Oh dear."

"Does that matter if I can ride a bike?"

"Well no, I don't-don't know, but I'd have to have a word with my-my wife and the two other riders, Mick and Dan, before I made a decision. Anyway you may as-as well try the bike and I can see if-if-if you can ride." He had a glint of hope that if I couldn't ride, then his problems would be over. Then he added. "Oh, there is no electric start on any of the-the-the bikes." He had another ray of hope.

I got on one of the bikes and gave an almighty kick, now determined to get the job regardless. The bike gave a throaty roar, which drowned the instructions. I had understood he wanted me to ride the bike around the field, set the throttle friction, and stand on the foot pegs. Taking my hands off the bars, I'd then kneel on the seat or ride side-saddle without holding the bike, then jump the ramp. Finally I was to bring the front wheel off the ground for as high and as long as I could. For the last two, I could put my hands back on the handlebars.

The only problem I encountered was jumping the ramp, as I had not jumped a bike before – only horses. I landed flat and it was somewhat painful – not that I would have admitted to feeling anything as I did not want to fuel Gerry's belief that a female could not take the same pain as a male. He came over and told me to ride at the ramp more slowly, accelerating as I came up, then to open the throttle as I approached the end of the ramp and pull the handlebars back. I tried his way; the bike cleared the ramp with feet to spare, and the landing was as soft as silk.

"Well I'll say one thing – you are de-de-determined," he said. "You can obviously ride a bike. I'll t-t-talk to my wife and the l-l-lads and give you a c-c-c-call."

After what felt like weeks, but was actually two days, the phone call came. I was accepted into the Team with Gerry Gooch. This was the biggest breakthrough in my life. I rode to Surrey, the following Saturday, for the first practice session with the full Team.

That season, the Team consisted of Gerry, Dan Hicks, Mick Maloney and me. Dan, who had ginger hair and freckles, worked as a minicab driver during the week. Mick was good-looking, slim and tanned with dark wavy hair, and I thought the best motorcycle rider … or perhaps I was biased. His star spot was to wheelie the BSA the entire length of the field, changing gear as his speed increased. Although most riders can wheelie a motorcycle, Mick was precise in when he would pick it up and when and where he would put down the front wheel.

Gerry agreed that now he had a Team sorted, he would plan the shows for the weekends ahead and let us know which venues we would be attending. He suggested another couple of practices to 'smooth out the creases' as he put it, but he already felt the routine we were developing was workable. He had worked on the choreography and sequences: all we had to do was put a 30-minute show together.

The idea was that we would enter the arena four abreast, linking arms with each other. The two riders on the outside would keep their hands out and give a wave to the spectators. The throttles were set faster than required and the speed controlled by the brakes. A lap of the field was ridden without touching the handlebars, then one rider would take a wheelie diagonally across the field.

Mick and Dan would then ride close together while I stood up behind them with one foot on each of their bikes. Halfway round the field, Gerry would appear, riding a small Monkey bike, wearing a clown's mask and waving at us. I would gesticulate frantically for him to get out of the way as it looked as though he would knock me off. At the last minute, Gerry would duck down and slip between the bikes and under my legs, while I covered my eyes in 'terror'. Gerry would then turn and ride behind us, again passing between us and under me, where I would 'fall off' the bikes and land on Gerry's shoulders. He would then continue the lap, carrying me round the field as Mick and Dan rode back to the corner.

As we reached our corner, I would jump onto a BSA and ride a lap of the field side-saddle, waving to the crowds with both hands.

As I returned, Gerry would start out riding a bike, very slowly, with a metal ladder attached vertically to the front. Dan would call out "Wait for me!", run after the bike and leapfrog onto the back, at which point Gerry picked up speed while Dan climbed to the top of the ladder, then fell gently backwards, holding onto the ladder upside-down, by his toes.

Then there were tricks with the ramp. One rider would jump the ramp and, on landing, two others would ride flat out across the landing end of the ramp, heading for each other, passing in the opposite direction very close, just as the wheel landed of the person jumping the ramp.

The shows with the Gerry Gooch Display Team started and every weekend was taken up riding at a fair, fête, horse show or any festival booking our act. The horse shows were fun as we always erected the ramp to enable us to use the water jump, when there was one. It reminded me of the days I had jumped the same obstacle on horses and I found myself 'encouraging' the bike to jump higher.

My pay for each display covered two hours of flight training.

Chapter 9

THE AFRICAN DESERT

My trial flight at Stapleford had whetted my appetite for learning to fly. I sold my Marcos sports car to pay for flight training, which I did in the afternoons, while taking a part-time job as a van delivery driver that I did in the mornings.

The Team had an exciting booking for Ndola Trade Fair in Zambia early in the season. My flying instructor, Fred Wells, suggested that when I was in Zambia, I should find a flying club and rent a local aircraft. He loved Africa and would talk for hours about the flying he had done there. He also ran his own motorcycle shop and was very interested in my stunt riding.

With a wink he suggested I say that I had my private licence and to quote my phone number for a licence number, as no-one would know the difference since I was from England. That way, he said, I could rent an aircraft solo. I was only a few hours short of taking my final flight test and felt confident, which might have been a different thing from feeling competent.

Bernie Taylor, our allocated motorcycle engineer, met us at Ndola airport to supply and modify the bikes. This was the cheaper alternative to shipping our bikes over. Bernie was a friendly man with a good depth of mechanical knowledge.

By sheer co-incidence, he had an aircraft of his own, a Tri-pacer. On hearing I could fly, Bernie suggested I fly with him after the bike practice. Once we were airborne, with me at the controls, he explained he hadn't got his licence yet so was pleased to be able to fly with me. He had assumed I was a qualified pilot: I didn't tell him otherwise or neither of us could have flown. He also introduced me to the Ndola Flying Club, where I managed to hire one of their aircraft, a Cessna 172 for a couple of flights. I had taken Fred's suggestion and given my phone number as my British pilot's licence number. It worked!

There were many problems with getting suitable bikes for the show, and further problems getting the brackets adjusted to Gerry's satisfaction. We had a variety of bikes with a Yamaha, Honda and two Suzukis. By the end of the day, they finally all started and we put together a practice-routine, modified for the slight difference in performances. Jumping the ramps proved interesting; the bikes seemed to shake out nuts and bolts on landing, which Bernie replaced each time.

The week in Ndola was perfect with lovely weather – sunshine throughout and extremely friendly organisers and people that we met. Our bike displays were well received on each day of the Trade Fair.

When I returned from Zambia, I took my general flight test, and then celebrated my Private Pilot's Licence with a large party-cum-barbecue at home in Chelmsford, where my mother and John were now living. It had been only three months from my first trial flight to getting my licence. When my parents saw the empty stable, they realised that although I was now a qualified private pilot, I had had to sell the Marcos to do it. I hastily explained that the Marcos had gone to fund the initial licence, but my immediate plans were to go to the US to 'build hours', return and take a flying instructor's rating. I could then teach flying.

The six weeks in Florida passed rapidly (there's much more about this in Part 3 of this book). I flew a rented Cessna 150 Aerobat and taught myself aerobatics, mainly falling out of each manoeuvre attempted, but from a safe height, which was fun and exciting. I also landed at 52 different airfields, including one called Naked Lady Ranch – just to be able to put it in my logbook. Flying to different places increased my experience, fun and excitement for every flight – and made sure I didn't forget how to navigate.

I returned to England and took my Instructor's rating – less than four months after I'd got my Private Pilot's Licence. I drove down to London to pick up my licence, taking all the flight test paperwork, medical report and logbook: I was issued with my licence within minutes. It was much faster in those days: now you can't get an instructor rating within a few months of learning to fly and anyway, you now need a commercial pilot's licence before being allowed to train to become an instructor.

I started instructing at Stapleford, where I had learnt to fly.

This worked out well because the stunt riding took place only in the summer, partly because there were more fairs, shows and fêtes in the summer months and also because Gerry stripped the bikes down completely during the winter months and rebuilt them to ensure they would run trouble-free for the displays.

To run old bikes like the BSAs and to expect them to never break down was a tribute to Gerry's engineering, I was impressed that in the first two years that I rode with the Team, a problem never arose with the bikes. There were many occasions where older motorcyclists would come up to our corner and say how wonderful it was to see the old BSAs being used, so it saddened all of us when, at the beginning of my third season with the bikes, Gerry informed us he was changing to Yamahas. He'd been offered the brand new Yamahas free of charge for the advertising. None of us realised that the Team was especially well heard of, even though Gerry had changed the name to Gerry Gooch and the *International* Team of Motorcycles, which sounded better, since the Zambia trip.

To be fair, there was nothing wrong with the Yamahas. They were reliable and much easier to kick-start; they had better suspension and were more comfortable to land after an especially high jump, over a ramp. The only thing missing was the nostalgia, the sound of the exhausts and the 'pride' of riding British bikes.

I had hoped to continue riding in the shows throughout the summers and did ride the first season with the Yamahas, but found fairly that all Flying Schools and most general aviation in small aircraft takes place in the summer and mainly at weekends. So it was with a heavy heart I had to leave Gerry's Team as I could no longer commit to any or every weekend for a show.

The flying instructing continued daily for many months and I amassed a few hundred hours of experience in my flying logbook. The next rung of the flying ladder was to take the CPL/IR (the Commercial Pilots Licence / Instrument rating).

I took the CPL/IR in 1980 and then spent the next few months flying a small twin-engine Seneca One for Tony Holmes, who owned Rexon Pumps. My task was to fly company personnel to any destination they chose, from the Sywell aerodrome in Northampton.

It was very different from instructing and in some aspects was more challenging as there would be different airfields or airports to find each day and the challenge of approaching in thick cloud tested my newly acquired skills of flying accurately on instruments with no outside or external visibility until the runway appeared ahead at the last minute.

Sadly, after a few short months, I was informed the aircraft was to be sold, due to the recession, so once again I was looking for work.

I spotted an advertisement in 'Wings Over Africa', a monthly flying magazine, from a company called KASAC, looking for pilots for a two-year charter contract, based in Botswana. I replied to the Box Number and after an interview and many forms to be filled in, I found myself boarding a 747 from England, during an exceptionally cold February to arrive some hours later to a heatwave in midsummer at Gaberone. You can read about my flying adventures in Botswana in Part 3 of this book, but here I want to talk about my decision to buy a horse – and a motorbike.

With my first month's salary, I bought a lovely thoroughbred ex-racehorse, which I kept at the local Pony Club five kilometres down the Bush. He was a seven-year-old light grey, standing 16 hands. and had a lovely temperament. I named him Kasac.

As the weather grew hotter, I thought about getting a motorcycle for longer trips in the heat – or just for enjoying in the Bush. I had been toying with the idea of taking part in a desert race and there was no shortage of encouragement as most of the KASAC pilots had a motorcycle and felt I should get one too. I was told to go to the local Polytechnic where I could find Haydn Beswick, who would probably help me start racing. He had won plenty of desert races and was considered the best rider in the country.

At the end of the second month, I took a trip down to the only motorcycle shop in Gaberone. I looked at the bikes on display and asked which was capable of winning the Transkalahari Desert Race.

"Well there's only one," said the 18-year-old salesman. "Obviously the Honda XR500R, since that has won with Charlie Tisson every year for four years – but you wouldn't be able to manage that much motorbike." He suggested I tried the 200cc Honda road/trial, then returned to the magazine he'd been reading when I walked into the shop.

I asked if I could take the 500 for a ride. He told me to help myself, if I could get it started and since it didn't have a key, I didn't need his help.

Fine. So I pushed it out of the shop, looked it over very carefully, and gave it the hardest kick I had ever tried. I was astonished to find it started immediately. I rode round the block, not convinced it had enough power to win a big race, then returning to the shop, I rode unexpectedly into a concealed ditch. The wheel was over half buried in the mud, but luckily the engine did not stall, so I gave it full throttle, dropped the clutch and nearly fell off with the result.

The bike responded to my brutal treatment by rearing out of the ditch and leaping into the air, then screamed up the street, only just stopping in the few yards outside the bike shop.

Totally flabbergasted by the unexpected performance and terrific feeling the 'boring looking Honda' had given me; I told the guy I would take it and asked for a clean one.

He was speechless, then muttered that he could have one ready in three days and asked how I would pay. I gave him a cheque, figuring he would wait the three days to clear the cheque anyway.

Strangely enough, when I returned three days later, my cheque was still there, not paid in. The guy was surprised to see me. I reminded him I had come for a new, clean Honda and he started muttering that it would be ready sometime soon. He then dialled a few numbers on a weird-looking telephone, chattering in a local dialect.

After hanging up, he turned his attention to me and confessed he had not thought I was seriously looking for a bike or had any intention of buying one. He explained he had not presented the cheque, as he didn't think I knew what I was doing – and he had never sold a bike to a woman. He thought he was being 'set-up' for a prank.

He apologised and agreed I could have a new, clean, road-ready Honda, which would arrive from Jo'burg the following morning.

As it was, I did not have to wait for the cheque to clear – no one bounced cheques, as everyone knew where everyone could be found. There was little robbery or violence in Botswana. That was in the early eighties and life was so good.

Although each flat was equipped with a garage, there was not room for both a bike and van, so naturally the poor new van I had recently bought had to live outside from now on.

After tracking down Haydn Beswick and explaining I had heard of his reputation with desert racing, I asked if he could brush up my riding enough to be able to race in the Trans-kalahari Desert race. Haydn had a laid-back manner and could come over as brusque, though I later learned that this was due to shyness.

Haydn told me to call him Bes and said if I wanted to ride with him, he would meet me the following morning at 6am at a roundabout by the KASAC Complex. After the ride, he would be able to tell me whether there was any point in my trying.

"You will crash several times and probably hurt yourself – are you sure you want to come?"

I nodded.

Then he added, "dress up warm – it will be cold at that hour."

It was a better outcome than I hoped. The next day was a Saturday, with no charters allocated and Kasac would be happy to be ridden later.

At 06am I arrived at the roundabout to find Bes already there.

"Follow me," he said, winding his throttle open on the short stretch of tarmac before we hit the sand of the Bush.

Bes rode fast on the road, which I had expected since there seemed to be no speed limit. Most people drove at sensible speeds, except in the evenings on the way home from a bar, when most drivers' speed increased. There were usually one or two cars in a ditch or upside-down on the wrong side of the road by the following morning. The cars were always cleared the same day, presumably to make room for more the following night.

As we touched the sand, it seemed that Bes became a maniac. I could not bear the thought of losing my chance of further tuition, so I wound my throttle wide open and followed his trail of dust. After only a few miles that felt like hundreds, I lost my bike on a corner. I picked it up and started kicking frantically, terrified that the dust would settle and I would lose the chance to follow the trail of rising sand. A few miles further on, I caught up with Bes, who was lying on a rock with his bike leaning against a tree.

"I wondered what had happened to you. Thought I'd better stop and allow you to catch up as there will be no sand for you to swallow for this part – it's just rocks, so try not to fall off, or it will be painful."

He got up, gave his 'Camel' one mighty kick and took off.

I was thankful that I had not switched the ignition off or I would have lost sight of him even before I could coax my bike to life. The rocky section was much easier than the deep sand. I noticed Bes rode his bike standing on the foot pegs, so I copied this and found it less effort to go faster as there was no feeling of being jolted or jarred as when sitting.

It was similar to riding a horse that was determined to buck its jockey out of the saddle. Try sitting down and leaning right back (movie style) and the first or second buck will probably send you flying. If you lean forward and take your weight on your knees, without your backside touching the saddle, you will probably not be dislodged.

After a few miles of fast riding over the rocks, Bes stopped briefly, turned his engine off and asked how I was doing. Although totally exhausted, I told him, "just fine – the rocky parts are so much easier than the deep sand – I could ride all day on these rocks."

Bes told me that there were no more rocks, only sand now until we arrived back, but at least I could follow his rising sand. Determined not to lose him this time, I just wound the throttle open.

I had a few near misses where I thought I had lost the bike completely but somehow I stayed attached. However after a few more miles, I fell off while trying to go round a bend in very deep sand. I managed to keep the throttle open but could see the trail was beginning to vanish. With many near misses round various dried-up riverbeds, (which contained the softest, most treacherous sand), I finally caught up with him.

This, however, was only because he stopped to wait for me, again. As I approached, Bes looked at me, sighed and took off again. Before I knew what was happening, the road came into sight – what a feeling of relief.

As we reached the road, a few yards from where we had started, I looked at my tacho and was surprised to see that we had covered 80 kilometres.

"Well done," said Bes. "You're a bit slow, but you do have hope. You'll have to get the hang of cornering in deep sand – speed up, don't slow down when there is a curve or bend ahead, or you will fall off every time. Same time, same place tomorrow?" He kicked his bike to life, not waiting for my answer.

I rode back to the complex, to a deep cold bath, after which I changed and rode the Honda to work to fly an unexpected short charter flight to Kang and back, barely a couple of hundred miles round trip, then rode to the stables to take Kasac for a leisurely ride. It was a delightful way to unwind at the end of the day.

The following Saturday after another sand trail behind Bes, and a long ride in the Bush on Kasac, I arrived home to find a note on my door from Bes, offering me breakfast after the ride finished the following morning.

There was a small postscript to the note to say eating food would be a change from swallowing his sand. That day, I rode over ten miles before taking my first fall so I was pleased with the improvement. Bes designed the route to give me a break halfway through the ride. After 50 miles of hard riding, there was an easy rocky section where I managed to keep up, stay the right way up, and recover some energy. As the rocks finished I could see in the distance deep, thick, heavy sand with twists and turns.

As he opened his throttle wide, I did the same and stayed level, on the thick sand. Suddenly riding on sand had become easy – all I needed to do was keep the throttle full and the bike would stay upright. Even round curves and bends, I kept pace with Bes. I felt I had mastered the brute beneath me and relaxed temporarily. The throttle must have slipped back a centimetre, as Bes surged ahead and I was back in the sand spray, taking a sharp bend in deep sand and CRASH.

This time, Bes stopped and rode back to me while I was still kicking the bike into life. He laid his bike down (no tree this time), ordered me to get off, climbed aboard my Honda and gave it one healthy kick. The engine roared into life immediately, so Bes handed me back my steed.

"Ride, don't cruise," he said.

Despite another fall, I finally caught up with Bes, who waited for me at the end of the sand with his engine switched off.

"Good timing," he said, looking at his watch. "Breakfast should be ready – follow me."

Bes introduced me to his wife, Christine, and their three young children: Helen, Matthew and James. Christine was very attractive, with a lovely oval face, straight brown hair and a good figure. She offered me a chair, into which I collapsed and found a feast of bacon, eggs, sausages, fried bread, mushrooms and beans; tea, coffee and fruit juice on the table.

Since arriving in Botswana I had dispensed with breakfast, usually having a slice of toast with peanut butter and jelly on a day off, or slices of Biltong (dried meat) and a flask of tea, during a flight. I told Christine it was my first cooked breakfast since I had arrived and it was terrific. She said, "if you two are going to continue your crazy rides every Sunday, why don't we make breakfast a regular routine? You must need it after the rides you are doing."

Bes told me he was building a boat in his garden – and asked if I would like to see it. Expecting a small dinghy, I was amazed to see a half-finished 45-foot yacht, which needed a ladder to climb aboard for inspection. It had a galley, six berths, toilet and a work area at the back for charts etc below deck with considerable room on the top. The workmanship was incredible, smooth teak being used for much of the craft and Formica tops in the galley.

"Are you doing this alone?" I asked. Before he had time to answer, I said, "I thought you were a welder not a carpenter?"

"Well both really, but I couldn't get a job teaching carpentry, so I teach welding and I'm building the boat to sail to England, going via America. Hey, I'll need crew, so let me know if you want to try your hand at crewing. She should be finished in two or three years. We're reckoning on taking a couple of years for the voyage. Chew it over."

I was both impressed and puzzled. After just a few rides and even less spoken words, he was now offering me the chance to crew on a two-year voyage.

"I will chew it," I said. "It'll taste better than sand."

"So you do have a sense of humour. I'm glad about that."

Chapter 10

THE TRANS-KALAHARI RACE

S unday mornings took on a routine, with a two- or three-hour hard, fast bike ride, followed by breakfast with the Beswicks; after which I would either ride Kasac or fly with a student.

After a few weeks, other people had heard about the crazy desert Sunday rides and occasionally another rider would join me and Bes – and for breakfast. Christine never seemed to mind however many people arrived.

After breakfast, the boys would chat together and I would talk with Christine, who always insisted on seeing my latest collection of bruises. She became a close friend in a short time. We discussed cookery books and Christine showed me her favourite, which she used almost exclusively since she had arrived in Botswana. She said she had been given a second copy and insisted I took it. I liked that book in particular because there was a colour photograph of each meal on the page opposite the recipe, plus all the recipes were traditional to Botswana.

After the first dinner where Christine and Bes came to my house, we soon fell into a routine. One week Christine and Bes would come to dinner with me and the following week, I would go to dinner with them. Since Christine and I had the same book we decided on which meal to ask the other person to prepare for the following week. We communicated in 'code'. She'd say 'page 32', for example, to let me know what her choice was. As far as I knew, Bes was never allowed into the secret of the 'twin books' and he did look puzzled at our numbering of the meals.

For the first time in my life, I found cooking interesting and exciting. Trying to make a meal look like the photograph, where the main or basic ingredients were not available, was fun.

The pre-breakfast rides were getting faster and less painful on a weekly basis, as I fell off less frequently. When other friends of Bes joined the rides, I felt as though I had improved significantly, since he and I would leave the others in a trail of sand, waiting at stages for the 'newcomers' to catch up. One Sunday, mentioning to Sven, one of my flying club students and a well-mannered Scandinavian, that I planned to take part in the Trans-Kalahari Desert race in a few months, he asked what the race consisted of.

I explained it was a 1,000-kilometre race spread over two days. There was a Speedway race, first, to eliminate the people who could not ride on sand, to keep the main race clear of too many fallen bikes en route. Then a timed Trial took place: that was a rocky section of vertical ascents and drops to be ridden against the clock, to determine the position on the line-up prior to the race itself. The race was then run over 500 kilometres, with the first one back to be the first on the line-up for the following day. The second day was to ride the same 500 kilometres in the reverse order, which was considerably easier as there were less fallen riders along the route.

Sven said he knew someone who would be interested in sponsoring me. I was overjoyed as there was a lot of costs involved in preparing the bike, the competition clothing needed, transport to the start of the race which was in Mafeking, plus the overnight accommodation and the fuel and spares required for the 1,000 kilometres.

Although I asked Sven on many occasions, he would never tell me who the sponsor was: they wished to remain anonymous. Having always thought that the idea was to advertise who was sponsoring you, I felt it must have been Sven but he never did admit it.

Before I knew where the time had gone, it was the day before the race. Sven and his wife Stella supported me as my ground crew. Stella was always relaxed and supportive, although whether she was supporting me in my race preparation, or supporting her husband for encouraging me, I did not discover.

They had also booked me into a hotel, which I retired to early after the race briefing. I planned to get a good night's sleep for the most important day of my life so far.

The biggest disappointment was that Bes was not taking part. He had told me that his 'Camel' was so far outdated that it would be pointless to take part. He would not enter without a good chance of winning. Had I been more sensible, I should have offered him my bike to ride and taken his Camel. He would have stood a serious chance of winning, whereas I only hoped I could win because I had one of the best mounts.

The following day was the speedway qualifier. This consisted of riding six timed laps round an oval track in deep sand. Sven insisted I should not try to go fast as I would waste energy. There was no point in risking falling off, as it was only timed to prevent anyone taking part in the race who could not ride on sand. There were no bonus points for coming first in the speedway.

I was by no means the first one home but was pleased with a respectable time.

Then it was the Timed Trials, which determined the start position on the grid. The sooner you got away, the less dust you swallowed from those ahead. Once again, Sven insisted I wasted no energy on the Trials.

"Since you would need to put all your effort in it to win the Trials, you may as well take it easy. Coming second is no different than second to last."

These were wise words that I heeded. The Trials were terrific fun, riding up and down almost vertical parts of terrain, which were all rocks and no sand.

Lined up for the big race, the Trans-Kalahari, I found myself being interviewed live on air by a TV crew. They were making a meal of the fact I was the only female entrant. The cameraman then told me (unkindly, I felt), "well as you know there was one other lady, but she broke her jaw on the Timed Trials, so we'll wish you luck."

Finally, it looked like action was about to happen. I was in a good starting position, at the signal, when all 125 bikes screamed off the line with wheelies, wheel-spin smoke and dust flying high. I concentrated on keeping the throttle wide open, knowing I had a chance of winning if I didn't fall off. The first couple of miles were straight and I was among the front-runners, then there were bends and deep sand in abundance. I probably made 75 kilometres before my first fall, in very deep sand.

I had a few more tumbles, mainly caused by catching up with other slower riders who had got ahead when I had fallen, then needing to brake as the overtaking places varied. As I had found out in the earlier training, the only way to ride in deep sand was flat out: as soon as I slowed, I fell off – simple.

After 100 kilometres was the first re-fuelling stop. Like everyone else in the race, I was wearing a litre bottle of water on my back, with a plastic straw in front of my mouth – available at any time. As I screeched to a halt, one guy opened my petrol cap, while peeling off one of my petrol vouchers from the pocket I indicated, without stopping the bike. Another guy poured petrol into the tank, while a third told me to put my head back and poured some water into my mouth and refilled my plastic bottle. While he was filling my bottle, the guy said,

"Well done lady, you're lying 25th."

The whole process took only eight or 10 seconds, then I found myself speeding along, full throttle: I still wanted to win.

Negotiating my way off the main track to avoid a fallen bike, I rode over some tree roots, which caused me to lose my balance, and I fell heavily onto hard ground with the bike on top of me. That fall was painful. The bike started, so the engine was undamaged but the handlebars were bent which meant I had to ride with one arm straight and the other bent right back. Suddenly the race had become painful and difficult, no longer fun or exciting.

Luckily, I was just 10 kilometres from the agreed meeting place with Sven. We had agreed if I needed help at that stage, I would stop; otherwise I would wave and carry on.

With relief I stopped and indicated the damage.

"No problem," he said and started pulling the bars back into shape with the assortment of tools he had brought. While he did that, I fled into the bushes for a comfort break. As I returned, Sven had just finished straightening the bars.

He saw me running toward him and said:

"But Tizi, you are hurt, you're limping. You had better stop."

I was annoyed with myself that it showed and told him I was going to continue but would love it if he would kick the bike into life. Which he kindly did and I was on my way again. However, the stop seemed to have affected me. It didn't seem possible to stiffen up in less than a minute's break but somehow the bike felt slower, the sand seemed deeper. I fell off again on taking a sharp turn, with no one in front to give me to give me an excuse. I now began to notice the heat.

Now I was sweating, sipping my water and feeling the strain. My body didn't seem to belong to me. I kept passing more riders sitting by their bikes who cheered me on. At first I was puzzled, wondering what they were doing – having a picnic during a race?

Then another fall in more deep sand and this time I found it a struggle to pick the bike up. I had seen another competitor sitting down close by when I hit the sand. Seeing my struggle, he came over and offered a hand. I couldn't understand it – he was in the same race. I said as much.

He laughed and told me he not only had two flat tyres but also was finished himself and waiting for the 'pick-up boys' who would be along collecting the non-finishers. He even offered to kick my bike over. I was amazed, delighted, and suddenly smitten. As I rode away full throttle I felt I was in love with the guy who had helped me in my hour of need. I didn't know his name and I never saw him again, but it felt good and gave me a new burst of adrenaline.

The next re-fuelling stop was equally rapid, but it didn't have the same impact as the first one, probably because I now knew what to expect.

Going over a hardened patch of sand, I hit a large rock, which I didn't notice among the loose ones and came off with a heavy landing. My helmeted head hit another large rock and I was stunned into temporary unconsciousness. Another rider coming from behind, stopped, laid his bike down and offered to help me. I was seeing double and cross with myself. There were only a few miles to go to the overnight stop. I thanked the guy, accepted his offer and asked why he had stopped when he could be in with a chance.

"It's too late to win," he said. "Might as well be last as second. You look finished yourself; you can ride back with me and I could help you if you fall again."

There seemed some sense in that. So, the race was gone: I accepted his offer.

Eventually lights came into view and the welcome bonfire for the Braai – the barbeque – was beckoning. There was a queue for food, so I lay down for a couple of minutes to relax.

I remember waking to a gentle nudge at my shoulder, from Sven. He had driven, via the tarmac roads, and was kneeling with a plateful of food for me. I felt embarrassed that I had let him down so badly. Poor Sven had organised the race for me, including the transport, the hotel and the servicing for the bike. I hadn't even been in the placing but he seemed pleased – not angry or even disappointed. He told me I should be proud to be the first woman to complete the course.

Perhaps I should remember the race as the biggest non-event in my life, or perhaps as a personal reckless record. It was the first time I had succeeded in falling off a bike 15 times in one day, with concussion on the thirteenth fall.

I felt slightly consoled when I heard there were only 18 finishers out of 125 starters. The winner was Charlie Tissan, riding an XR 500 Honda. He said that because of the drought and therefore the condition of the sand throughout the course, it was the hardest race-ride they had ever experienced.

I do freely admit that riding the Trans-Kalahari is a man's sport: the only thing that will change my views is if a woman ever wins it.

Me aged 8 in our house in Kingstown St, London

Toto (on the left) and me in Primrose Hill Road, nearby

Jumping Candy at a local show in 1964 when I was ten years old

*Riding side-saddle on my beloved horse, Spook, in 1969. Spook
(real name Silver Ghost) was a dappled grey. He loved me as
a dog loves its master and followed me everywhere*

With my sister Toto at a local gymkhana in London, aged 10

Sword of Justice was the best horse I have ever ridden and was owned by Bill Johnson. The bridle was made by me and was unique

A 'glamour' photograph of me, 1976

My stepfather John Cramphorn with my mother Anne, and Finn

Despatch riding on Kawasaki 900cc ZI in London, 1975

The Wall of Death in Germany, where I joined on a whim as a rider, eventually conquering the Wall on a Zundapp motorbike and leading a gypsy way of life

Me on my Honda XR 500 which I bought in Dalby, Australia, the same model that I used when taking part in the Trans-Kalahari Race in 1982

Stunt riding with the Gerry Gooch Motorcycle Display team in 1980

Me flying a Stampe in 2010

The bike I am riding over the water jump is a BSA 500cc. We developed a 30-minute routine and performed this at fetes, fairs, horse shows and festivals every weekend. My pay for each display covered two hours of flight training

*My dog Finn, at the controls of a PA28 Cherokee GAXTB
in which I flew my first solo in June 1977*

Greeting a client at Tiger Airways with Foxy, our first biplane, 2001

At my mother's in France in 1995, on a short break from Air UK

In France at my mother's house in 1995

Despite her ferocity, Xarra loved me enough to let me hold her without a glove

Me with Buzz, a Ferruginous Hawk

With Popeye, a snake given to me because he was apparently
too vicious to handle. He became my best friend

With my Kestrels, Xraysay and Xoisi

Chris Rollings, my partner of 20 years, holding Xraysay. I'm in the Tiger Moth biplane, part of our Tiger Airways venture that we started in Staverton, Gloucestershire, in 2002. That's my dog Aski in the background

It had always been my dream to hunt my hawk on horseback. Here I am in Scotland on Snowy with Xarra, a golden eagle, in 1997

PART 3

FLYING INTO THE UNKNOWN

Chapter 1

LOOPING THE LOOP

It was while I was clocking up my hours of flying in Florida, that the idea of aerobatics first came into my mind. My original intention had been to rent the cheapest aeroplane I could find to gain the required 90 hours' flying experience that would allow me to take my instructor's rating.

In a motel room phone book, I found a Flying Club in North Perry airfield, where a guy called Tom offered me a Cessna 150 for $10 per hour, dry. With an exchange rate of two dollars to the pound, that was £5 an hour. I agreed to book the Cessna for 90 hours over a six-week period.

It was going well until one day, arriving at North Perry, Tom said he had some good and some bad news.

"Fire away," I said impatiently, "and start with the bad news first."

"The bad news is, we've sold 'your' aeroplane."

"But you can't sell him – I've fallen in love with him," I cried in despair.

"The good news is we are going to give you another one – a brand new Cessna 150 Aerobat, for the same price. But it doesn't have any gyro instruments, if you can cope with that."

This excited me.

"An Aerobat? Does that mean I can fly aerobatics in it?"

"Sure you can. Treat it like your own for the next six weeks. Do anything you like – anything you can, or even anything you can't." Tom laughed.

I had never even flown any aerobatics, so now was a good time to start. I had been desperately keen to try even just a loop but there was nothing aerobatic at Stapleford.

After a careful inspection and tying everything securely, I took off and climbed ahead, then thought 'now where?' I looked at the chart carefully folded for North Perry and the surrounding area and picked La Belle as a nice-sounding name. Barely more than an hour away, this gave me a chance to try a loop or something en route.

149

I looked at the checklist, which gave recommended speeds for the manoeuvres the little Cessna was capable of. Then, pointing in the direction of La Belle, I set on a climb to some 6,000 feet. 'Safety in altitude' had been drummed into me from the early stages. When at last I reached the planned altitude, I tried my first loop. I lowered the nose to the recommended speed and pulled back on the control column. Geronimo! Over the top and back facing the same way, although some hundred feet lower than the starting point and at a higher airspeed.

So, I've looped the loop and I'm still alive, I thought, then climbed again and tried several more. They seemed to improve with aiming at less height-loss each time and hoping for a lower speed at the exit point.

The next manoeuvre to attempt was a roll, with disastrous results. At the inverted part, all the dust flew out of the aeroplane and the microphone fell out of its socket. I got the rudders confused and ended up tumbling tail over cockpit. Just in time, I remembered what I'd been told:

"If you're ever silly enough to try aerobatics on your own and it all goes wrong, just pull the stick full back and kick in full rudder."

So I applied full rudder, pulled the control column full back and held it. The Cessna started to spin, so I used a normal spin recovery, which I was familiar with, then checked my altimeter. The height loss was three thousand feet.

Another lesson learned. There really was safety in altitude. Had I started at the recommended altitude for aerobatics of 3,000 feet, it would have been my last flight. I figured it was time I tried to find someone to teach me.

On arrival at Le Belle, I taxied clear of the runway and parked by the fuel pumps. A guy called Marv walked up and asked if he could help. I told him some food for the aeroplane (pointing at the fuel pumps) would be good and some directions as to where to get food for myself.

Marv was a steady, elderly man with a slow drawl and a very laid-back attitude. He handed me the fuel nozzle, then a set of keys. As I started refuelling, he gave me directions to the nearest hamburger shop. He reckoned it to be out of walking distance but to help myself to the airport car, indicating an enormous half-house/half car, that I was getting accustomed to seeing in America.

I reflected on the fact that with prices less than half those in England, and with so much more space everywhere, it was no surprise to find everything bigger. Here I was in this enormous motorised contraption, about to eat an elephant-sized burger that was cheaper than a normal hamburger in England. My thoughts roamed to emigration, perhaps at a later stage in life.

Returning to the airport, Marv enquired about my length of stay at La Belle, what my intentions were and where I planned on staying. I told him for a day or two, that I was looking for someone to teach me aerobatics and that I planned on using a sleeping bag in the Cessna.

In genuine horror, Marv said, "but you cannot possibly sleep in that tiny craft – you can use a bed above the hangar over there. I'll give you the keys. I have a friend, Johnny, who is an ace at aerobatic flying. I'll give him a call and see how he is fixed."

I thought once again that life was amazing.

After a telephone call I was told Johnny could fly with me the following day if I flew to his home near the airport at Pahokee. That evening, I settled down and plotted a trip to Pahokee.

There was a knock at the door and a young woman came in, introducing herself as Jenny.

"Marv told me you were sleeping alone here. Well you can't possibly do that, so my husband Ron is cooking dinner for us all tonight and you can stay with us. Fancy expecting you to sleep in a hangar like a piece of metal – oh, that man Marv needs locking up!"

How could I explain that I was actually looking forward to a pleasant night with a lovely view of some splendid aircraft beneath? I had discovered earlier, by using a screwdriver, which was on the end of every fuel strainer, I could remove the end-plate at the tail of the Aerobat. I then had enough room to stretch out full length, while in the sleeping bag.

Jenny locked the hangar with her key, telling me she worked part-time as secretary for Marv and lived in the trailer 'over there'. 'Over there' was barely fifty yards from the edge of the airport, in a lovely area surrounded by a massive rockery and secluded from sight by towering fir trees.

"How beautiful!" I voiced my thoughts.

"I'm so glad you like it. Ron and I made this yard when we moved here. Ron's a truck-driver but he's at home for a while between jobs."

I felt it strange that Jenny and her husband thought I shouldn't sleep in an enormous hangar, when they were living in what looked like a caravan. But, on entering, I realised why they are called trailers. This one could hold a British three-bedroom-semi, with space over.

"Hi love," Jenny called to Ron "I've rescued the English Damsel in Distress. She must be starving. How's dinner, honey?"

"Any time now," said Ron, "Hi Tizi, pleased to meet you. Please feel at home. Jenny will get you a drink. You look starved – when did you last eat?"

"I'm fine. I had a slice of bull, the size of a small elephant, wrapped between two loaves of bread for lunch."

The following day, I took Jenny for a flight in the Aerobat before I planned to set course for Pahokee and Johnny. She loved the flight, even with a couple of poorly executed loops thrown in, which I could not resist.

The forecast was for hurricanes scattered around the place. Having not come across hurricanes in England, I asked someone what speed hurricanes attained; the answer given was 'about 60 knots'. Since the little Aerobat could cruise at 80 knots, I figured if I saw a hurricane in front, I could turn round and return without a problem, so I set off.

At Pahokee I looked for somewhere to tie down the Aerobat, then went in search of Johnny. No sign of the man himself, but I did find a pilot called Carl, who told me Johnny had been around earlier expecting a lady from England to meet him. With forecasted hurricanes between here and La Belle, he knew she would have more sense than to come, so he had returned home.

With the little Cessna – named Five Eight Alpha – secured, I walked down the track, hoping to come across a hamburger store at some point, preferably before anyone noticed the 'dumb English lady' had arrived despite the forecast. Not five minutes after I started walking, the heavens opened.

I looked around and saw a large truck parked up, so hurried underneath and hung onto bits of the truck as the worst storm I had ever seen passed through. I was shaken at my mistaken belief that I could have dared attempt to fly through it or away from it. The countryside seemed flattened and eerily quiet in the aftermath.

Forgetting the hamburger, I returned to the Pahokee Airport to check on the poor Aerobat. It was glistening as though it had been through a 'plane-wash' and none the worse for wear. I took my chart out and looked for somewhere to go. Pompano Beach seemed a good place, less than an hour away, so I set course for the shores of Pompano.

The sun began to set as I arrived at Pompano – or I assumed it was Pompano. There was no sign of life or habitation: not an aeroplane in sight, or even a tie-down, but just a large expanse of clear, clean salt water. As there was no one around, I took a long swim in my underwear, relaxing in the complete tranquillity of the place.

I decided to sleep under the wing of the Cessna – it would be my first night sleeping 'rough' since arriving, yet this was a paradise. For dinner, I feasted on part of a large block of cheese I had bought at the beginning of my trip, in case food was difficult to find. I ate the cheese with my legs dangling in the water. Life was good.

As the day turned to evening I realised I was not alone in liking large expanses of water. In no time, I was being eaten alive by every mosquito in Florida. I tried to hide in the Aerobat, but the mozzies were lying in wait.

There was nowhere I could run, nowhere to hide. As I tried in vain to sleep inside the Cessna, I lay scratching all night and heard the gentle buzz of all the migrant vagrants that had joined me to squat, uninvited and unwanted.

I awoke early, took another dip to freshen up, but that was painful. I had forgotten the effect of saltwater on the red blotches of mozzie-eaten flesh.

I flew to North Perry to top up on fuel and reassure the club I was still alive.

The next airfield to try was the Everglades. I had already heard tales that the Everglades were abundant in alligators. Should you come across one of them, the safest thing to do was to toss them a marshmallow, as that would apparently keep them sweet while you turned and ran. Game to try most things, I had bought a packet of marshmallows, hoping to tame an alligator, given the chance.

Chapter 2

JOYRIDES

A t Everglades I landed, cleared the runway and parked in the only space I could find. Yet again, the place seemed deserted. While I was having some more cheese for my lunch, a car drove toward me, stopped and two of the occupants got out. One asked if I would take them up for a flight. I was surprised, as this had never happened in England, but quickly realised that if I took them up on the offer and only ask for the cost of the fuel, I could fly for longer than planned on my original budget. As there would be no profit, it would not be illegal.

The lady who approached me said, "I know the price is $5 a ride but both the kids would love a go. Can you take them both?"

"Yes, but not together. Which way are you heading when you leave here?"

"We're headed for Naples."

I knew Naples was a half hour flight from the Everglades, so I suggested I took one of the lads for a half-hour trip, return then fly the second lad to Naples, where I could re-fuel. The family could follow by car and we could all meet in Naples. This was agreed, so I taxied off for the first flight, and then noticed the sign I had unwittingly parked behind: 'Joyrides, $5 per person'.

As I departed with the second 'ride', I saw a green Cessna 172 land and proceed to park in the only spot behind the sign. He was probably the legitimate 'owner' of the sign, so I was naturally concerned. I set off toward Naples and put it out of my mind. Shortly after I had taken off, the same Cessna appeared behind me and overtook without difficulty, since he had a larger engine. He seemed to be going to Naples too.

In any other situation I would have turned and aimed for a different airport, but I needed fuel – and I needed to deliver the son to Naples to reunite him with his parents.

There was no escape. I had to own up to this proprietor of the sign, who would probably want to prosecute me and take my licence away – even my passport. I felt I deserved it.

At the airport, I met the parents of the boy and could see the pilot of the green Cessna watching as they handed over the $10 bill. I refuelled and went to pay at the counter. As I turned, I faced the pilot of the green Cessna.

"Hi, how are you? What are you doing here?" he asked.

"Refuelling," I said. Wasn't it obvious? Then he asked me to join him in a hamburger.

Is this how the undercover agents work, I wondered? I agreed to a hamburger, thinking I'd rather be convicted on a full stomach than an empty one, as this could be the last meal for a while.

The Cessna's pilot was John Byers. He seemed cheerful with an innocent expression on a good-looking face with a square jaw. He had short brown hair and blue eyes. He ordered the hamburgers, adding a couple of chocolate shakes, and mentioned thinking he had seen me at Everglades. I said I'd met a couple of friends and gave one of their sons a ride here as I was coming for fuel. John then admitted he had been hoping for a spare 'ride or two'. He often rented a 172 on his days off, to blow the cobwebs away and perhaps make a few dimes extra by dropping in at Everglades. He then wondered if I owned the 'sign'.

I burst out laughing, releasing all that pent-up worry, explaining that I'd been terrified, believing I was going to be prosecuted. John saw the funny side and joined me in laughter, then asked again where I was heading next.

I told him I was building hours going nowhere in particular, not even in a straight line, but wanted to learn some aerobatics.

John said if I was going nowhere in particular with nowhere to stay, I was welcome to stay at his house, if I didn't mind a sofa. Provided I cooked the dinner, although he was happy to buy the ingredients.

'I've landed in butter', I thought, then suggested duck in an orange sauce – my favourite meal.

We went shopping and I faithfully cooked the duck.

"That was good." John sounded surprised. He told me that he was an airline pilot for Naples Airline, flying DC3 Dakotas for his full-time job.

I offered him a flight in the Aerobat on the following day.

"It may be little, but it's a whole bunch of fun," I told him. He agreed to come up, despite having said earlier that he didn't like aerobatics.

The following day, after climbing for altitude from Naples, I asked John if he wanted to try a loop. He agreed, but only if I did it. So I tried a couple of loops, which had improved from the first attempts.

"What's next?" he asked.

I explained about the roll and what had happened on the last attempt.

"Get some height then, gal," he said.

After what felt like hours, climbing to six-and-a-half thousand feet, I made another attempt to roll. This also was destined for disaster. The engine stopped when the aircraft was upside-down then tumbled like an autumn leaf. I again resorted to pulling the stick back after applying full rudder, recovered and apologised to John.

Far from being terrified, as he should have been, he enjoyed the whole thing and was laughing his head off.

"Well smarty, if it was so funny, why didn't you help me recover when it all went so badly wrong?" I was angry, more with myself for getting it wrong but especially for being laughed at.

"No need, Tizi, I thought you handled the situation very well. Anyway, what do you mean 'when it all went wrong'? I thought that was deliberate and I was highly impressed with whatever that manoeuvre was. Bet you couldn't do it again."

"All right I will."

I put the Aerobat into a climb, wondering whether I should apply the same inputs to the controls as the last time, to get the same output. With a proper Airline Pilot next to me, how could anything possibly go wrong? If it did, John would obviously take control.

"Check your belts are tight and hold on," I said, as I put the nose down to gain speed.

"No, Tizi, Stop. I was kidding. Might I suggest we fly, the right way up, back to Naples where I will offer you a picnic on the beach?"

Two hours later, we walked along the beach on a lovely warm day with a light overcast, which sheltered the sun a little. After a refreshing, long swim, followed by the picnic, John suggested a game of chess.

I agreed to a game, which went on for four-and-a-half hours, ending in a stalemate.

"After all that, no-one wins," I said. "Another?"

"But no-one lost." John pointed out the obvious. "Besides, you are getting somewhat pink. It's time to go in."

I looked down at my unprotected legs that had been clad in shorts all afternoon and agreed.

The following morning, I was indeed raw and peeled, so asked John for directions to a chemist – or, as he termed it – a drugstore.

Ten minutes later, at the drugstore, I was diagnosed as having third degree burns and was offered bandages to protect the raw and peeling flesh. I thought bandaging burns did not seem sensible, but as I walked out of the door without buying anything, an elderly lady remarked on the burns.

"It's Aloe juice you need, my dear, and you'll be fine."

I looked puzzled. She pointed out some of the plants in pots by the sides of the road.

"Take a leaf, break it and rub the sap on the sore areas, but be careful no-one sees you as those plants are protected." Then she vanished inside the store.

I picked a couple of the leaves, took them back to John's house and applied the sap to all the burned areas. The pain eased almost immediately and by the following morning, all the red areas had turned brown. As John was due to start work again, I bade farewell and decided to continue my travels.

Getting airborne, I reached for my chart and wondered, where next? I flew to Sun City, which was barely an hour away, but with some loops and plenty of rolling practice, it stretched the time somewhat longer. My rolls were progressing: at least I came out the right way up, not ending in the usual spin to sort it all out.

After landing, a woman came up and introduced herself as being Ruth Lummis. She was a small fair-haired woman with a gentle manner. She asked if I knew Sheila Scott, being from England.

I did not point out that England is quite large, since it's barely double the size of Florida. Like most budding pilots, I had heard of Sheila Scott, but had not met her. She was very famous for flying her Comanche around the world. She wrote a successful book about her flying, called Barefoot Around the World, and had been my idol for years.

Ruth invited me into her caravan by the airstrip where, after introducing me to her friend Jerrie Cobb, she made a pot of tea for us all. Jerrie was equally small with tanned skin, blonde hair and blue eyes. She had dazzling good looks, although she spoke very little and was very quiet.

We chatted about aircraft and I asked Ruth what they both did for a living. Ruth told me they were missionaries, flying down to South America and teaching the locals basic survival skills, in addition to providing them with medicines and cures for the diseases brought in by the visiting 'white man'.

"Jerrie is the flyer – I just tag along to help," Ruth added.

We chatted for a long while and eventually Ruth suggested I stay with them for the night – she even had a spare hammock. The following morning she asked me if I would like to see their house in Moorehaven. I suggested I fly her there.

On arrival, we went into her house and she offered me a glass of fresh orange juice. She asked me to find a vase behind a curtain, for some flowers she wanted to arrange, while she made the drinks.

Drawing back the curtain, I saw an incredible sight. There were more trophies than I had ever seen before – some reaching a height of three feet. I read the inscriptions: 'Awarded for the Greatest Gain in Altitude in a Piston Engined Aeroplane.' Then: 'The First Woman Successfully Trained for Space Travel.' There was also: 'The First 1,000 Miles Flown at an Average Speed of 220 Nautical Miles per Hour.' The list went on.

"Have you got the vase? Your juice is ready," Ruth called.

She had picked the oranges from their trees, squeezed the juice, added ice and claimed it had to be the freshest juice I had ever tasted. It was.

"But all those trophies." I was lost for words. "Jerrie didn't say anything – I only knew she was a pilot when you mentioned it."

"Oh, that's Jerrie. If you knew her for months, you still wouldn't know she had achieved anything. She's a private person and only interested in helping others. Her only interest is to help other people less well-off and to spread the word of God. I'll give you an example.

"She set up a foundation and bought an Islander that she uses to help the poorer people, especially the natives in South America. She helps them with education, medicines and seeds-to-plant, to help them become independent. She knew when she embarked on this that she'd be going into the deepest jungles where 'white man hasn't been' and should there be a problem with the aeroplane, she would have to fix it herself. She took an engineering degree before starting out – she's a fully qualified aeroplane engineer. Why, one time, we had to land in a small clearing with only one engine working. Enough to make the average male pilot worried, trying to land a twin-engine Islander, with one engine out, in a space barely long enough to land a single-engined Cessna.

"She then set to work cutting down a tree to use as a workbench, removed the engine and repaired it on the 'workbench'. Then continued on her way, by foot in the jungle, looking for the indigenous people who needed her help."

I was amazed. Jerrie was probably the most qualified aviation person in the world, yet when we had talked the night before, she had not given me the idea she even flew. People were still exclaiming about me being a qualified pilot because I was female, which in 1978 should not really have been something to remark on: if only they knew about Jerrie!

I asked if Ruth had the same qualifications as Jerrie.

"Oh no, Tizi. I'm a mother of two children who are only just off my hands. I have never even had the time to learn to fly. I just help Jerrie 'spread the word', help with the foundation, and organise the fundraising events. We need dollars to keep going, but Jerrie has no interest in money, or in making it – she thinks it unnecessary. So I guess you could say we make a good team."

Jerrie arrived later with their truck, having driven over with some heavier items I could not have taken in the Aerobat. During supper, she asked if I would be able to drop off some photos to Sheila Scott when I got back to England, as long as it wasn't 'out of my way'. She lived in London, so I must go there often if I was from England.

Assuring her I would love to, she gave me the photos, which I treasured carefully for the rest of my trip, as it was an introduction to one of my heroines.

I stayed a few days with Ruth and Jerrie at Moorehaven with their vast number of orange trees, flying daily either with Ruth or alone. Jerrie was always too busy to fly for fun. She was either scheduling her programme of where to go next or when and what to take.

Time to move on. I bade my farewells and headed for Immokalee, for no particular reason other than a new airport to visit.

Chapter 3

MY FIRST JUMP

After departing from Immokalee, I flew to Wauchula then to Bartow to pick up some fuel, and onwards to Arcadia.

At Arcadia, I fell into conversation with an outgoing guy called Arch Deal. He introduced himself to me as 'Arch Deal of the Falling Arches' and then told me the best feeling in your whole life was experienced when you skydive from an aeroplane. I gave him the usual remark about not seeing any sense of jumping out of a perfectly serviceable aeroplane.

"That's where you are wrong," he said. "There may be a time when you have to jump when an aeroplane is on fire or whatever. Wouldn't you rather know how to cope?"

"Well that would be different. I'm sure I could cope. Besides, what happens if your parachute doesn't open?" I asked.

"We always carry a reserve. If that doesn't open, you can still survive, if you learn how to freefall."

Arch then told me how he had experienced exactly that above Cypress Gardens in Florida at 2,000 feet. When his reserve parachute failed to open, he steered his body toward a row of bushes, which helped break his fall. Although he broke almost every bone in his body, he was jumping in displays six weeks later.

Naturally, I was intrigued. The worst thing that could ever happen had happened to this guy, yet he was here and talking to me. Of course, I had to try.

"We train every weekend, at Tampa Downs. Since that's tomorrow, why don't you come for a jump?" Arch suggested.

While we were talking, we'd been joined by Tom Ferguson, another of the Falling Arches.

"No time like the present," said Tom. "Why doesn't this young lady try her first jump today?" He stared at me with piercing blue eyes that were waiting for an answer. He was tall, dark and handsome and seemed to be daring me to try.

"Err, you haven't said the price?" I asked quietly.

"You can have the first one on us," Tom offered. "I can borrow an aeroplane here and we can go now. I'll come with you and tell you how and where to exit – we'll even throw in a crate of beer if you can land standing up." That clinched it.

Tom went through the 'first jump drills'. The canopy would open automatically, so I needed to know how to exit, check the canopy and open the reserve if nothing was open above my head by the count of five. Then, most important, which was how to land with a PLF (Parachute Landing Fall).

I interrupted him. "What's the point of showing me how to fall, when I'm going to land standing up?"

"Tizi, that was a joke," said Arch. "Not even one person in 600 with a round canopy has stood up on their first landing."

"Then give me a square canopy," I said. A square canopy was one that relied on the parachutist to pull the ripcord, whereas a round canopy opened automatically.

We went up to three thousand feet and Tom told me where to get out, and not to forget to 'land into wind.' I jumped and far too soon the canopy opened. The feeling was tremendous. I had never felt so high, or so happy. This was better than flying in a plane. I forgot about the wind direction until I was about thirty feet from the ground and heading directly downwind. I looked at the windsock, realised my mistake and started frantically pulling a toggle to turn round.

From below, Arch could see that I had only just noticed and what I was attempting to do.

"Don't try to turn.," he yelled. "Just roll over."

The result was an excessively hard landing. Arch came over asking how I was and whether I'd enjoyed it. I'd loved it, although I would not admit to any pain from my dumb mistake. I had not won my crate of beer, but a beer was the order of the day for the three of us when Tom returned.

Arch said, "Well we'll be off now. Shall we see you at Tampa Downs tomorrow?"

"Of course." The only answer possible.

The following day I flew in early to Tampa Downs, having previously visited another drugstore and been diagnosed with a badly sprained ankle. This time I bought the bandages and strapped the ankle up tightly to be able to ignore the throbbing.

At Tampa I met a girl called Cindy who had arrived for her first jump. She was extremely pretty with dark blonde long straight hair and was wildly excited, plus a trifle nervous. I told her I had tried one the day before, not mentioning my ankle. We had a long wait while other people arrived and found we had so much in common. On learning that I was sleeping in the aeroplane, she insisted I stayed in her apartment.

Cindy went first, landed into wind and had a good PLF. I went after her and very carefully landed into wind with a respectable PLF, which did not hurt at all. I was worried about aggravating the injury but the padding worked and I felt terrific.

Cindy then joined me in a long flight in the Aerobat. I let her try the controls. This was only the second time she had ever been up in a small aeroplane. I then flew a very respectable loop on Cindy's request. She asked me if she could try one: I didn't see why not. After a few attempts, always with plenty of spare altitude, Cindy had it cracked.

We landed and felt as close as sisters. I told her she just had to learn to fly: she promised somehow, some day, she would but we were never to lose touch.

From then on, it seemed natural to make Cindy's place my home base while staying in Florida. She worked fulltime as a teacher, but as this was vacation, she had plenty of free time.

The following day we went for a picnic with Cindy's friend David. The picnic venue, Antonio, was delightful; thickly wooded with streams and a river criss-crossing the paths. David, being the only man, had naturally volunteered to carry the picnic hamper that he'd brought. He looked strong enough, towering over me and Cindy. In the hamper were salmon sandwiches, salads, slices of watermelon, exotic fruits and three lobsters.

Returning home, there was a log precariously balanced across a narrow but deep part of the river that we needed to cross. David happily walked across it with the now-empty hamper basket, followed by Cindy. I stood on the log, trying to balance enough to take one step in front of another, with the water some four feet beneath. I felt terrified.

Cindy, shouting encouragement, told me the log was safe, not wobbly at all and the stream was the same one in which we had all just bathed.

I still could not cross. I felt pathetic. Cindy was embarrassed as she had been bragging to David about various things I had done in the past. David saw nothing strange about a normal girl being scared to cross a log laid over a stream and eventually Cindy and David returned over the log and we made a detour round to get back.

After a few more days with Cindy, I decided it was time to fly on – I was trying to avoid landing at the same place more than twice, other than for fuel, for no reason other than wanting to fill in more columns of my flying logbook of places visited.

We bid our farewells and I flew to Arcadia, then to Airglades and on to Tampa Downs for fuel. Walking out to 58Alpha, I saw Tom Ferguson, who said he was visiting a friend and would I be passing Zephyr Hills, as he was headed that way?

Pleased for company, we departed at last light. As we approached Zephyr Hills, it was very dark. I asked Tom if there were any lights on the airport. He told me there weren't but he often 'jumped in' and would I mind dropping him off, after which I could land further away at somewhere that had lights? Since Sun City was within my fuel range, I agreed.

I offered Tom a few loops and rolls en route. This time we came out the right way up and even facing the same direction. While I was chuffed, Tom said I was nuts to do aerobatics in a single-engined aeroplane at night.

"But you accepted."

"Haven't you noticed I'm wearing a parachute?"

As we came over Zephyr Hills, Tom jumped out, deployed his canopy and floated down, while I orbited awaiting his promised 'wave' indicating he was OK. I looked at the small hand waving a torch, some two thousand feet below and wondered which of us was nuts.

Over the next few days, I visited many more strips and airfields before the end of my 'business-holiday'. I had the necessary hours for my instructor's course but I was not looking forward to leaving the Sunshine State. I was feeling pleased with the improvement in my aerobatics and felt my flying had improved a good deal. So, with a heavy heart, I flew into North Perry to say goodbye to the wonderful bunch of people who had given me such a great start to my flying career.

In the office, Tom asked where I was going now.

"By bus to Miami International Airport, to return to the cold and rains of England, on a large jet. To sit as a passenger and think about the wild times I have enjoyed over here," I said sadly. Tom then offered me a dream.

"I don't think your vacation is over yet. How would you like to fly your Aerobat into Miami International, to meet your plane? I could come with you and fly your plane back here."

I could not believe what he was saying. No one can land a Cessna 150 at Heathrow without paying hundreds or thousands of pounds in fees. Surely, the same applied to one of the biggest airports in Florida? I was informed there were no charges to land anywhere in the States – even at the big airports.

With the bills settled, I loaded my suitcase, sleeping bag and what was left of my original elephant-sized lump of cheese into the back of 58Alpha, tied down securely. I had a memorable flight into Miami, naturally with some loops and rolls en route, then landed and taxied among the 747s and Airbuses. I kissed Tom goodbye in my excitement and he shouted,

"Well, I won my bet."

This puzzled me but he would not tell me what the bet was.

On board the 747, I asked the hostess if I could visit the cockpit: I had to ask another three times before she finally agreed I could take a quick look.

Overwhelmed by all the buttons and dials, I asked where the carburettor heat was.

The flight crew both laughed and the Captain, who insisted I called him Geoffrey, asked what had I flown. I told him about my Cessna and he asked if I would like to sit on the jump seat for part of the journey.

After breakfast – served to me in the cockpit – Geoffrey asked if I would like to try the controls and offered me the right-hand seat. I was on cloud nine.

However, just as I was feeling awfully pleased with myself, a stewardess knocked at the door and said passengers were complaining about the bumpiness! Geoffrey immediately put the autopilot back on and my head shrunk considerably.

Chapter 4

MEETING SHEILA SCOTT

Back in England, at the end of a cold and wet March, just three weeks away from the start of my Instructor's Course, one of my first priorities was to meet Sheila Scott to deliver Ruth's photographs.

I drove to London, with my dog Finn, in my trusted, rusted Renault 4. A stern-looking woman answered my knock, asking what I wanted. She was formidable to look at, with her brown/grey hair tied tightly in a bun. She wore a smart well-tailored suit, with small heels and dark glasses.

I nervously said, "I have some photos from our friends Ruth and Jerrie in America. I told them I would deliver them to you. Err, bye." I quickly walked away. Sheila called for me to come back and insisted I had a cup of tea. She wanted to hear about Ruth and Jerrie and thanked me for bringing the photos.

Since starting flying, Sheila had become my idol. She had done everything I would love to achieve. She was commercially qualified and had flown *'Barefoot Round the World'* as she had entitled her book, based on her solo round-the-world trip in her single-engine Comanche named Myth Too.

I could never have imagined or hoped that she would be so friendly or so helpful to a complete stranger and a beginner pilot. We chatted for hours. She told me many stories about her aviation life. Sadly, she no longer flew solo as she had lost her medical on grounds of damaged eyesight, hence the dark glasses, which she even wore inside her flat.

When I told her I badly wanted to learn to fly aerobatics and enter competitions, she said I should join the Tiger Club. It was the only way to progress in Aerobatics; in fact she would take me there and introduce me to the owner, Michael Jones, the following day.

We talked into the early hours of the morning. She cooked a quick snack for the two of us and even found some food for Finn. Food was a sure way to Finn's heart, so they were both firm friends in no time.

The next day, I drove with Sheila to Redhill, home of the Tiger Club. Everyone there gave Sheila a very warm welcome. Most pilots compared the Tiger Club, the most exclusive Flying Club in the world, (obviously Jerrie Cobb was a member), to an Inner Temple of Temples. People like me would not be able to enter, never mind join and fly their exotic, vintage tail wheel, wood and fabric bi-planes and single-seat Turbulents, Fourniers and everything available to the Members.

To join the Club, you needed to know at least two Full Members for over two years, one of whom must propose and the other must second you. At the following club meeting, the new prospective Members were voted in (or not) on the strength of the reasons put forward. The lucky ones selected were then allowed to hire the Tiger Moth G-ACDC, (the oldest flying Tiger in the world) and learn to fly it, accompanied by a check pilot. Any prospective Member must already hold a private pilot's licence and have done at least 100 solo hours.

That wasn't all: after having satisfied a check pilot that they could fly the Tiger, the candidate was then put through a gruelling flight test with the senior check pilot. If they failed, or if they took too long to get the hang of the Tiger, the candidate was politely asked to leave the premises and not return.

Once they had passed this test, the successful candidate would then have to fly the Tiger Moth for five hours solo, to gain further experience. Only then was free rein given to fly any other aircraft in the hangar, with only a verbal checkout. The reasoning for the stringent conditions was that all the aircraft were irreplaceable; the club could not afford sloppy flying, a possible bent or broken aircraft, or a slack attitude to airmanship, punctuality or flying ability.

Eventually, the candidate would become an assistant member for a year, after which they could request an upgrade to full membership: again, a panel had to decide whether that person was a good pilot.

To join had been my dream for a long time, though I'd planned on gaining more flying experience before I ventured down to take a visit. Yet, with not much over 200 hours of flying experience, I found myself applying to join. Ron, an old friend of Sheila's, agreed to propose me and she seconded me. That secured my application and a few weeks later, I had the news I was now an assistant member of the Tiger Club.

*

While awaiting news from the Tiger Club, I was summoned to start my flying instructor course.

The course was terrific. It was run by Edward Clack at Southend, and the other trainee Instructors were Danny Wolfe, Ray Evans and Brian Andrews.

At the end of training we all drove together to Rhoose Airport, Cardiff, to take our graduation test with Captain Hubbard.

Captain Hubbard looked frightening to all of us, as any examiner does. He stood very upright and solemnly took our names, then proceeded to set us all at ease by telling a couple of light-hearted jokes. We gave him our 'briefs' individually. This is where you are given a subject to brief the student on for the specific lesson they will learn that day. I was lucky as my brief was on 'spinning and recovery'. After that, it was time for a test-flight, and a group debriefing.

"Before I debrief you all, I would love to know who gave your ground lectures," Captain Hubbard said.

Silence.

"Well, I will tell you that everyone has passed, but the interesting part is that I counted the word 'OK' 35 times in your speech, Danny. Ray, you had 42, and Brian, you had 38. Tizi, while you had only 25 'OKs' during your brief, the whole thing only lasted 15 minutes instead of 30 minutes. But I'll allow a margin for nerves, as you seem to speak quickly."

None of us had noticed the word OK at all. But later, whenever anyone said it, one of us shouted.

We stopped during the return drive for a really hot curry, to celebrate being now qualified as Assistant Instructors. Each of us tried conscientiously to avoid the word OK.

Having started flying at Stapleford Flying Club near Romford, it was only natural to commence instructing there. I wanted to be able to instruct on every type of aircraft the Club owned, so I within the first week I returned to Edward Clack, starting by instructing on a basic Cherokee, then adding a Cessna 150, a 172 and a Condor D62 to my instructor rating.

Fred Wells, my Chief Flying Instructor, welcomed me back as an Instructor, having finished teaching me to fly only a few weeks ago. He allocated me my first student, a lovely 80-year-old woman called Jean Kurti. He told me he was giving me a challenge, as Jean had already flown over 80 hours but had not gone solo.

She was keen to qualify as her husband was a PPL holder and they flew together on many overseas trips, but her hang-up was spinning. In 1978, unless a student was signed out in their logbook as being able to put an aircraft into a full spin and recover, they were not allowed – in most clubs – to fly solo.

I thanked Fred for giving me a student so soon.

"There is a catch," muttered Fred. "You have five hours to get her ready to pass the General Flight Test or you're out; but if you manage, I'll take you on full-time."

I decided there and then that Jean would be ready. I went in to find her and told her I was taking her on until she obtained her licence. She was so pleased and thanked me profusely. Jean was not the typical student, being into her late seventies when she had started to train. She looked rather frail with pearl-white hair, a slender frame and trusting blue/grey eyes.

"Oh, this is such good news," she said. "I must have been up with every Instructor and have flown so many hours. I thought I was just going to end up with a different Instructor every time and never finish. Fred did tell you I am learning in the Condor, didn't he? Most of the other instructors are trying to persuade me to learn in the Cherokee as it's easier."

"No, he didn't," I replied, "but that's wonderful news as it's my favourite aeroplane."

I read through Jean's log-book and found, she had had 21 instructors, a good number of hours on the circuit and countless hours flying cross-country. I mentioned there was no spinning.

"No, I really cannot face spinning. It seems no one else wants to take me for the dreadful spin detail either."

I told her that would be the first thing we did and I would personally guarantee she would not only come back as an ace at spinning, but that she would love it. Spinning was the best part of the flying syllabus and she was missing most of the fun.

I suggested she took me for a flight in the area she knew best. I would put the aircraft into a spin and recover, then talk her through one, or even two; then she could try her own.

Poor Jean looked a little apprehensive at first but agreed to listen to my thorough briefing. Using a model to demonstrate, I explained what the aircraft would be doing as it approached the stall, then entered and developed the spin and why it was doing it. Then I wrote out the spin recovery and insisted she learned it by heart before we flew the lesson.

While Jean was having a cup of tea while learning the recovery formula, I went to pick up the keys to Fox Charlie.

"Oh, I'm glad you picked my favourite aircraft, Tizi," she said when I returned. "I'm actually looking forward to my flight now."

Jean got in the little yellow Condor – there were three Condors at Stapleford – and taxied it over the grass to the holding point. By the time she had reached the edge of the runway, I was already wondering what the problem was. She had a firm, authoritative manner and gentle touch with delicate controls. She looked both ways almost every five feet and was totally relaxed. By the time we were airborne, I could not see how she could have a problem: Jean seemed to be part of the aircraft.

"Well here we are at three and a half thousand feet. I'm ready to spin," she told me, while giving me control of the aircraft. She had completed the pre-aerobatic checks. I suggested a steep turn both ways, maintaining altitude before we spun, to which she agreed and demonstrated two very respectable 60-degree banked turns, one in each direction.

Then she showed me a stall without flaps and a second with flaps. The recoveries were excellent. Jean prevented a wing from dropping by careful use of the rudders.

I wanted to spin the aircraft as gently as possible, but one thing a Condor will *not* do is spin gently. So I started by stalling, at which the wing dropped immediately. The Condor has this tendency, to which I recovered and asked her to try. She did, perfectly, so I felt the next step was a full spin. Approaching the stall, I eased the stick back and gave full rudder.

At the same time, Jean collapsed completely, her head thrown back uttering a slight gasp, followed by silence. Her head lolled to one side, which convinced me she had died of a heart attack.

While recovering from the spin as soon as it had started, I wished I had started lower, so I could land sooner and administer artificial resuscitation. There was no time to return to the airfield so I set the aircraft into a glide for an approach to the largest field around, into wind.

Jean asked why I wasn't climbing for height, for another spin practice.

I couldn't believe what I heard. She was alive, looking very well and apologised for being so silly. Could she take control, climb back up and would I show her once more, so she could try the next time?

"Now I know exactly what is going to happen, I am no longer afraid," she said, sounding determined.

I talked her through another. She asked for a further demonstration, after which she tried her own spin. It was successful and I decided that would do for the day. Jean insisted she try one without any help, including the recovery – having learned all the theory, she wanted to practise.

I agreed. It was good, although the spin over-rotated on the recovery and we ended up spinning in the other direction.

"That wasn't good. I'll try another, since we are here with the height which would be silly to waste."

The next one was perfectly acceptable to pass a test. I was delighted and told her it was flown to a pass standard. We returned with a lovely landing and decided to fly again in two days and cover some practice forced landings. These went well, so the next flight in a couple of days would be the last flight prior to Jean going solo and taking her final General Flight Test.

Meanwhile an acquaintance I had met while learning to fly, called Harry, (nicknamed Big H), asked me if I would teach him to spin. Although he'd got his licence, he said he still didn't feel confident he could get out of a spin on his own.

I gave Harry my spinning briefing and insisted he learned the recovery by rote before flying. Harry was a large man – well over six feet and very well built. He had a short, spiky hair cut and looked rather formidable. He was known to come from a rough background, but all I knew about him was that he had lovely manners – he pulled out chairs and opened doors for women and paid all his bills on time. I liked him. As we strapped ourselves into the delicate Condor I wondered how he would fit inside the tiny cockpit. Then I felt a sudden apprehension.

What if he should freeze on the controls when we spun? I would not be able to overpower him with my pathetic eight stone of weight. Perhaps he would panic and thrash about? It was too late to turn back.

He taxied the aircraft slowly, completed all his checks and took off. He asked what altitude I would like. I would normally have suggested 3,000 feet, but this time I decided to go to 6,000 feet, thinking that I would have more time to wrestle the controls if it became necessary.

After he did the pre-aerobatic checks, he sat back and folded his arms.

"The checks are now complete, so you have control," he said.

I pulled the little craft into a spin, recovered and offered him the stick back.

"Not yet. I think I have it, but I'd like you to do it again, while I watch and then I'll try one."

Which I did, then gave him the aircraft, by which time we were down at 4,000 feet. He executed a good spin and an excellent recovery – no signs at all of any fear. I felt highly embarrassed at my previous thoughts.

"Brilliant!" The praise was honest, "and we are still above 3,000 feet."

"Well I'll try another from here, if you're happy?"

The next try was just as good. He then set course toward the airfield and a few minutes later we taxied back to the parking lines. His handling of the aircraft was gentle and firm. I couldn't help comparing his handling with that of Jean's; both of them had such different personalities yet they both flew with such natural grace and poise, combined with firmness.

Harry insisted I join him for a cup of tea during the de-brief. I noticed a letter tattooed on each of his fingers and asked him, as a joke, which lady owned the letters. He seemed embarrassed and put one hand under the table. I thought no more about it.

That evening I asked Edward Clack to remove the 'instruction of aerobatics' restriction on my teaching ticket. This consisted of a five-hour course and an aerobatic instructional flight test at the end. Edward asked if I could fly aerobatics: I told him I had done plenty in the States in an Aerobat and was quite happy. I was fairly conceited.

We flew the first detail of a loop, barrel roll and slow roll. I came out on the wrong heading after the barrel roll and fell out of the slow roll.

"So what happened to all those hundreds of aerobatic hours in the States?" Edward teased, then proceeded to teach me the basic manoeuvres.

Edward had had more hours instructing in Cherokees than anyone else in the country, some 10,000. He was not only experienced, but extremely patient and thorough. By the end of the course, I wished I had done it prior to going to Florida – I could have practised and improved there, rather than uncomfortably falling out of everything, by self-teaching.

On returning to Stapleford and informing Fred that I could now teach aerobatics, he pointed out that nothing on the fleet could do more than spin.

"But," he said, "you can do the spinning details for all the students here – none of the other Instructors want to teach that detail."

I was delighted. It was worth the cost of the course.

My next flight was with Jean and we ran through a short practice run for the flight test and finished with a few circuits in different configurations, with and without flaps, with and without using the engine.

"Well, Jean, you are readier than anyone to go solo, so I am afraid I'll have to put you with a full instructor for your next flight, as I am only an assistant," I said. The next day she found a full instructor to take her for the required three circuits to prove she was safe. I was overjoyed. She was well ready for her test. After completing all the necessary hours solo on the circuit, she was ready to fly her solo navigation trip. She insisted on taking a trip with me first. Apart from my checking her log before take-off, she flew the short triangular navigation trip totally unaided.

"You might just as well have been solo, for all the help I gave you," I exclaimed in delight.

Jean competently flew her first solo cross-country flight, and then a longer navigation flight with me, before flying her final qualifying cross-country flight. When she returned, I told her I was booking her in for her flight test the following day, to which she happily agreed.

I had flown 4 hours and 55 minutes with her. The last flight was up to her and my future depended on it. I don't know who was more nervous, Jean or me.

She passed and was almost in tears.

"Oh, Tizi, how can I thank you? This means so much to me!"

She did not realise quite how much it had meant to me.

Later that evening I found Fred to tell him the good news – Jean had passed within the five hours so I was now a full-time instructor, surely?

"Hey, Tizi, I hope you didn't take that seriously – it was a joke. I just wanted to put you under a little pressure so you took life seriously for a change. No hard feelings, eh? Of course, you have a full-time job; I always look after my students."

I was astounded. My future was in the balance – but it had been a joke. Suddenly I doubled up with laughter, buying Fred a beer and joining him with one. I told Fred about Harry and he warned me to be careful – he said he was a strange lad with an uncertain past. I re-assured Fred that Harry was a real gentleman and that I would trust him with my life. Yet, how wrong could I be?

A couple of weeks later, after dinner with my parents (John Cramphorn was now officially my stepfather), my mother asked if it was the same man, Big H, that I had been teaching to fly whose picture was in the daily papers? Apparently, Big H was the most wanted man in the country: he was a contract killer, shooting people then taking their bodies, mincing them in a large machine and hiding the remains in the M11 that was under construction!

I remember declaring Harry's total innocence: there was no way he could be guilty. He flew the Condor so beautifully and his manners were so polished. He was every inch a gentleman.

"It says here," said John, pointing to an article in the paper, "that he's got 'F-U-C-K – O-F-F' tattooed on his fingers. Is that true?"

I remembered asking Harry about the letters on his fingers and him hiding his hands under the table. I thought he was shy to talk about a jilted love. Over the following days, it appeared he really *was* the most wanted man in the country. I had also heard direct accounts from people I knew, who were Harry's 'friends', that he had offered 'to do away with' various troublesome spouses 'as a favour' – for no charge.

Chapter 5

A PEA-SOUPER

L ife at Stapleford improved even more. I was soon flying every slot available: the only irritation was being a lowly assistant instructor.

I needed a minimum amount of instructional time – which I obtained rapidly. The next step was to hold the instructor's rating for a minimum time, which did not pass swiftly. I quickly passed the IMC qualification (a ticket enabling me to instruct flying on instruments, as opposed to visual flying). Now all I needed was for the required time to pass.

I was excited about booking the required flight test with Barry Tempest, the examiner, at Sywell, Northampton.

The next day dawned with reduced visibility, low cloud and rain, but it was forecast to clear up in the early afternoon. I asked Fred if I could take a Cherokee to Sywell, as there were seven or eight Cherokees parked on the grass and with the miserable weather, none were flying. He told me I could use 'my aircraft', G-ARVS. Even if the weather cleared up, no one flew that one from choice, except me.

G-ARVS had no radio, no navigational aids and no gyro instruments, but apart from that, the engine was 160 hp whereas all the other Cherokees had 140 hp engines, so it was faster. A radio was not a necessary requirement then, so long as one avoided controlled airspace; it was easier to have no 'background interference' from a radio while talking to a student.

I set off northwest toward Sywell. Initially I flew at 1,500 feet, but the cloud base gradually lowered the further I went. By the time I was three-quarters of the way there, the cloud base had lowered to 600 feet. This was the altitude above sea-level, not the ground that I flew over.

As the weather was forecast to clear up, I stupidly pressed on. The visibility reduced with the cloud base and I was more intent on seeing ahead and around and keeping the compass heading, than I was on paying attention to the altimeter. It was well past the point at which I should have already turned back. Devastated, I turned through 180 degrees and headed towards home, but on turning round, the cloud base and visibility was the same, equivalent to pea-soup … and thickening.

Suddenly, some pylon lines appeared slightly above me. Too late to get beneath, I pulled the control column back, disappeared into cloud, paused, then eased the controls forward again. Clearing the lines, I had not realised until then how desperate the situation had become, so I decided to land – anywhere. An airfield would have been preferable but now my sense of orientation had left me unsure of my position. For the first time, I wished I had a radio, or a radio aid to help navigate. Passing a stretch of tarmac gave me a 'fix' on my position: I was over the drag strip at Podington. I glanced at my chart and saw that Cranfield ought be just ten miles due south.

Soon, another piece of tarmac appeared almost beneath me. As I was skimming the earth's surface anyway, I just closed the throttle and landed. What a relief to be back on the ground! The visibility had deteriorated even further and I could not find an exit off the runway. After taxiing for what seemed forever, a building came into view. I shut down the engine and entered the building, which happened to be the Control Tower, so I decided I may as well pay the landing fee and find out what was happening to the 'improving weather' that never improved.

The Air Traffic Controllers were quiet when I entered.

"Where are you planning on going and when?" I was asked.

"I've just come in, so I need to pay someone," I explained.

"No-one has landed here for hours – it's been fogged in and closed for the last two hours."

By now I was totally confused. I went to the next building, which was a flying club and asked if there were any tea facilities.

A man called Mark pointed to a kettle and told me to help myself, asking where I was bound. Mark looked like all instructors, wearing a white shirt, black trousers and black tie.

Making a tea, I explained I had started from Stapleford, tried for Sywell but the weather had forced me back. He explained that I'd landed at Cranfield: I was surprised as I'd expected it to be further south.

Another instructor asked what I had come in, then the whole crew room seemed excited, agreeing somebody had heard something land but thought they had imagined it. When Mark found some updated weather reports, I realised I would reach neither Sywell nor Stapleford that day. He very kindly said that I could stay over with him and his girlfriend and try again the following day.

The day dawned bright and cloud-free, with a gentle breeze. I flew to Sywell and was met by Barry Tempest, a very good-looking blue-eyed man, who said that he'd heard me attempt to come in and turn around again. He believed I'd only been a mile away when I turned around. I told him I had learned a good deal the previous day and I would not get that far again before turning back.

By early afternoon, the flight and briefings were successful and I flew home as a QFI – Qualified Flight Instructor – no longer a mere assistant. I enjoyed the flight back, feeling pleased, happy and proud.

At Stapleford, I was told Fred wanted to see me. That was natural. He was obviously pleased to be able to welcome yet another full instructor onto his fleet, and probably wanted to congratulate me.

"Hello, Tizi. I'm surprised to see you back, after the weather you set off in. That was hardly an example to set to your students. I doubt you even had 1,000 feet of cloud base to start with." It was not the greeting I expected.

"It was higher to start with and it was forecast to improve." I bleated in self-defence.

"I will not put up with that sort of reckless, irresponsible attitude, especially among my staff. You should have waited until the weather cleared before taking off. I was going to ask you to leave, but instead I have decided you may stay. However, you may *not* exercise any of the privileges of a full instructor. Nor will you receive the wage increase that should accompany it, as I don't think you have shown that you deserve it."

I was knocked out. From feeling so pleased and proud, I now realised what a terrible thing I had done. Later that evening, I offered Fred a humble apology and a beer. He accepted both and we had a good evening. I didn't even ask for a change of mind on my punishment: as he said, I deserved it.

As the months passed, I amassed more flying hours and flying friends, who suggested I studied for my CPL (Commercial Pilots Licence). I duly sent off for the home-study notes and decided to study whenever the weather was too bad to fly a normal detail.

In the meantime, Stapleford Flying Club's owner, John Chicken, offered me the use of an old caravan to live in, since I was at the club over 12 hours a day, seven days a week. He would not take any rent. So I moved in, which reduced travelling time and costs to zero. Food became almost the only requirement for living.

John was an amazing man. Almost as broad as he was tall, with short dark hair and a round face, he owned the airfield, all the aircraft and also kept many ponies and horses at the side of the airfield, many of which he trained for trotting races. He regularly won all over the country with his fabulous team of ponies.

After an instructional flight, a student often offered the instructor a cup of tea, which I always declined in favour of a glass of milk – containing more calories than tea. If, after the last flight I should be offered a beer, I would decline in favour of a cheese roll. Over a period, John Chicken noticed I was eating nothing but cheese rolls. He told Phyllis, who worked behind the bar and in the canteen, to put any leftover rolls at the end of the day in the freezer and I could have them for breakfast, dinner, lunch or tea.

Additional protein came in an unexpected way. At night, when the aircraft had finished flying, I took to driving my little Renault 4 around the airfield, with the lights on full beam. Within a couple of minutes I'd feel a bump, which meant I had driven over a rabbit, as the airfield was rabbit infested. I would pick up the dead rabbit and cook it on the stove in the caravan, sharing it with Finn who seemed to prefer fresh rabbit to dog food.

With food and accommodation taken care of, my outgoings were so far reduced that I could spend almost all my wages on aerobatic competition practice. My goal now was to learn contest-style aerobatic flying and the obvious place to do so was at the Tiger Club.

I took a day off to visit the Tiger Club, expecting to be intimidated by anyone and everyone, especially as I was on my own this time, but the atmosphere was welcoming and friendly. Everyone wanted to help me find my way round the buildings and the aircraft, especially the Tiger Moth – G-ACDC. I was then assigned to check-pilot Jim Alderton who agreed happily to commence my 'familiarisation' flight that day. Jim was a short stocky man with a reassuring manner to set anyone at ease when they flew with him.

He helped settle me in with the numerous straps and went through the basic differences of flying a Tiger. The first time in an open cockpit aircraft was more comparable to a motorbike, with the wind in your hair. It felt like having learned to ride a small pony and then being told to go out on a large, heavy Shire horse. I needed two hands to taxi the aircraft – it was heavy, but I needed one for the throttle.

There was no forward visibility while moving on the ground. It felt like I imagined it must have been like in the 40s. Jim demonstrated how to weave the nose left and right in order to see obstacles and aircraft ahead. The same applied when flying at low speeds. The long Tiger's nose would rise ahead of the pilot's vision so the view ahead was nil. After a short flight in the local area, I returned to the circuit to learn how to land the brute. It was heavy and demanding but fabulous.

I returned to Stapleford and told Fred I had just fallen in love with the best aircraft in the world, a Tiger Moth.

"Oh, you must have been down to the Tiger Club. Well, I'll tell you one thing. When you get to fly the Stampes down there, you'll be calling the Tiger a dog and not wishing to fly it again."

I told him he was completely wrong and nothing could be as good as a Tiger. I just couldn't wait to fly it solo. Whenever I found a few hours spare, I drove to Redhill for more flying on the Tiger.

I was flying almost every slot, every day with students at Stapleford, so I had to work out some way to visit the Tiger Club without losing the revenue from teaching. By finishing flying the Tiger before 9am and then returning for the first slot at Stapleford by 10.30am for a few days, I managed to take enough time off to fly the Tiger with a check pilot until I could finally take the flight test.

At last the final test was taken, followed by the required five hours solo on the Tiger before being allowed to try any of the other aircraft.

All Tiger Club members were shown where the key was kept, so anytime I wanted to fly an aircraft I could open the hangar doors, fly an aircraft, return it to the hangar and go home.

The first different type I tried after completing my five, solo enjoyable hours in the Tiger Moth was the Stampe, G-ATKC, known as TKC. I had spent a long time reading the Stampe's checklist and found most of the speeds and handling techniques were identical to the Tiger.

Well, Fred was right: the Stampe was so much nicer than the Tiger. It was gentle, responsive, forgiving and kind. There were two Stampes; the other was WEF, but nothing like as nice to fly, although both were head-and-shoulders more fun to fly than a Tiger. I soon found that if the Stampes were both booked, I would avoid driving down to the Club, rather than to take a Tiger up instead.

I asked Jim if he would teach me aerobatics in the Stampe. He told me aerobatics were not his scene and pointed me toward Pete Kinsey, Ian Senior and Harpo, who all came up at various times to improve my aerobatics and handling skills.

I set my new goal of reaching the stage where I could practise over the airfield. This had one main advantage, which was that fellow competition pilots would critique each other whilst recording their opinions on a tape recorder. The mistakes made during practice could be heard after landing.

To practice over Redhill aerodrome, sited under the outer part of Gatwick's control zone of 1,500 feet in height, I needed to have 'cleared to fly aerobatics down to 1,000 feet' stamped in the Tiger card. This meant some considerable improvement on my part.

Back flying seven days a week at Stapleford, I had to find spare time to fly the Stampe, daily, despite Redhill being a good hour's drive away. The 'bunk room' at the Tiger Club was available to any Member for 50 pence a night. I set a routine of taking Finn and an overnight bag and driving to Redhill once the last student had left.

During the day I would request the Stampe to be re-fuelled before being put back into the hangar: as the last aircraft in, it would be the first one out.

Arriving at the Club, I'd check the oil, fuel levels and the aircraft. Having slept in the bunkroom, I would get up very early, pull TKC from the hangar and depart for an aerobatics practice at first light, returning to the hanger with time to drive back to Stapleford by 9am.

Life was fantastic. I felt I had everything anyone could possibly desire. My life was almost constantly airborne. After a few weeks, I begged Pete Kynsey, another check pilot, to take me through an aerobatic check ride to reduce my height restriction to 1,000 feet. He accepted my aerobatics were safe, so I was cleared to the magical height to be able to fly directly over the airfield.

There was an additional advantage of flying over a runway: should the engine fail there was a runway to land on, rather than having to put down in a field, which might not be as smooth a surface as it looked from the air.

Over the airfield, aerobatics could only be flown during a one-hour window in the evenings and a two-hour period in afternoons at the weekend. Both Stampes were used during the slot times, with a pilot ready to start their 'sequence' as soon as the earlier pilot rocked the wings to signify the end of their sequence.

Usually 10 people managed to fly a sequence in the slot, although often we could fly more than once each. It was exciting to be able to watch a fellow pilot fly the correct 30- and 45-degree angles, then to recite into a recorder whether the lines were too steep or shallow. These 'critiqued flights' were of much benefit.

To improve my aerobatics, I needed to buy an aerobatic aircraft, but money was short because I'd spent every penny on practising in the Stampe. A friend at the Tiger Club, noticing I was driving back-and-forth to fly 'my' TKC, suggested I bought a single-seat Turbulent, for cheaper transport. That seemed reasonable, so the following week I acquired a Turbulent aircraft: a slight drain on the insurance money but a good investment, I thought.

The Turbulent, G-AWBM, (WBM for short) was a wood-and-fabric, tail-wheeled aircraft with a 1,700cc VW engine, instead of the standard 1,100 or 1,300cc engine. It also had a canopy, which meant flying in winter was considerably warmer, but it was not cleared to fly aerobatics.

The plan was to fly to Redhill at the end of the day, stay overnight, then after flying TKC I could return by plane instead of car, to start the day's work. I had missed the fact that I always finished at last light: there were no lights fitted to the Turbulent, neither were there any lights at Redhill.

When I was invited to a barbeque, somewhere in Oxford, I asked if there was room to fly in with my Turbulent, which was kept on a permit – to-fly basis. This meant I could land in any field, without it needing to be an airfield, airport or runway.

"No problem at all," I was told and given the precise directions to locate the field on my flying chart.

Arriving overhead, I could see the field, as there was a fire already lit, but WBM was coughing and spluttering. On reaching the overhead, I circled to look at the landing space available and the engine died. The only option was to glide down to land on the field. When the aircraft stopped, I jumped out, put the tail over my shoulder and 'carried' WBM to the action end of the field.

A chap called John asked if there was anything wrong with the engine, told me he was a mechanic by trade and offered to check it.

I was delighted because, apart from having brought the usual 'bottle' with me, (which I had no intention of drinking) I had no cash, credit cards or chequebook. Between mouthfuls of burnt sausage and hamburger, John took the engine apart until he found my problem.: a blocked carburettor. This he cleaned and told me it was now running smoothly. I wondered how to thank him for his life-saving deed. He told me he had flown gliders before but never tried an aeroplane, although that was his next intention.

I could not suggest he flew the Turbulent without a licence but saw nothing wrong in offering him a 'hop' – to taxi at high speed down the field, get airborne and land immediately. John thought the idea exciting, so I helped him in, swung the propeller for him and pointed at the beginning of the field.

John put on full throttle and got airborne quickly. He went higher and higher. I was in a panic, wondering why he had done such a foolhardy thing: I had not even told him the stall speeds so he wouldn't know at what speed to try to land it. I worried if he crashed it would be my fault, as I had offered him the hop. Then I remembered he'd told me he had done some gliding – I vaguely wondered whether he had flown solo in a glider.

As I watched in horror, expecting him to come straight round to land, he started climbing in circles above the field. Then he seemed to slow right down, high above us. Soon, he started making an approach. The aircraft seemed to be under control and he looked to be coming in at the correct speed. He judged the approach well and closed the throttle when he was about 800 feet above the field, the standard height to glide in from. A few small bounces and he landed – in one piece.

I ran up to WBM and without thinking I found myself congratulating John on a lovely approach. He apologised for taking off when he only intended to hop. He told me that although the aircraft was quickly airborne, there didn't seem enough room ahead to land again. Instead, he flew up to a safe enough height to stall the machine, so he could find at what speed to make an approach. I had to admit I was impressed as heck as that was his first ride in an aeroplane, especially when he confessed he'd never flown solo in a glider.

Chapter 6

FLYING THE AVALANCHE

The next event on the aerobatic calendar was the Icicle Trophy, held at Redhill – always the first event of the year. Held in February, it was named for obvious reasons.

I had been practising hard all winter and was hoping to be able to take part in the Intermediate class of the Icicle Trophy, an aerobatics contest held in February at Redhill. The only options were classes of Intermediate or Advanced. For the Intermediate class, in addition to 'known' sequences, there was also an 'unknown' sequence. This was a series of manoeuvres put together by the judges but not shown to the pilots until just before the contest, giving no chance to practise.

At the pilots' briefing, the sequence was drawn on the blackboard. A friend and fellow pilot, Brendan O'Brien, asked me if I knew how to fly the first manoeuvre; I admitted I had no idea even as to what it was called. Brendan was a popular extrovert who flew brilliantly.

"That's no problem," he said. "It's an Avalanche; a fairly simple manoeuvre. You're flying the Stampe?" I nodded. "Put the nose down for 130 knots, then pull up …" He paused and asked me to make a fist to feel my muscles. "… with *both* hands, as hard as you can, watching the speed. As soon as you see 70 knots on the clock, pull the stick full back, kicking full rudder at the same time. You'll see a kaleidoscope of stars … and when you are 90 degrees from the inverted, apply full opposite rudder before easing the stick forward at the same time as centralising the rudders. That's all there is to it, I swear." He reassured me that it was no more than a one turn spin from the top of a loop.

I couldn't help thinking how lovely it was to be offered help from another pilot in the same contest. It had not been like that when I competed with horses in earlier days.

When my turn came, I did exactly as instructed. The lovely Stampe responded as if being read instructions from a textbook, coming out on the right heading in the right place. I got a treasured 9 out of 10 for my first Avalanche. Although I was fairly low down in the final placing, suffering on positioning, I felt as happy as if I had won the whole contest.

At every contest, there were usually as many as 15 pilots flying the same aircraft, TKC; sometimes people would also fly WEF and there would be other competitors with their own mounts. Lots would be drawn as to which competing pilot would fly the competition aircraft to the destination. The other pilots would make their way by car, train or even in another aircraft rented from the Tiger Club. On the occasions I did not win the 'lot', which was most of the time, I flew there in WBM.

The next contest was the McCauley Trophy, held at Little Snoring. There was a tailwind forecasted, but it was the longest stretch I could make on one tank of fuel so I decided to stop at Seething, for fuel.

The Turbulent was not fitted with a radio when I bought it, and as the Tiger Club was proud that none of the aircraft in the hangar had a radio, there was no option to fit one. Flying round the London control zones and overseas made navigating more demanding and challenging. There was, however, a handicap for the average female when flying non-radio, which often irritated me.

When flying into controlled airports you have to phone the airport to request permission to come non-radio (usually granted) and to give an accurate estimated time of arrival. Since the typical female is liable to change her mind for anything, including the destination once airborne (and I was certainly no exception), this became impossible. Should the 'booked in aircraft' not arrive at the destination within a reasonable time, Search and Rescue was initiated.

For Seething, it was not necessary to book in first, so I departed with plenty of time and kept a careful eye on the fuel gauge. This was a cork bobbing on the fuel level with a straight piece of wire attached, protruding out of the cowlings. I had been told by the man who sold the aircraft to me that when the wire was level with the cowlings, there was a further 30 minutes of fuel. However, he told me he had not put it to the test.

When I was less than 30 minutes from Seething, the wire reached the bottom. I assured myself there was another 30 minutes remaining and less than 30 minutes to Seething. Then I remembered, '*he had not put it to the test*'.

I worried a little for five seconds then looked around. The countryside seemed friendly enough; the fields were large enough. Checking my chart, I was somewhere around Laxfield, about 15 miles south of Seething. Deciding to err on the side of caution, I landed in a small field, which had a building next to it.

As usual, I carried WBM's tail over my shoulder to the side of the field, lest someone else should want to use the field, and walked to the building where there were a couple of guys working on some machinery. I explained I had parked in a field and asked to use a phone.

I called a local garage and asked if anyone could come to meet me in the field with five gallons of two-star fuel. The kindly garage owner agreed to come out straight away. He helped me fill the Turbulent, telling me he had not had to 'rescue' an aeroplane for over ten years when a Tiger Moth last landed in his field without any fuel.

He asked if I could give him a 'flypast' before I departed. Of course I agreed and he waved frantically while I circled around him after taking off. He had refused to take any more than the price of the five gallons, which I thought was very sweet of him.

TKC flew well for me in the McCauley Trophy, helping me to second and third position in the standard and the intermediate classes. After more determined practising at Redhill in the 'slots' and over the reservoirs, my placing improved by the end of the season.

I was still instructing full time at Stapleford and I had been allowed to use my privileges of the full instructor rating a couple of months after obtaining it. This improved my life so much.

Stapleford, like many flying clubs, had a rally each year and this one was scheduled for September 1st. It was to encourage other pilots to fly in and meet different people. Fred asked if I could bring a Stampe from Redhill and fly some aerobatics overhead for the day. There would not be many people there, being just a friendly day, so I could treat it as a slot practice.

However, the Tiger Club had both Stampes booked on the day. I felt terrible, having promised Fred I would bring something, so spent all my free time trying to find someone who had an aircraft that would fly upside down and which I could borrow. With a week to go, I had drawn a blank everywhere, then someone told me to try Nigel Brendish, whom I had heard of but not met. I explained my dilemma and he said he would find an aircraft if I wasn't fussy as to what it was.

With two days to go, Nigel called to say he had found an old Chipmunk, G-ALWB, that had been standing for some months or years behind a hangar at Southend Airport.

"Have you flown a Chipmunk before?" Nigel enquired out of curiosity.

"No," I replied, "but there'll be a checklist with it, for the speeds."

His answer was that apart from a bunch of rust, there would be nothing with it. Nigel gave me the necessary speeds and suggested I took it up for an hour or two to blow the cobwebs off and get acquainted. It was a refreshing approach, which reminded me of the American's attitude to lending aircraft.

The following afternoon, finishing early, I drove to Southend and tried out the Chipmunk, which after about fifty swings to get started, turned out to be a sweet-natured aircraft, gentle, and very forgiving. After going through a sequence a couple of times, I flew back to Stapleford. The engine coughed and spluttered quite a few times and quit every time I turned it upside-down, taking a long time to restart, with plenty of smoke once erect. I put this down to rust in the joints.

The following day, I flew the same sequence I had practised, with the long silences every time I turned over. Each time the engine re-started there was a series of backfires, pops and black smoke. The effect on the ground was apparently startling and awesome. People were betting as to whether the coughs were deliberate stage effects.

On landing, I had a lovely surprise. A man called Andy had flown in with a Stampe he had recently bought and he had seen my flying. He asked if I would like to fly his Stampe over the airfield, as he had not started flying aerobatics, but would love to see his aircraft fly. This was a wonderful offer, too good to turn down. I asked Fred and he was delighted to have 'more to offer' for his rally. When flying inverted, the engine ran sweetly, so as an ending I flew the Stampe inverted the full length of the runway.

Feeling more at home with a Stampe than with any other aircraft, I naturally thought the 'strung-together-manoeuvres' must have looked far more polished in the Stampe. But everyone told me the Chipmunk was so exciting to watch with the engine cutting out so often and all the fireworks following me around. I thought there was nought so queer as folk!

One of the people I taught to fly was Jane Speight, who was later to become a close friend when I stayed with her in her pub in Romford, Essex. When she was ready to fly her first solo cross-country, she said she was scared to go alone and that she would only fly if Finn could come with her. I agreed. She flew the route with Finn beside her and on her return I asked why taking Finn had given her such confidence. She told me she knew I wouldn't have let her take Finn unless I was 101% sure that she would get back safely.

Three months later, an old friend, Nigel Harris, offered me a twin-engine rating (so I could fly twin- or multi-engined aircraft) on his Aztec he had just bought as a business venture. I told him I could not afford that sort of luxury. He asked if I had a Visa card. After a nod, he offered me a complete twin rating, including the test, for £400, which could be paid by Visa. That was too good an opportunity to miss: I'd thought it would cost £1,000.

Nigel was an interesting entrepreneur who started up many companies of his own over the years I knew him. He was another tall, dark and handsome pilot with a very persuasive manner. So a couple of days later, I found myself multi-engine rated, but without a hope of renting a multi-engine aircraft to fly anywhere.

On a very windy day in December, I had a student booked for instrument flying training in his own Rallye. As there were some 40-plus knots of wind blowing at the surface, any instrument training would have been a waste of time. He asked whether there was anything at all he could do, so I suggested a Backward Square Circuit. I explained he could take off, using plenty of flaps, climb vertically, then hold the lowest speed possible and hover down to land.

He agreed readily but only if I accompanied him. The take-off was almost vertical, then with about a knot difference from the lowest safe speed and the wind speed, we took almost 20 minutes to fly backwards over the runway and hover gently down to land. On exiting the Rallye, we were told that 'locals' were phoning in to say there was an aircraft behaving like a helicopter and asking what was happening.

Life was fun.

Chapter 7

'YOU'RE FIRED!'

There was a fair amount of fog during December 1979, making flying impossible. With spare time available, I painted my Renault 4. Using a paintbrush and a few cans of paint, I converted my rusty old car into a shiny new Tiger with black and yellow stripes. I drove straight to the Tiger Club, where I had a strange welcome. The reactions varied from 'horror', 'different', 'terrific' or 'embarrassing'. On the occasions I drove to London, friends would shout and wave as the Tiger gently prowled the streets.

I also obtained the necessary textbooks to study for the commercial pilot's licence. It was called the CPL/IR exams because it was combined with an instrument rating: going anywhere in the UK with its typical weather would mean that you couldn't fly for more than a few days a year without an instrument rating. I locked myself into my caravan and started the long, entertaining and fascinating study. Meteorology *(why not call the met-men on the phone before flying? It's what they're paid for anyway)*. Instruments and how they work *(a waste of time as a separate engineer licence is required before being allowed to repair an instrument – even if it is obvious what's wrong and how to repair it)*. Navigation and Forms of the Earth *(I know the Earth is round – I really don't need to go to school to be told)*. Air Law *(as there are no cops up there, why bother?)*. Principles of Flight *(The aircraft flies itself. To know the mathematics and principles of how and why it flies doesn't make the plane go faster or cost any less)*.

It was hard work, which made me regret leaving school at fifteen. I began to wish I had studied harder; at least taken mathematics, algebra and geometry to help with the 'sick' radios – which is what I called those that could be repaired – especially the calculations of the speed of light and sound. The weird ways the radio waves travel, bending round mountains, dancing up past Concorde's altitude and shooting back down again, reflecting off water and

186

crawling over the ground's surface, at speeds so much faster than the fastest motorbike I'd ridden.

Having finally finished the studies over the winter and passed the horrendous exams, I felt I could now get on with instructing and taking more ratings.

With the arrival of my pass results, Fred asked how it went. I happily told him I had passed the written tests – now there were only the flight tests to do, so I was delighted.

"You are fired from here," he said.

"But I passed – what do you mean? Have I misunderstood? What have I done wrong?" I blabbered.

"I don't need you round here anymore. You've done nothing wrong, but I want you out of here by the end of the week."

John Chicken was my employer and was Fred's too. I asked John if I could stay, as I loved working at Stapleford – it felt like my home. Poor John was in a difficult position. He sympathised with me but understood that I was now a threat to Fred as he had not taken his commercial exams. It was either keep me on and let Fred go, or let me go and keep Fred.

Fred would probably still be at Stapleford in ten or twenty years' time, whereas I was young and was highly likely join an airline or go abroad for a better job when an offer came. Then where would he be? Would I commit the next 15 years to working for him? He would not be so unkind as to ask me to do that.

Although shocked, I could see the sense in what John was trying to explain. I loved him for being honest and for the first time, disliked Fred with the same intensity.

I telephoned Edward Clack at Southend and asked if I could instruct for him at Southend Flying Club and told him what had happened. He was delighted and told me I could start any time. I agreed to start in a month and encouraged my students to change their club to Southend, which they all did. With a spare month, I decided to get my Instrument Rating and to take the Commercial Flight Tests (called GFTs 1,2,3 and 4).

DF Aviation at Leavesden agreed to take me immediately and suggested using the simulator instead of an aircraft for the training. The choice was £6 an hour or £100 an hour, with the same result. The aircraft was expensive because it was necessary to train on a multi-engine aircraft, rather than the single-engine option.

After plenty of simulator training, I flew a practice route in the aircraft, then successfully took the final Instrument Rating test. The next hurdle was the GFT tests, which were about general handling flight and navigation. The last of these had to be flown at night and to do so, I rented a small, twin-engined Apache aircraft.

Less than a month later, fully qualified with a new commercial licence complete with instrument rating, I started instructing at Southend Flying Club while waiting for my certificates to arrive in the post. On June 7th 1980, my commercial licence arrived.

It was the same day as an aerobatic contest at Leicester Airfield but this was a contest with a difference. The only mount allowed was a Cessna Aerobat and anyone could enter. I took a day off to compete. To fly a simple aerobatic sequence is less natural in a modern aeroplane with a control wheel, than it is in a bi-plane with a stick. As I was more familiar with the bi-plane, I wasn't disappointed to finish somewhere in the middle.

The trip was worth the effort as I saw Barry Tempest who was also flying in the contest: Barry had been my examiner when I'd taken the upgrade from assistant instructor to full instructor. At the post-contest party, he offered me a dance and asked what I was doing. I told him I had started instructing at Southend and added proudly that my commercial licence with instrument rating had arrived that morning.

"Did you get a first-time-pass for the instrument rating and are you looking for a proper job, flying a multi?" asked Barry. He knew that most pilots pass the commercial first time, but very few have a first-time pass in the instrument rating test.

I nodded to both, as I would have to move up to larger aircraft to justify the new ratings, despite enjoying instructing so much.

"You can have my job, Tizi." He explained that he wanted to move but had promised his boss that he would find a suitable replacement before leaving.

"I've known you for years, competed against you in many aerobatic contests and tested you for your instructor's upgrade in the past. I would be more than happy to suggest you fly for Tony. Call in to my office at Sywell Airfield on Monday – I'll show you round the paperwork and the aircraft G-BAIG, which is a Seneca One."

I was stunned. The ink was hardly dry on my licence and I could soon be flying live passengers in a Twin Seneca.

Although I had a twin rating and had flown one circuit at night in a twin, my experience was almost non-existent. I had not yet saved for the rating to teach multi flying. Added to which, I would be leaving Southend, having hardly even started.

"Can I tell you this evening, after I've thought about it?" I asked.

"Of course, there's no rush; Monday is two days away."

I had a few more dances and drinks with friends I recognised, and some I didn't. At the end of the evening, Barry saw me again and asked if I'd thought any more. I agreed I would start on Monday.

On Sunday I called Edward to explain the events at Leicester. I expected him to be angry, but to my amazement he was delighted. He then added there would always be a job with him, instructing, if I found any spare time on my hands.

After packing a few garments and rags, I rode my bike to Bedford to find some accommodation. I took a B&B adjacent to the airport and thought about the following day.

Monday morning at 6am found me meeting Barry, the Seneca and the mounds of paperwork: technical logs, airframe and engine logbooks, weight and balance sheets all had to be completed before every flight.

The good news was that Barry would fly with me that first day, taking off at 7.30am to Liverpool, with two people from Tony Holmes's company Rexon Pumps, returning after two hours on the ground.

'Two hours – just enough time to fill in the paperwork', I thought to myself.

The flights went smoothly and when Barry left, he said if there were any problems I could give him a call anytime. I stood there for a long while thinking of everything that might go wrong the following day, when I was doing the same trip but with different people on board. What if the weather was too bad, or the people did not turn up, or the Seneca got sick or I got sick or – worse – lost?

I refuelled G-BAIG and thoroughly checked him over to leave less for the morning, then tried to do a weight & balance and realised I didn't know the weights of the people coming with me or how many were coming. Then I went home to worry a little more.

The next morning, I arrived at 6am, despite not needing to be there until 7.30am as the two passengers were due to arrive around 8am for an 8.30am departure. I needn't have worried: my first commercial flight was glorious. I felt light-headed as I rode my yellow Norton motorbike, Peril, back to the B&B. What a wonderful life!

For the first few days, I flew back and forth to Liverpool for Rexon Pumps and on the third day, I met the boss, Tony Holmes. He was charming and a pleasure to fly with.

He had a private pilot's licence, so could could have flown his Seneca himself but explained that he did not have the time for all the paperwork and needed to be fresh when he arrived.

Three months after flying with Rexon Pumps and my friendly Golf Bag, as I referred to the Seneca, I felt permanently settled. Flying an average of three or four days a week gave me plenty of spare time. I used the time instructing at Southend Flying Club and caught up with a couple of hobbies; calligraphy and making leather goods, mainly for horses. Michael, a colleague of Tony Holmes who owned G-BAIG, asked if I could paint the name of his girlfriend – 'Kerrigold' – on the nose.

Using an Olde English script in gold paint outlined in black, the name looked smart against the white nose of the green-and-white Seneca.

Michael was pleased with the result and having heard I worked with leather, asked if I could make him a cricket bag, as his was falling apart. I used the metal frame of his old cricket bag, bought some leather in London and spent a few weeks working on constructing the bag. I felt pleased with the finished product especially as it was nothing like the basic straps I was used to making or repairing.

Michael asked what I would charge. Although it had taken a long time, it had been good work experience and I had enjoyed making it. I told him he could have it as he had supplied the major part – the frame – and my time was effectively his.

I still loved instructing in my spare time and felt that I was improving in value to my students as my flying horizons broadened. It was time to invest in taking the rating required to enable me to train other pilots to fly multi-engine aircraft. Edward Clack agreed to fit me in for training and, as it happened, there was a week when no flights were scheduled for Rexon Pumps. Tony agreed that I could hire the Seneca for that week and he would let me know the cost.

After an enjoyable few days at Southend, flying with Edward Clack, I obtained the twin instructor rating and flew back to Sywell.

Michael, the Seneca's owner, called and congratulated me on my multi-instructor rating. He joked that I should teach him to fly, to which I replied I would love to. I then asked him how much I owed for the hours flown in his aircraft.

He would not allow me to pay him a penny.

"You wouldn't take anything for my beautiful golf bag, which I use regularly," he said. "Call it a swap. Perhaps I will take up flying sometime. Then I will take your offer to teach me."

I was lost for words.

Two days later, I was asked to take three people to Cork in Ireland, returning the following day. My hotel was a few miles from the airport and it was an enjoyable walk in beautiful surroundings. As I approached the hill that led to the hotel, I saw a stable lad walking next to a horse. I crossed the road to walk with them, asking the lad why he was not riding up the hill.

"I've finished my ride, so I'm taking a break," said the lad, who turned out to be called Mick. "You want to ride ole Ginger up the hill?" He asked this matter-of-factly, as if it was quite normal to offer a horse to a stranger.

"I wouldn't say no."

Mick said I could leave Ginger tied to a tree at the top of the hill if I got there before him. Naturally, I walked Ginger beside Mick, to the top.

Everyone in Ireland seemed friendly, courteous and helpful, without the peculiarity suffered in England of having to have the necessary introduction before talking to anyone.

On my return to England, I had a phone call from Tony, with terrible news. The Seneca was to be sold, as the company could no longer justify its occasional use when other means of transport were far less expensive. It was all part of the recession that the country was suffering. I no longer had a job.

I couldn't believe what I heard. I hadn't even noticed England was in a recession. Not reading newspapers or listening to the radio and having never owned a TV there was not much chance of noticing a small thing like a recession. This was a bombshell. Tony sounded so distraught for my sake that I found myself consoling him. I told him about the terrific trip to Cork and how much fun I had had, which was surely the best way to have a job end – on a fabulous note.

*

The following morning I called Edward Clack asking if he needed any instructors. He told me he would be delighted if I returned but warned me that things were very quiet, being in a recession and October, so not to expect to do a great deal of flying. He added there might not be a full-time job until the spring or summer but there would be freelance instructing, with possibly the occasional charter in his twin Aztec.

I rode my bike to Chelmsford to stay with my parents and be reunited with Finn, while sorting out accommodation nearer to Southend. In the evenings, I wrote to various job advertisements asking for pilots to fly anything anywhere, not really expecting to hear from anyone.

After a couple of weeks, I received a phone call from my old friend, Olly, whose bike I had crashed on the Wall of Death in Germany, a few years ago. He was working as a security guard on night patrols. He suggested I travel up to see him in Newcastle and look for instructing work there as he thought the flying clubs were all busy despite it being winter.

"Bring your tools and leather with you, and you could make and repair saddlery items when you're not flying," he suggested.

Since I had not travelled anywhere much further north than Sywell, apart from flying trips, it seemed as good an idea as any. So I packed a large suitcase of tools, a small one of clothes with a few 'butts' of leather, loaded Finn into my little car and headed toward Newcastle.

All my visits to the flying clubs and charter companies at the surrounding airfields proved to be welcoming and friendly, but none of them could offer any work.

But fortunately, having spread the word that I was thinking about returning to saddlery, I found I was soon receiving orders that kept me busy twelve hours a day. I loved working with leather and especially making a vast amount of harness for large Shire horses, using black leather, yellow thread and attaching shiny horse brasses. Among my customers were Ann and Ken Playle, who I had worked for when I first left school.

After barely a month in Newcastle, stitching daily, I had three possible flying jobs to pursue: one with Kalahari Air Services and Charter (KASAC) in Botswana, one in Carlisle where I would be running a flying club and operating a Cessna 310 on charters, and one at Luton Airport flying charters in Piper Aztecs and Chieftans and also running a small flying club. The Carlisle one sounded ideal and the African one the least exciting.

Chapter 8

CHANGING MY MIND

The following week, I packed everything and returned to Essex to discuss the job offers with my parents. It was all academic, since not one was even a definite offer yet.

I travelled to London for the interview with Jan Bakker, operations manager of KASAC, but was not impressed with him. He came across as a male chauvinist who was trying hard to be civil to a potential female employee whom he already disliked. He was tall and slim and looked frighteningly formal and intimidating. I could not help wondering why he had travelled from South Africa to bother interviewing me. He gave the impression that a woman's place was in the home, preferably limited to the kitchen and bedroom. I completed the interview with disdainful courtesy although with extreme politeness. My nerves naturally vanished as the job no longer held any interest for me. Although with Gerry Gooch's motorcycle team I had really enjoyed Zimbabwe, Jan Bakker was enough to put me off the potential job.

A few days after the interview, the phone rang and it was a firm offer of the Luton job, with a starting date in two weeks. I was amazed. It was 1980 and most people were still surprised to be approached by a female who wanted to fly at all, much less commercially. Barely an hour later, a telegram arrived from South Africa notifying me I had been successful in being selected to fly for KASAC. As soon as the work and residence permits were organised, I would be sent a ticket to my base of operations in Gaberone, Botswana.

I stood, holding the telegram, thinking what a relief Luton had accepted me. I told my parents that I had accepted the Luton job, though they both thought I should opt for a chance to travel, see the world while I was young and unattached and to make some money in Africa.

During lunch, with my mind churning over which was a better move in life, the phone rang again.

"That'll be for you, Tizi," said my stepfather.

I took the call. My dream had come true: the Carlisle job was mine. I accepted immediately and was told I could start in a week.

My mother told me it would be even colder further north and she thought I would prefer the warmth of a hot country; my stepfather thought I would be better going to Africa, to travel and earn some real money. KASAC was offering a gratuity at the end of the two-year contract, which meant I could buy my own flying club when I returned.

Undecided, I returned to finish stitching a head collar, thinking about the three options, while my parents went out. My heart was crying out for the 310 in Carlisle, while my head debated the advantages of the remoteness of Botswana.

When I had finished the head collar, I noticed that I'd concentrated so much on the job options that I'd sewn a cheek piece back to front. So I spent another hour correcting my error.

My parents arrived back with presents for me: a cassette-radio that I'd been wanting for a. long time, and a fully automatic Kodak camera. My mother explained that I needed a good camera as there would be a wonderful opportunity to use it on the wildlife in Africa. She then told me the gifts were 'farewell presents' but they would both have the presents back if I decided not to go to Botswana.

That settled it: Africa it was to be. I wrote an acceptance to KASAC then called both Luton and Carlisle to say I had changed my mind, which is what women do best anyway.

*

My parents drove me to Heathrow to see me off or, was it to make sure I really did go?

My stepfather casually asked if I had any cash. On checking my purse, I found a fiver. He then insisted I take some cash with me: it would be a month before my first pay and I would need food, maybe uniform, certainly appropriate clothing and perhaps even some blankets and cutlery before the month finished and my fiver had been extinguished.

My first reaction was to refuse, as I liked to be independent, but then I realised I might not get far with my fiver. He pointed out that I had mentioned company housing was supplied, with only hard furnishing; was I to wait a month for a blanket, pillow, soap, shampoo and a knife and fork?

He bundled £200 into my hand and told me not to even think of returning it until I was settled.

So, on that freezing day in February, I boarded the aircraft wondering what lay in store in Africa.

As the aircraft arrived at Botswana, at four o'clock local time, a message was relayed that the temperature was 35 degrees. Perhaps it would not be as bad as I'd feared, I thought as I stepped onto the tarmac wondering where to go.

Dudley Barlow, the Chief Pilot of KASAC with his wife B (Belinda), was delegated to meet me on behalf of the General Manager, John Byron. Dudley was a tall, grey-haired, very good-looking man who always looked at the brighter side of life and helped everyone he came across. B was equally bubbly, some years younger than Dudley and with a striking figure.

Dudley told me they were taking me to the Holiday Inn, where I was to stay until given a company flat within the KASAC complex. First, they would offer me a 'toot' at their house and let me settle in and relax.

As we entered their house I was introduced to their two young daughters, Pippa (8) and Hailey (6). Pippa and Hailey were both beautiful blue-eyed, blonde, children with better manners than any other children I had met.

Hailey disappeared rapidly and returned in seconds with an ice-cold Castle lager, which she pressed into my hand.

"You'll need that," said Dudley. "What a time to arrive! We are having a heat-wave. Anyway, welcome to Botswana." Then he added, "There are only two beers available in Botswana – Castle and Lion – but no-one drinks Lion because it's a Kaffir beer, made by the natives from millet."

Then he asked if I would like a swim since the heat was oppressive and they had a pool in their garden. Having checked the map for Botswana, before leaving England, I'd noticed there was no water within hundreds of miles, so had not packed a swimsuit. B saw my hesitation and told me to come upstairs where she would find a suit to fit me as she was taking a dip anyway.

In a few minutes, lying on my back relaxing in the warm pool, I couldn't believe what was happening. I didn't recall walking through a Looking Glass, but this seemed on a level.

As B was telling me to relax, Pippa appeared with a plate of sausages, pineapple and cheese and fruit of all varieties that I had not seen before. Setting the plates down at the edge of the pool, Pippa said, "Mummy told me you would be hungry having come all the way from England, so this is for you."

The fruit was delicious – fresh mango, paw-paw and bananas. B warned me that she would be giving me some dinner soon, before taking me to the hotel. I told her I would be more than happy with the fruit, which was fabulous. But so was the kudu steak she served for dinner. I had to confess I wouldn't even have recognised a kudu if I'd seen one.

A little later Dudley drove me to the Holiday Inn, telling me to sleep and rest well and he would call for me at lunchtime to meet Mr Byron.

Sleep was about the last thing on my mind: everything seemed so unreal and I worried that if I fell asleep, I would wake up in freezing England again. But did sleep come, followed by a beautifully warm morning, which I used to walk around the locality.

Most of the houses were something called a Rendavel, a round dwelling place made of mud, reeds and sticks, with the door being either bits of wood, a blanket or sheet of some kind. After a brief enquiry at the bank, where I discovered I needed a letter of employment in order to open an account, it was time to return to the hotel.

At Botswana airport, I met Mr John Byron, who addressed me as Hodson every time he spoke with me. I thought that was sweet, but later discovered he had not wanted to employ a female, so tried to avoid admitting to himself that he had done just that.

The meeting was brief. He told me I could relax and get myself acclimatised to the weather. When I was ready, I could take the necessary written exams, then the flight training required to pass the flying tests qualifying myself to hold the Botswana commercial licence and instrument rating.

He then told me to go out and buy myself a car, preferably a new one, as I would need reliable transport. He stated I should keep the risk of breaking down alone in the Bush as low as possible, and if money was a problem, I should go to the local garage and buy one on Finance – KASAC would stand as guarantors.

While he was talking about the car, a pilot walked in to put a piece of paper on Mr Byron's table. I was introduced to Mark Sampson, who seemed pleasant enough, but as soon as he left the room, Mr Byron told me to stay well away from all the pilots who had wives or girlfriends. Obviously, according to Mr Byron, every female was out to trap any male. I vaguely wondered why he felt that way, but instead tried asking if there were a company flat available for me, as I had understood accommodation would be provided.

At this, he got very upset and asked what was wrong with the best hotel in town, to which I told him there was nothing at all wrong with it, but I did not want to cost the company more than was necessary and would feel more settled in a home of my own than living out of a suitcase.

I was then dismissed so had the chance to ask Dudley about the possibility of a flat. Apparently this was a big issue: Mr Byron felt it was not fair for 'a little girl from England' to be shoved into a flat as soon as she arrived, when she would no doubt be suffering from heat exhaustion. I wasn't sure how long I would last if he treated me like a china doll forever.

That afternoon I walked to the car dealer and bought my first new car; a white panel van on a two-year lease. It was the cheapest new vehicle in the showroom. Since I had no interest in cars, apart from hoping they would start when the key was turned, slow down when the brakes were applied and give reasonable fuel consumption, it wasn't a difficult choice. The van was delivered late the same afternoon, which gave me a good feeling of independence.

I drove round to Dudley's house to find out where I could obtain the reference material to study for the necessary exams, but Dudley was more concerned that I should join him in a beer. However, I did find out the address of the Department of Civil Aviation (DCA) in Gaberone.

The following morning found me at the office of the DCA loaded up with all the reading material that I might need for the air law and the type rating exams for a Beechcraft Baron and a Navajo Chieftain.

The inspector supplying me with the books seemed to know who I was when I introduced myself, so I asked if I could book in a date for the exams. He told me not to worry but to return when I was ready and then I could take them immediately.

On my return, I stopped at KASAC's company doctor, a charming man by the name of Dr Letsunyane, who told me he could see me immediately. I passed the medical, returned to town and bought a swimsuit. After a few hours swotting the air law, I drove round to Dudley and B's house, changed into my new costume and walked toward the pool. B thrust a cold Castle into my hand, telling me I must need one with the heat and the amount I was doing.

I placed the can on the side of the pool and after a few lengths to relax, floated on my back, taking a sip every now and then. This seemed like a fairytale life.

Chapter 9

THE 'CHINA DOLL' TREATMENT

I returned and stayed in my room for the next couple of days immersed in the borrowed books and then returned to the DCA office for the exams. I was happy to show Dudley the written exams results and ask him when I could start flight training. I also dropped another hint about the empty flat that needed a tenant.

After constant persistence, I eventually finished the training and testing and was ready for my first passenger-carrying trip. I was also allowed the front door key to my flat, so life seemed to be improving.

My first few flying trips were with another pilot 'to show me the airfield for the first time'. For the first one or two flights that made sense, but when it came to the point where I thought I was going to be accompanied on every route before I could be trusted to find an airfield alone, I thought this was taking the 'china doll treatment' too far. When I told Dudley how I felt, he apologised saying Mr Byron worried that he couldn't cope with adverse publicity should a female pilot get lost over the Bush as sole captain of the aircraft.

I was furious and asked what the purpose was of employing an extra pilot if each trip would be 'two-crew' on a single-crew aircraft. In fact, I was a burden, an expense and a liability with no financial contribution to the company – worse, I was taking up precious space of an extra seat for a fare-paying passenger on every trip I flew.

Dudley must have spoken to Mr Byron, explaining my feelings, as I was soon rostered for my first solo charter, followed by a rostered day off. I presumed the day off was to recover.

The next chartered flight was accompanied as I had not visited Maun before. In fact Maun is straight up the only north / south tar road in Botswana, which runs for a couple of hundred miles to the top of the country, which then turns into Zimbabwe and Zambia. Since Maun had radio communication, plus the airfield was sited on the edge of the tar road, any novice pilot who had just completed their private licence could easily find it. That left me understandably infuriated.

The day after the Maun trip, Mr Byron summoned me into the office. He was in a dilemma as two Americans had arrived unannounced. They wanted to charter an aeroplane and pilot for 10 days to take them into south-west Africa visiting ranches they owned or in which they had an interest; flying into airstrips, not large airports.

Having heard the problem, I suggested I should take the charter, since I had recently taken my first solo charter without a problem. Mr Byron could hardly be expected to throw away the chance of 10 days' worth of considerable profit for the company by saying there was no pilot available. I even tactfully pointed out that I was being paid the same as the other pilots.

"Do you think you could manage to find these small ranch strips?" he asked. "I have not even asked the two gentlemen if they would even agree to having a … female pilot flying them in the first place."

He had no option, since he could not throw away the potential long charter, so he asked the clients, Kent Crane and Paris Theodore, if they would have any objection to being flown by a woman. They were both delighted. Unleashed at last for my first solo charter (with passengers), into the unknown lands and skies of south-west Africa, I drove home with an hour to pack.

As it was hot, I decided I could wash everything on a daily basis, rather than carry unnecessary weight, so I grabbed an overnight bag and returned to Gaberone Airport. There, I checked my allocated aircraft, refuelled it, filed a flight plan and took off for G J Strydom Airport with the two passengers before Mr Byron could change his mind.

Kent, a large American with very short black hair and small piggy eyes, took the front seat and chatted happily on the way to Strydom. He asked casually if I had been on a hunting safari before and whether I could shoot – also if I had brought any suitable clothes?

I guessed he'd noticed my very small bag, so I answered no and yes, mentioning I had a shirt, slacks and a wash bag. He then discovered I had no boots or even shoes – just the sandals I was wearing at the time.

"Well, the first thing we'll do tomorrow morning before we leave Strydom, is to get you dressed up properly for the real Bush," was Kent's reply.

I was kitted out with shorts, two long-sleeved cotton shirts (for the thorns), desert wellies, (which were felt shoes), a bush hat and two pairs of long thick socks. He told me I could ditch the uniform, but I needed to keep it to fly back to Gaberone in.

After the shopping trip, we returned to the airport and I asked where he wanted to go. The next stop was a small ranch owned by the Sparrows, which was not marked on a chart. I had a one-and-a quarter-million chart of Botswana, which went into south-west Africa, then stopped. This was a typical flying chart that gave little detail, with no villages or airstrips marked on it – just the large airports (the maps used by beginners show airstrips, villages, lakes, forests, wood and even pylons). I asked a few pilots if anyone knew of the Sparrows' ranch and sure enough, someone had been there.

My directions were to head due north for 45 minutes, at which point I would see two very high hills: mountains resembling women breasts, whereupon I should turn due east for thirty-seven minutes and the ranch would be beneath me. I would need to check the airstrip carefully before landing as, not being fenced, game may be grazing.

With Kent and Paris aboard, I followed my strange directions and came upon the airstrip for the ranch. As per the warning, there was a small herd of giraffe on the runway, so I buzzed them low, expecting them to go. However, as I turned onto the final approach, I saw a baby giraffe walking down the centre of the runway, so I had to fly another circuit. At the third approach, I saw a distressed looking larger giraffe at the side of the runway, which seemed to be calling the baby.

After landing, we were met by Mark Sparrow and I was shown to a hut, complete with a personal (outdoor) shower, I changed into my new Bush clothes and met Kent and Paris to go on a shoot. We were offered a choice; the tame area, where the game were friendly, would come up to you and perhaps take titbits; or the hunting area with 30.06 rifles supplied by the Sparrows.

Kent and Paris both opted for the hunting area, while I took directions to the tame area, where I had the time of my life making friends with zebras, giraffe, kudu, gemsbok and wildebeest. That evening I felt like Alice having stepped through the looking glass.

Kent insisted I went with them the following day on a 'proper' safari, not another 'picnic in the park.' I had been looking forward to another few days on my own, but I could hardly be so impolite as to turn him down. I sat in the back of the Landcruiser – the locals called them 'Landcruises' – with Paris, while we bumped and bounced at high speed over the desert terrain. Kent was in the front with Gibson, the game tracker/driver.

Paris was such a contrast to Kent, with a quiet, gentle voice and a slender build. Of the two, one listened to Kent but talked with Paris.

Behind us were two boys chatting away in a totally unintelligible dialect with different clicks preceding most of their words. I asked Paris what language the boys spoke. He told me they were Bushmen, and were talking Bushman, although he had no idea which tribe they were from as there were many and the languages were completely different, but they all contained clicks.

Soon we stopped to allow Gibson, a professional tracker to track the spoor of a particular kudu – an antelope – which Kent wanted to shoot. Gibson was trying to read the tracks, which had been crossed with another kudu. The sun was being generous with its rays and I was feeling drowsy, so I lay back with the constant chatter and clicks behind me whilst enveloped in the sun's warmth. I was now pleased I had opted to be social with Kent and Paris.

Soon the Landcruiser was trundling forward again, although much slower. Kent seemed excited, turning round to say we had almost reached 'his kudu' and the last part was up to him. I vaguely wondered what he meant but wasn't bothered, as the scenery was fantastic. The sand all around changed in shades with the locality.

Soon the Landcruiser stopped and I looked ahead to see what was happening. Apparently, Gibson had tracked the kudu to within a few hundred feet. All Kent had to do was walk (or crawl) until he was within a comfortable range to shoot the brute.

He seemed to take a long while to get unnecessarily close, considering he was using exceptionally high-powered telescopic sights. He finally fired and the magnificent beast went down with a loud cry of pain, but only to its front knees. It then tried in vain to rise, uttering a pathetic lowing sound at each attempt.

Kent stood a few yards away, watching and beckoned for us both to come, shouting, "it's OK, he's perfectly safe – the back is broke."

"Then finish him off!" I screamed, hating to see the poor animal in such unnecessary pain. I knew Kent had two bullets in the rifle and had only used one, so one shot to the head would have removed all the pain immediately.

But the 'Brave Macho Big American' had other ideas. He waited for several minutes while the poor brute, badly wounded but not dead, was still trying to get up in pain and terror, until it collapsed with exhaustion. Kent just watched.

I tried to get past Paris, out of the truck. He asked what I was hoped to do.

"To take Kent's gun and put that poor beast out of that totally unnecessary agony," I told him.

Paris seemed genuinely worried and held me back.

"No, you can't touch Kent when he is hunting. Just leave him be."

"Let me go – it's still alive and yet better dead." I struggled but couldn't get free from Paris' grip. I tried not to watch, but there followed another desperate cry of help from the dying beast. Unable not to look up, I saw Kent sticking a knife into the beast's shoulder. He seemed to be on a bloodlust hunt, twisting the knife to no good effect.

Poor Paris was now holding me in his arms and I could see he was almost as sickened and upset as I was. He tried to explain there was a shortage of ammunition in Zimbabwe and it was a sign of a poor hunter if you needed more than one bullet to 'drop' any game.

I told him between sobs that to shoot a poor innocent animal in the back was not hunting anyway – it was murder. I think Paris privately agreed with me, that hunting was fine but backstabbing and cold-blooded murder was unforgivable.

During the remaining days, I spent my time in the tame area, trying to forget the bloodbath. Kent had tried to explain to me the kudu had 'record antlers' with over three-and-a-half twists and that it would go down in the Book, which is why he couldn't risk a head shot: it would ruin the trophy. Yet, when the beast had finally succumbed to its own moment of peace in death, Kent had said the trophy was not as good as he had thought earlier and didn't want it mounted after all. How I had hated him when he told me that.

When it was time to go, Kent asked if I would take him to a different airstrip, which he owned. I was given directions from the Sparrow family and set off happily for the new ranch. This strip was somewhat shorter but not a problem to the Beechcraft Baron, which was a good short-field aircraft and nicknamed the Desert Ship. Kent remarked that the strip seemed too short to get airborne from. I agreed it was short and that I would be happier if I could measure the actual distance and then check it on the performance graphs. Then I could tell him if temperature or weight limited us to get airborne in complete safety.

He left me a Landcruiser and a driver who he instructed to bring me to the camp when I had finished. After driving the full length of the available strip, I measured it and calculated at what weight and temperature we could all get airborne. I found with the small amount of fuel we had on board, even with the three of us, there was no problem getting airborne in 28 degrees of temperature, which was almost midday. The driver delivered me to Kent's camp, where I gave him the good news but either he didn't trust my calculations or didn't believe me capable of the calculations (the latter I think). He said that 'just to be on the safe side' he was going to ask his men to cut down a further length for use as a runway.

The morning came for our final departure to G J Strydom. The plan was to stop for the night there, prior to clearing customs and return to Gaberone. It was a cool morning with a couple of knots of breeze down the runway, so there would be no problem with the take-off, even without the extra length cut down. However, as we approached the aircraft, Kent asked about the nearest airfield where we could refuel. I told him there was an airfield 10 miles in the direction we were heading.

"Well, you fly there, fill up and I'll meet you there. I'll go by truck – I still don't like this little strip. Paris, you wanna fly or ride?"

Paris said he trusted the pilot's judgement and wouldn't like to be bumped, rattled and rolled for an unnecessary 10 miles when there was a comfortable aircraft right here.

We both watched Kent get into the truck beside the driver, who made no attempt to depart, which meant he wanted to see our take-off. When the doors were closed, Paris asked if there was plenty of slack or whether it was still a bit tight on length. I assured him there was no problem at all: there was more than sufficient room before extending the length, but just to wind Kent up, I planned on making a 'short field departure', if that was OK with Paris.

He was delighted with the idea, so I taxied to the absolute beginning of the strip and applied full power with my feet on the brakes. Then as I released the brakes I let the speed develop a little and took two notches of flap. The aircraft was airborne in less than half the original length. Although I was busy flying the aircraft, Paris shouted in excitement as he could see Kent raising his fists and jumping up and down on his seat.

Finally back at G J Strydom, I topped up the tanks again and cleared customs, then tried to find any usable weather forecast for Gaberone. That was about as hopeful as finding a cool ice-cream sitting on a sand dune. I tried to hurry Kent, to arrive in Gaberone before nightfall: it was a three-hour trip and night flying was to be avoided in summer, unless the aircraft carried a serviceable radar. It was not possible to see the vicious clouds or potentially dangerous thunderstorms at night.

Kent had fully recovered from his previous worry about the airstrip and was now being obnoxious, throwing his weight around and insisted on eating a complete meal before departing, followed by a drink or few.

As three o'clock approached, I told Paris of my concern about night flying over the desert in summer – could he somehow get Kent to leave now or postpone the departure until the following day? Kent agreed to come right away.

Somehow, more time elapsed with paying the bill, using the bathroom and packing the aircraft. When we set off heading for Gaberone, it was gone four o'clock. I would be out of radio contact with anyone for well over two-and-a-half hours, until I could reach VHF reception with Gaberone.

The scenery was beautiful consisting of sand followed by more sand, rippled in places and flat in others. The colours changed from the lighter sand in the southwest to the darker variation as we flew further east. There were no dwelling places, trees or vegetation – just the sheer beauty of space and freedom.

I had a vague notion of how fabulous it would be to get on an uncontrollable horse, allowing him to gallop forever, as fast as he wanted, in any direction, until he finally ran out of steam and slowed. In the midst of my daydreaming I noticed the blue sky we left behind was beginning to become scattered with cloud, which was building up rapidly. Cruising at 10,000 feet was still clear but in a few minutes I needed to descend to remain in clear skies. This was unexpected, as the forecast had indicated a clear passage back.

With the clouds getting closer, there was no option but to descend. I could not risk entering cloud without being in radio contact with a controller, somewhere close enough, who could tell me who else might be in 'my' present piece of sky. I have never spoken to any pilot who has collided with another aircraft in cloud, and I am sure no one else has.

Shortly after commencing the descent, I could see a heavy build of possible thunderstorm clouds to the right and to the left of me. I only hoped I could get through the middle, but darkness was approaching and with it came serious streaks of lightning to the right and left.

There was no option but to turn back. In the darkening sky it was not possible to see a safe passage through. Both options to go round the storm were out , with the lightning appearing like fireworks ahead and around.

I explained to Kent and Paris that due to the storm and lightning ahead, we would have to turn round and return to Strydom. We had no radar and I could not risk entering storm clouds in the dark. I then tried to communicate with anyone on the radio: there was hope that another pilot might be listening in on the standard frequency so I could get some idea of the weather at Strydom. Kent asked who was I talking to, so I explained. He went ballistic.

"You mean to tell me we are flying over the desert in the pitch black, out of communication with anyone, and I don't suppose you even know where we are," he said. "Just now, you're gonna tell me we're running out of gas. I want to get out. Anyway, I need the bathroom, so I want you to put this little aeroplane down, anywhere, like now, and I want to get out alive." He was shaking and I felt sorry for him.

All I could do was to assure him we were fine on gas and – a little white lie to make him feel comfortable – that I knew exactly where we were and showed him by pointing to a part of my chart. He asked how I knew we were just there. I explained I had calculated the wind from when we had left and been tracking with the elapsed minutes on my watch.

Then I showed him the exact place where we had turned around. I just didn't mention it was dead reckoning, and where we actually were might be quite a different position. Kent started jabbering non-stop about everything and anything. That was fine since the more I reassured Kent, the more I seemed to reassure myself.

At least Paris seemed to be totally calm in the back seat. Kent seemed to take a sudden turn for the worse and again demanded we land.

I started talking into my microphone as if holding a conversation. Kent noticed and asked if it was Strydom I'd been speaking to. I said it wasn't but I had contacted another pilot who had departed from Strydom where the weather was fine. He settled a little at this and then he started telling me what he planned to do when we landed. He would find the best hotel in Windhoek and he would treat us all to the best meal of our lives.

Finally I heard a crackle on Strydom's approach frequency but they could only read me intermittently. After waiting a few more minutes I not only had a bearing on the airfield beacon but a clear reception with approach, who gave me the weather and helpful assistance to guide me onto final approach.

We were all glad to be down and Kent, true to his word ordered a taxi, asking for the best hotel in town. When we arrived outside the rather glamorous-looking hotel, he suggested after a 'freshen-up' we should meet in the restaurant.

Arriving a couple of minutes early, I studied the menu. Paris approached saying he had hoped I would be early, as he had wanted to ask me if I really knew exactly where I was when I turned around. Did I really talk to another pilot on the radio before speaking to the airport? I admitted the 'pilot' had been an invention.

The meal was one of the finest I can recall, starting with lobster, followed by a kudu steak then a lovely fruit salad of fresh paw-paw, mango, cashew-nut fruit, lychees and fresh cream and truffles.

The following day we landed back at Gaberone, where Kent and Paris bid their farewells before making their way back to America. Luckily for me, Kent sung my praises as a pilot to both Dudley and Mr Byron, so it was announced that from now on I could take any charter unaccompanied, even to airstrips I had not been to before.

Chapter 10

MERCY MISSION

With a quiet day and no charter flights booked, I was anticipating a leisurely afternoon when there was a knock on the door. It was Mr Byron, who asked me if I could take a mercy flight to Bokspits as soon as possible. I would take Colin, the local doctor, who was needed urgently at the Clinic.

"Well, of course I can," I said, looking at my watch. "There's no problem if I leave now. There's three hours of daylight and it's three hours away. Has the aircraft been fuelled?" I asked as I picked up my flight bag.

Mr Byron looked worried and told me he had to give me bad news – that the only aircraft free was ACS, but that it was full of fuel, already checked and the doctor was waiting right now to go. All the Barons cruised at 180 knots, except ACS who could only manage 170 knots. I had to hurry.

On a Mercy flight, everyone helps – the doctor was delivered to the aircraft and another pilot came to do the pre-flight checks. I started up, doing my seatbelts up and checks while taxiing at high speed. Once airborne, I turned onto an approximate heading, and then got out the plog (the pilot's log) to double check the heading, route and timings. I looked at my watch and groaned. It had only been five minutes since I'd been talking to Mr Byron, but there was a headwind and no chance of making Bokspits before nightfall.

I looked at Colin and re-introduced myself. He was middle aged, with slightly receding salt-and-pepper hair and wore a permanent frown, of worry or concentration.

We had met briefly in the crew room a few weeks ago and I remembered he held a private flying licence. So I asked him if he would like to pole the aircraft en route to Bokspits.

"No," he said firmly. "I know we have the slowest aircraft and it will probably be dark before we get there, and I have been warned that should you decide to turn round at any time, I must accept your decision. Since it's important to me to get there, I'll leave it to you to gain the last extra knot possible."

I then asked the nature of this mercy flight.

"It's a woman in labour, but the child is positioned badly and is likely to die if I cannot get there to deliver it, probably by suction, tonight."

He had emphasised the 'tonight.'

I pondered the implications. There were no lights at Bokspits: it was a sand strip barely five nautical miles from a small village, with the usual bottlestore-cum-general stores, a bank and a post office. There was a small clinic run by a handful of nurses with an occasional visiting doctor.

Not difficult to find, even in the failing light, as I had been there before and marked the proximity of the village to the airfield on my chart. It could be tricky, though, if I couldn't make out the short strip, should it be pitch black. Unlike the fading light of the British sunsets, when the sun sets in Africa it goes from bright light to pitch black – no twilight.

Still within VHF range of Gaberone, I called up the controller and asked if they could send a message to Bokspits, asking for a few vehicles to park in front of the runway with the headlights on full. I was told they would try to relay messages through Johannesburg and back to Bokspits. I explained there was a small life at stake: they said they would try harder.

The trip seemed to take forever. Fifteen minutes short of the ETA the daylight went. Colin told me there would be a bright light in the clinic, so we both started looking for any signs of life.

I had told Colin that because there was a life at stake; I was prepared to try one approach to land. If I couldn't find the runway – it was pitch black – or if the approach did not feel right, then I would simply go around and set heading straight back to Gabs.

Colin told me he was grateful for me to even have come this far, as the other pilots would not take the trip with such low odds of success. A strange time to find out that the pilot who helped pre-flight the aircraft had refused to take the trip!

Suddenly the light of the clinic came into view. Although I couldn't see the runway, or the village, I could calculate where it should be. After four minutes, I turned slightly to the left, which should theoretically have put me onto a right base leg of a runway I still hadn't seen. There was a full moon and no cloud. As I turned onto what I thought should be base, I lowered a stage of flap and reduced the throttle. I then saw two small lights facing each other across, not down, the runway, dazzling rather than assisting any landing.

After turning onto what was hopefully the final approach, I lowered the last flap and descended through 300 feet: with the aid of the moon, the runway came into view straight ahead. I felt like shouting with relief. As I touched down, I realised the lights shining toward each other across the runway, one on either side, were the lights I had requested to be shining down the runway, so that I could see it. We both laughed. I was glad Colin had a licence – he could see the funny side of it.

"They meant well," I said.

A Landcruiser met us as I slowed down in the middle of the runway. Colin was busy thanking me. I stopped him short by saying, "Look, I've done my bit. Your bit is more important. Why don't you go to the clinic now, and I'll follow when I've put the plane to bed?"

I parked the aircraft, turned everything off and secured the controls with a seat belt. By the time I had picked up my flight bag, the car was already heading back toward me.

What a reception I had! The local people couldn't have treated me better if I had been royalty. A bottle of cold beer was pressed into my hand and a bed was being prepared for me at the clinic. No one yet knew the outcome of the pregnant woman.

Shown to my 'room', just a bed between two partitions, I finished my beer swiftly. There was an eight-hour rule between bottle and throttle and I had no intention of breaking that one.

He arrived shortly, looking happy.

"A success?" I asked. He nodded and thanked me again and told me the woman also wanted him to thank me from her.

I then gave him the bad news; of my required presence at Gabs at dawn for an early charter – did he want to come or wait for the next plane? He agreed to join me and ordered the car for 2.30am.

The return flight was beautiful. There is always something special about seeing the African sun, rising with the entire sky ahead, turning from black to a deep, rich, red before daylight breaks and the day had started.

After running my charter flight, for the Ministry of Education, I found a note in my pigeonhole to see Mr Byron on my return. I knocked at his door, expecting he was going to be pleased that the mercy flight trip was a success and that the child was delivered alive, and perhaps pleased that I had made an extra effort to get back in time for my charter.

Far from being pleased, he started reprimanding me about the foolishness of the flight. He told me I should never have left in the first place, when I was aware I could not have arrived before dark. He then told me I had no business risking the aircraft and the life of the doctor by landing in pitch blackness on a remote sand strip, but more especially – having put the whole company at risk – I then made a foolhardy decision to take off the following morning, again in pitch black, just to cover an ordinary charter which could have been done by another pilot.

"But there was a child's life at risk," I muttered pathetically, when I thought the onslaught was over.

"That 'child' as you call it, was *black*," he stated vehemently. "In fact I have decided to suspend you from any further flying as I don't think you are fit to fly for KASAC as a sensible company pilot. Captain Barlow would like a word with you when you leave here."

I couldn't believe what I had heard. What had the colour of the child to do with whether one should try to save a life? I hadn't known, asked or even cared whether the child was white or black.

Crestfallen, ashamed and embarrassed, I arrived at Dudley's house, wondering whether Mr Byron would have felt the same had it have been his wife likely to lose a baby if a pilot couldn't be bothered to try to help.

Dudley was smiling when I entered. "Well, Tizi, you really have set the cat amongst the pigeons. I was told to give you a rollocking, but since I've only heard one side of it, just take your time and tell me what actually happened. To start with, how did you ever find the place?"

I told him events as they were, including the full moon lighting up the strip and warning Colin that I was only prepared to make one approach then return had everything not felt totally comfortable. I told him Byron's comments, which disgusted me even to repeat them.

Poor Dudley, he was so wonderful. He told me that he was totally on my side and thought I had done a wonderful job.

"As far as the suspension goes," he said, "yes, you are suspended for tonight – you look like you need a night's sleep. But over my dead body will Mr Byron try to give you a bad name, when you deserve a medal for what you have done. There was another pilot who could have gone but wouldn't try because he didn't think he'd have a hope of finding the place if it got dark, so naturally he feels very bad because you succeeded. I'm not telling you who it was, but unfortunately he has been mouthing to Mr Byron about the implications with regard to any insurance, had anything gone wrong. He is trying to justify himself for not taking the flight, so naturally Mr Byron is thinking well of him and less of you in the light that was painted. I told him I'd talk to you first before he was to do anything. Anyway he'd have to fire me first if he wants to fire one of my pilots, so have a toot and calm down."

It was Dudley's answer to everything: a toot. It was Botswana slang for an alcoholic drink, but generally meant a beer. Pippa had arrived from nowhere, bearing the ice-cold toot. Relief flooded over me as I took a delicious sip of the most refreshing beverage I had ever had.

Chapter 11

A MIXED BUNCH

The pilots flying for KASAC were a very mixed bunch. Dudley, tall and lean and in his late 50s, was popular with everyone. He originated from Rhodesia, was efficient and an excellent pilot who worked hard and seemed to know how to make people want to do their best for him.

Mark Sampson, from South Africa, was an incredibly bright individual, who was perhaps the best pilot. Although very much a people's person, he was happy in the Bush with the Botswana lifestyle. He also rode a motorcycle very well, so I liked him as a person and respected him as a biker. His girlfriend, Sandy Wetton, was to become a close friend of mine.

Blicks Bakkers was a typical Afrikaner, well over six feet tall and with a face that gave the impression he was not to be crossed. He was also a complete male chauvinist who thought he was better than anyone else. Unfortunately, he was the training captain for KASAC so I'd had to endure my earlier base training with him.

Blicks had a beautiful, petite, adorable wife, Rose. She was a brunette with a heart of gold who would never say a bad word about anyone, especially Blicks. This was strange as he beat her up fairly regularly, which meant she would rarely swim in her neighbours' (Dudley and B) pool, and was always covered up to hide the bruising. B told me she often heard Rose's screams in the middle of the night, accompanied by shouts from Blicks. They had a foul, spoilt, four-year-old boy, called Carlos, who spent his entire time shouting, screaming and crying or bullying their obnoxious Airedale terrier.

Les Sacks was a very quiet man. He was South African born and bred and hated the Bush of Botswana. I had often wondered whether he even enjoyed flying. He disliked night-stops and loved my arrival as he gave me all his night-stops and told me I had improved his life considerably. He was a good pilot and certainly knew his way round the Bush. He had a pleasant laid-back manner and nothing fazed him. I liked him. He was more of an owl then a lark and found early morning departures difficult. He would usually arrive in the crew room ten minutes before his charter was supposed to depart. He never joined any of us partying, yet as soon as he was rostered off for two days or more, consecutively, he would fly or drive to Jo'burg, where he kept his girlfriend (who none of us had met). He would then arrive back in Gaberone about 10 minutes before his charter, hoping the aircraft had already been refuelled.

One morning, he arrived a little late, to take a charter to Mopipi, some 220 nautical miles north-north-west from Gabs. Seeing me in the crew room, he asked if I had been there before, to which I nodded. He told me he had overslept and did I happen to have a plog for Mopipi? I searched my bag, pulled out and passed him a prepared but used plog. He thanked me profusely and walked out to his aircraft. I watched in amazement because I carefully plotted, planned and prepared a flight the night before when it was a first visit, scrutinising the 1;1,500,000 chart for anything I hadn't seen before but I would not have dreamt of 'going cold' on a charter with a plog prepared by someone else.

Dave Wilmot, also from South Africa, was about five feet tall, with dark blond hair and blue eyes and was very quiet. Like Les, he avoided socialising with anyone after flying. He disliked the Bush so much that he stayed for half of his contract and left after a year.

Russell Newby was another South African, who preferred the 'proper civilisation' of South Africa to the 'filthy bush' of Botswana. He was tall and lean with brown, wavy hair and blue eyes. He often mentioned that he couldn't wait for his two-year contract to be finished, to return to civilisation again. Yet he was a good pilot, popular with everyone, but not conceited. He had a motorcycle and I liked him.

I was given the flat next to his, so I saw more of him than the other pilots. We took to teasing each other about anything and everything, although I cannot remember which of us started it. He disliked the night-stops intensely, until I arrived. Of course, I told him I was doing him a favour by swapping rosters but he knew I enjoyed them.

Ben Bowles, originally from England, had come to KASAC from South Africa, where he had met and married Michaela (who was South African). They were a terrific couple and both Ben and Michaela became lifelong friends to me. Ben was quiet and unassuming, extremely efficient and a no-nonsense pilot. Some years later, after eventually returning to the UK, he became a training captain and fleet manager for Air Contractors. Their first child, Chay, was born during Ben's two-year contract with KASAC. Chay was the first tiny baby I had seen close up, so it was a memorable event for me as well.

Dave Knox, another pilot from England, was very much a dark horse. No one knew much about him. He smoked a pipe – very English. It was acknowledged he kept himself to himself, speaking to no one unless asked a question to which he would give a very long, thoughtful, intellectual reply. He was a generation older than all of us and was very much anti-apartheid; so much so that although he was divorced, he had adopted two black children at birth. The youngest, Ellie, was sweet-natured; her dream was to ride a horse, so naturally I took her to ride Kasac. She fell in love with Kasac immediately and I demonstrated how to get on and off. Before I had a chance to help her up, she had vanished to the wrong side for mounting, somehow managed to climb aboard, but faced Kasac's tail! Fortunately Kasac stood still, looking puzzled. The next attempt had Ellie facing forward, holding the reins, with me walking beside her in the Bush.

Although I took her several times, she had no hope at all of ever feeling comfortable or relaxed on a horse. When Dave asked about her progress, I found it difficult to be honest without being rude. I eventually suggested that, although she was more than welcome to ride Kasac, perhaps she should ride at the Pony Club: a pony would feel less intimidating, being nearer the ground.

The older son, Francis, was a real no-hoper. He was always in trouble with the police and on many occasions Dave would return from a charter to have to go to the police station to retrieve Francis. On his 21st birthday, he got wildly drunk, stole a police car and drove round the town until he crashed. The car was totalled but Francis was unhurt.

*

My next charter looked interesting. I was rostered to fly five passengers to Tsau, with Dudley flying a further five passengers. It was an afternoon departure with a planned night stop, returning around lunchtime the following day. This was my favourite type of charter. There was plenty of time to have a fun ride on Kasac before going, and a gentle unwinding, relaxing ride on return.

Dudley and I taxied our Barons down to arrivals – though it was a little presumptuous to call the tiny meeting area an arrivals terminal. I was astounded to see the amount of baggage the passengers were intent on taking. I looked anxiously at Dudley, who seemed to read my mind.

"Don't worry, Tizi, it's mainly clothing, which takes up a tremendous space but weighs next to nothing. We can carry what they can cram in."

I marvelled at out little 'air-ships of the desert', the trusty Barons. Such delightful little aeroplanes to fly: so forgiving, so fast, so strong, yet able to take such an incredible load out of such tiny short sand strips.

We arrived at Tsau two minutes apart. After parking the aircraft, we were all collected by Landcruisers and driven to camp, via the bottle store to stock up on cool beers.

I asked Dudley if he would like to join me in a walk, but he politely declined and explained he was halfway through a crossword in the newspaper.

Since this was my first trip to Tsau, some 320 miles north-west of Gabs, I was keen to see the area and the wildlife. It had looked totally deserted on the way in and the more remote the place, the more game there was to see.

The trip was unbelievable. I found a large pan of water after an hour or so of walking and settled down to write some letters. So many creatures came down, taking their turn to sip, lap or drink the water. I felt so much a part of the desert that it seemed almost wrong to get back into an aircraft to fly back to civilisation.

Back at the camp there was a general commotion and unrest. The passengers were unhappy about the beer being warm. People were getting louder and more irritated. I could see a group of people clustered around Dudley who was sitting with his newspaper, a can of beer in hand. When he saw me, he called me over and asked if I would mind flying over to Maun to fetch some ice.

"I've already had a beer, Tizi, so I can't fly, but I thought you would like an extra flight, so I have volunteered you for the 'ice trip'. It's up to you if you think there is enough daylight to get there and back."

"You mean you'll approve it?" I was amazed.

"No, Tizi, I was joking, but you'd better hurry if you want to go."

I had already grabbed my bag and was walking toward the nearest Landcruiser, which the driver had started in anticipation. Dudley joined me as far as the airport to finish briefing me on the trip to avoid wasting daylight. He explained I was to fly to Maun and turn off the runway, where a Landcruiser would meet me with a large box of ice. It would be loaded into the back of the Baron while I waited – there was no need to shut down the engines. Then I was to return directly. If I found no one waiting with the ice, it was because they'd been unable to get through on the radio, so I was to take off immediately and return empty handed.

I looked up Maun from Tsau; east-northeast and just 56 miles. At the thumbs-up from Dudley, I started the engines and set off for my first solo flight in a Baron, in Botswana.

I used a higher power setting than usual to gain a few more minutes. There was no wind, and with an extra-light aircraft keen to gallop, I couldn't help laughing aloud. Life was so good.

I looked at the speed – over 190 knots, although I had commenced the descent. I couldn't resist the temptation of a gentle victory roll in sheer happiness. The aircraft was more than strong enough, so I gently pulled up into a roll, feeling I was the luckiest human being on the planet enjoying life so much. Just as I was about to return to level flight, there was a loud CRACK accompanied by a whistling noise, sounding as though an aircraft was rapidly depressurising.

I looked round and saw that the back window had opened. The loud crack was noise of the window knocking against the metal latches and the whistling noise was what always accompanied flying with a window open. Pilots do not generally fly with windows open, not because it damages the aircraft, but because the noise is distracting. I decided there and then, no more aerobatics unless they were planned before setting off. A rapid arrival at Maun was met as planned by the 'ice wagon' and I was airborne again in a couple of minutes.

I couldn't help thinking, on the return journey, what a waste of money this all was. I didn't know the price the group were paying for this charter, but hazarded a guess at around 1,000 Pulas. It was a lot of money for ice that would melt not long after arrival back at camp.

On another charter to Tsau, the people organising it were clearly disappointed when they found they had a woman pilot. I asked what the problem and they told me there was nothing for dinner and no-one around could use a gun. They assumed because I was female, that I would be no use. I protested that I was very accurate with a gun, and they handed over a 30.06.

I went off in the Landcruiser with a driver – and the gun. The driver asked me how many yards I wanted to shoot from. I told him 200 yards would be fine, so we set off in search of edible quarry. Soon a duiker, a small antelope, was visible, so I got out of the Landcruiser, knelt down and shot the duiker: it went straight down with a clean shot through the heart.

I was especially pleased as I knew Mr Byron would have been delighted to have had another reason to prove it wasn't worth having a female pilot. In fact, if it hadn't been for my concern about being so unpopular with my boss, I would have probably settled for vegetables for dinner.

The following week, when I arrived for a charter to Kang, I noticed a strange atmosphere around the offices. I wondered what had happened. Mr Byron saw me entering the crew room and said in a worried voice that Russell had reported on the radio that he was unable to find Ghanzi.

Trying to re-assure him, I chuckled and said, "he can't miss Ghanzi, even in this terrible visibility; it's got a beacon."

He replied the beacon was unserviceable and the purpose of Russell's flight was to deliver the new replacement beacon, which was in the back of his aircraft. As he had been gone several hours and there had been no further communication, the worry now was how much fuel he had left. He might even be forced to land in the desert where it was difficult to locate anyone.

The poor man really looked quite distraught. Trying to throw in a little humour to relax him, I told Mr Byron not to worry as he had stated the aircraft was insured.

"Hodson, how can you say such a thing? I don't even care about the aircraft, or the beacon in the back. I just hope Russell is OK."

I apologised and returned to preparing for my own charter to Kang, which was a short flight of less than 1½ hours. It was a drop-off only, returning empty. There were two ways of flying to Kang; either in a straight line, or the longer, safer way of flying to Mosopa, then to Moshaneng, then simply following a small dirt road that led to Kang. New pilots were encouraged to take the slower, safe route. Until this flight, I had always taken the slower, fuel-burning route. Studying the map, I thought that heading direct would lead to the small airstrip.

Should the airfield not appear, there would be no problem as there was a road that crossed in front of the airfield, which meant turning and following the road in whichever direction it was felt the airfield should be, until the airstrip came into sight.

I set off and took note of the wind direction while in range of the VOR at the base airfield, which was useful for about 15 minutes before going beyond the radio's range. I calculated a time for the road to appear and with about ten minutes to go, I started looking for the road.

No sign. The little dirt road, according to my watch and calculations, should have been beneath me. All I had to do was to turn left or right. No road. I kept going. It had to come up eventually. After a further 30 minutes, there was no road, so I decided to turn back: I must have missed it.

To go much further on would mean I would not have sufficient fuel for returning to Gabs – there was no fuel available at Kang.

I explained to my passengers what I was doing, thinking they would be hot, bothered and cross, or even hot, bothered and possibly frightened by a pilot admitting she cannot find the airstrip. No one seemed unhappy.

I was not worried, since I must have missed the road somehow on the way up. On the return trip, I watched like a hawk for the road: there was no road at all. I wondered if either the road had vanished or perhaps my compass had been 90 ° out, which would have meant not crossing any road.

When I finally picked up the VOR's range and bearing to Gaberone, the heading was as expected for a normal return flight from Kang, of 124°.

Still baffled, and embarrassed on account of my poor non-complaining passengers, I taxied to the fuel pumps and filled both wing tanks, while my four passengers had a quick comfort break, then again set off for Kang. This time I took the 'slow safe route', which naturally had me thinking a little about the tortoise and hare race.

The visibility was similar to peering through a glass of soup, which made me think as I made my turn onto final approach that this was not a sensible day to have tried to fly there direct.

I opened the door for my passengers, apologising profusely for taking double the time. Still feeling terrible about not finding the strip first time, I asked one of the local ladies if she had been worried or uncomfortable.

"Oh no, I could never get worried when you are flying me, Buana," she said simply, and then explained. "I was in the Clinic at Bokspits when you flew our doctor in. It was night and black when you arrived. We had given up hope of you delivering the doctor to us. The others also knew you had flown that trip. How could we worry?"

Back at base, I parked the aircraft and picked up my flight bag very slowly. I went into the crew room, hoping it would be empty and I could crawl home unnoticed but of course, Mr Byron was there, waiting for me at the top of the stairs.

"Hello Hodson, are you OK?" He sounded concerned, not like someone about to send me back to England.

I apologised and admitted I had not found Kang by flying direct, so had returned, refuelled and re-flown the route via the longer way, which had gone as planned.

Mr Byron then told me that since the passengers were not upset and if I wasn't worried or upset and hadn't had a fright, then he was happy with the result and there was no more to say; but would I be happy to fly the following day? Or would I like to be accompanied again for a few trips to get my nerve back?

I was flabbergasted. There were no threats of dismissal or reprimand for the second-worst sin in aviation – getting lost while carrying fare-paying passengers (the worst sin was to run out of fuel). Surely I should be dismissed, grounded, or re-trained at the least?

"But Mr. Byron, I have just cost the company twice the amount of fuel to deliver four passengers to their destination. I'm embarrassed and ashamed that I have let KASAC down."

He then went on to re-assure me that everyone had been lost once and that a few litres of fuel was a small price to pay to find out you cannot get complacent when flying over the desert.

Relieved I left the building, only to meet Russell at the top of the balcony, outside our flats.

"Oh boy," he said. "Was I relieved to hear you missed Kang when I got in today! I thought I'd never hear the end of my goof, missing Ghanzi."

He invited me in for a beer and we then spent the evening sharing each other's experiences of getting lost in the desert. I made his day when I told him how Mr Byron had reacted to my joke about the aircraft insurance.

*

One evening, having flown a charter earlier in the day, I was working on some new drumbeats, using a beautiful set of silver Premier drums. I had recently bought the drum kit from a student called Jeff Owen, who became a close friend. As I had neighbours, I covered the drums and cymbal with leather skins, which muffled the sound but gave a better feeling than playing on rubber pads.

While practising on the drumkit, I heard a knock on my door. It was Mr Byron. I was surprised, as it was only his second visit to my flat.

"Good evening Hodson," he said. "Have you had a drink today?"

This seemed a weird question but it didn't look as though he was about to offer me one either, so I replied in the negative.

"Good. Then I must ask you to do a mercy flight now, to Johannesburg. There's no other pilot that hasn't had a beer. I will run you to the airport if you get your bag."

"OK I'll come now now." I used the local slang for immediately. ('Now' meant sometime soon, whereas 'just now' meant probably tomorrow). "But I'll take my bike. I keep my flight bag at work."

"It's raining hard, which is why I said I'll run you there."

"Thanks, but I'll take my car. I'll need to get back here when I return – I can hardly expect you to wait all night." I was halfway down the stairs already.

"I'd forgotten you had a car – you never seem to use it. I will see you at the airport, which is being opened for you. The aircraft will be refuelled by the time you arrive." Mr Byron would not use any slang: he was very British.

Five minutes and five kilometres later found me changed and at the airport. I met Mr Byron at the entrance to the crew room.

"But I saw you get into and out of your car, Hodson. When did you have time to change?"

"On the way. What's the history?" I was referring to the mercy flight, as I picked up my bag and walked toward the aircraft that had a person on a stretcher being loaded inside.

"It is a young lad, knocked off his motorbike and is likely to lose one of his legs. A nurse is going with you to give him a transfusion on the way. A flight plan has been filed and there will be someone to meet you at Jan Smuts. You will need to stop the night as Gaberone will be closed before you get back."

I departed immediately and noticed, once airborne, that only ten minutes had elapsed since Byron visited to my flat. Everyone helped everyone with a mercy flight. I glanced behind and asked the nurse how her patient was. She smiled and said, "he is sleeping now. We can only hope and pray."

On arrival, although it was approaching midnight, Jan Smuts was still open. I taxied to the nominated stand and saw an ambulance waiting. As soon as the second engine stopped, the back door was opened, the stretcher, patient and nurse were removed and the ambulance had gone.

I dialled up the frequency on the radio to ask for transport as no one was allowed to walk unescorted around the international airport. I removed my flight bag and waited. A camouflaged tank drove up and a soldier apologised for the only transport available at that time of night. So I crawled into a small gap by what seemed to be a cannon protruding out of the turret, opposite two more soldiers holding machine guns. I was surprised at how comfortable and peaceful it seemed inside.

Arriving at the airport exit, the door was opened by the driver to more apologies for the mode of transport. I laughed and told them I had enjoyed it, but I thought it might be pushing my luck to ask them to drive me to the hotel, so I decided to walk. As I disembarked, the driver asked where I was heading. When I said the nearest hotel, it was suggested I got back in and he drove me to the doorstep.

The receptionist, having watched my arrival, looked terrified as she took my details and handed me a room key. I smiled and wished her a good night, not wanting to disillusion her that I wasn't an armed hi-jacker.

The following morning I decided to walk back to the airport, to see a bit of the local area before returning to Gaberone. It was unattractive, with concrete houses squashed together, cars covering every bit of road, robots (traffic lights), parking meters and circles (roundabouts): just like London. No grass and no sand. I hurried on to the airport. One night in 'downtown Jo'burg' and I missed the sand already.

After I had landed at Gabs, I checked the roster: I had no planned trip until the following day, which was to Orapa and back.

I took Kasac for a long, gentle ride in the beautiful Bush. It seemed a cleansing tonic after the horrendous traffic noise of Jo'burg and the ugly tall office buildings without a blade of grass or bucket of sand. I wondered how dogs existed down there.

The following day, at Orapa, I marvelled at the beauty of the place. Not far from the dirt strip of Orapa's airfield was a gold mining camp. Security was strict with checks on everyone coming out, and no one was allowed in without a security pass. The whole camp was surrounded by a high wire fence. The few houses were simple and small with plenty of space between. Even with the high security fence surrounding the whole place, it still radiated freedom and tranquillity, unlike the feeling of being imprisoned, as it felt in Jo'burg. Outside the camp, there was infinite space, sand and Bush with the odd, leafless, tree and occasional traditional Rendavel house or other tented dwelling place.

On returning to Gaberone, it almost felt overcrowded: a town with its own shopping mall. It would have been better in a way to have just contained a general stores, post office and bank, like the other villages we serviced.

A while after the Jo'burg mercy flight, Mr Byron told me that he had been asked to pass thanks on to me, from the young lad who had apparently been spared the feared amputation. It had been touch-and-go – another hour would have been too long. Mr Byron also mentioned that should I have drunk a beer that evening, the lad would have been minus a leg.

Strangely enough, when I reached for a cold beer that evening, I had a haunting vision of the lad with his white bandages which had turned bright crimson as the blood visibly seeped through, fresh in my mind. I put the beer back in the fridge and put the kettle on.

Chapter 12

END OF THE CONTRACT

On the trips to Ghanzi, I had met a lovely Nharo Bushman by the name of !re!ey, pronounced with a click at the start of his name and another in the middle. When we first met, he asked if I would like to see his horses, as he had heard I was a keen rider. !re!ey was tall for a Bushman, although barely 5' 8", with a natural bronzed skin colour and thick, wavy black hair. He wore grey slacks with a fawn long-sleeved, open necked shirt and grey desert wellies (felt shoes for the Bush).

On the various trips to Ghanzi over my two-year contract, I had spent quite some time on his farm. I had also spent my first month of leave breaking and training six of his ponies to enable his young lads who worked on the farm to be able to ride ponies instead of donkeys.

!re!ey would drop in to say hello whenever he drove through Gaberone on the way to Lobatse, which was a regular trip, taking cattle to the Lobatse abattoir. Unexpectedly he had proposed to me shortly before the end of my contract. He'd knocked on my door and I'd offered him tea and toast as I usually did to anyone visiting. After he'd drunk his tea, he knelt down and asked if I would marry him. This came out of the blue: in all the time I'd known him, there had been no physical contact between us – not even a kiss. I asked him why he wanted to marry me as we hardly knew each other and were not in love. He said his mother, !raa, had suggested it when he'd told her about the lady pilot who had broken in his horses and seemed capable of anything. He found he got more work done and had more enthusiasm for his farm when I was there.

He went on to say that he could see that animals were more important to me than people, and he was happy for me to have as many horses, snakes and birds on the farm as I wanted. He would never ask anything of me physically and if we did ever end up being attracted to each other, that would be a bonus for us both. He wasn't able to employ me on the farm because he had no money, and anyway he would rather I was his wife than an employee.

I told him I would think about it. I mentioned it to a few of the pilots who though I was nuts, especially as Ghanzi was the most isolated part of Botswana (but it was also my favourite part). On visiting Bes and Christine over a Sunday breakfast, I asked their opinion. Bes told me he thought I should go for it. He'd known !re!rey for many years and found him likeable, honest and friendly. Christine, however, thought I was nuts, especially when I proudly showed her the ring !re!rey had given me: it was shaped like a cobra with a wide open mouth, with impressive large fangs and small diamonds for eyes. She looked at her own expensive gold and diamond ring.

"I'd prefer to find someone who could give me nice jewellery and smart clothes rather than offer me snakes and birds," she said. "Anyway, if you isolate yourself in Ghanzi, there'll be no parties, dances or entertainment of any kind."

Strangely, it was Christine's response that decided me to accept !re!rey's proposal: I wasn't attracted to money, jewellery, clothes or nightlife but I did love the beauty and peace of the desert. Also, !re!rey had been honest: he hadn't said he loved me. I found that people tended to tell you either what was expected or polite, but probably not what they really felt or meant. Animals were important to me for their honesty and so I admired that quality in !re!rey.

There was no rush on either side to get married: !re!ey wished to tidy up his farm and get it to his satisfaction before I would move north and I also preferred the idea of saving a little more before I stopped flying for KASAC.

With a month before my contract was due to expire, I had assumed I would automatically renew for a year, as this was a possible clause in the contract. However, I was informed that HQ in Jo'burg had told KASAC to thin down on pilots by not allowing anyone to renew at the end of the two-year period: I would be the first casualty. I wondered if the knowledge that I had agreed to marry a Bushman had anything to do with the non-renewal of my contract.

Despite feeling heartbroken, I started looking for other flying positions, preferably in Botswana, although anywhere in Africa would be acceptable. I exhausted all the charter companies, which was simple as there was only one other in Botswana. However ,an extra pilot was not required. On my next charter to Lansaria Airport, Jo'burg, I checked with all the charter companies, of which there were several, but none needed any additional pilots.

I then came to SAAS (South African Aircraft Sales), where I was directed to the boss, Pat Hewitson, a smartly dressed man in navy suit and white shirt. I asked if he needed more sales staff for the Mooney aircraft, for which SAAS held the franchise. He told me they were always on the lookout for experienced sales staff who lived locally. I told him I would be available in a month, could move anywhere and although I hadn't much sales experience, it was the one thing I had always wanted to do. Plus, since he said the company threw in the training for a private pilot's licence whenever anyone purchased a new Mooney, I would be able to train the customers, as I was a qualified instructor.

Pat sounded interested. We chatted over a few cups of tea and he agreed if I would be prepared to move there, he was sure he could find me a sales position within a month. I was amazed to have found success on my first day of looking. Although I disliked Jo'burg itself, the area around Lansaria had few houses, shops and people and was beautiful. I thought I could probably adjust to the civilized farms and farmland.

Two days later, I flew the taxi to Ghanzi, I met !re!ey and told him Kasac had gone to Francistown to live an easy life with Sue and Charlie before retiring. I'd met them on a night stop in Francistown when I'd gone to Charlie's motorbike shop to pass time and look at the bikes. We'd chatted and Charlie had said his wife was looking for a horse. They'd driven down to see Kasac and Sue had fallen instantly in love with him.

"Well, let me drive you down to Jo'burg, with all your belongings," he said. "You have a lot to move with the bike, drums and your car."

I had not even thought that far ahead – there were over two weeks left, but I would have had a problem moving everything south. This was an answer to a prayer I hadn't even thought about.

There was little need for my Renault panel-van in Jo'burg and as it was now paid off, I traded it for an open-topped bakkie – a pick-up truck – in another car-shop in Gabs. There was further work to be done on the car, so I agreed to pick it up in a week or two.

Some two weeks later, true to his word, !re!ey arrived in his 10-ton Leyland, to help me to up-sticks once more.

The trip was uneventful and early afternoon found us at Lansaria Airport. !re!ey parked the truck and suggested I check whether I still had a job waiting and try to find some accommodation, so he would know whether he could return to the farm. He gently reminded me it was a month since I had spoken to Pat Hewitson; nothing in writing had been received, offering me a definite job – not even a contract.

With the sun shining hard as I walked toward the airport and with green grass around, I found I could not worry about anything that might go wrong.

Although Pat Hewitson had left the company, luckily he had mentioned me to Hew Hodgson, who was actually the owner. Hew happily took me on and introduced me to Antoinette and Shelly. Antoinette was the bubbly, small, attractive receptionist and Shelly was PA to Hew. She looked and dressed like a model with never a hair out of place.

I agreed to start the following day and was promptly found some local accommodation by Antoinette. This was on a farm less than two miles away, owned by Meggie and Robert Hawson, who ran a dairy farm with a few cows, but mainly chickens. There were several enormous buildings used by egg-laying chickens. As Meggie was showing me round, she mentioned casually to 'help myself daily to fresh milk and eggs' and showed me where they were kept. It was all included in the rent.

It was a wonderful way to start my new life.

!re!ey helped me unload the truck, then, after a refreshing swim, I made some tea to drink by the pool while thinking about my first day in the office.

Antoinette and Shelly insisted I bought some smarter clothes and started to wear make-up, which I did to fit into the Sales Rep image. It was fun and challenging trying to find clients and turn them into a prospective purchaser for a Mooney aircraft.

After a few months with SAAS, Hew paid for me to attend a sales course, where I was taught for the first time about 'buying signals' and 'how to close a deal'. This made the job so much more exciting, as I was hoping to make many more sales.

My first sale had been to a farmer in Lobatse, who had been looking at Cessnas. I had suggested a Mooney for better fuel consumption, quieter flights, faster speed and better retention of the hull value (the term for the value of the aircraft a few years after buying it).

In Hew's office was a large poster of a very different Mooney aircraft. I asked him about it and he replied it was to be the fastest single-engined aircraft available, capable of 300 mph about to be launched by Mooney.

He showed me more drawings of the proposed Mooney 301. It was a beautiful design with a strange feature: it had a conventional tail. Every single Mooney built until now had the trademark 'backward tail', which we at Mooney called the 'forward facing tail – eliminating drag'.

Not being a design engineer, I could not comment on the reduction or otherwise of drag, but the new Mooney looked, if anything, better with the conventional tail. It featured a constant speed propeller, retractable undercarriage and was fully pressurised enabling it to fly above the weather at a speed in excess of most twin-engine aircraft.

I asked Hew if I could start marketing the 301. He encouraged me to do so and told me he was going to the States to watch the inaugural flight. Although I was hoping to be invited and prepared to pay my own passage to see this first flight, he told me it was necessary for me stay behind to look after the sales. I took this as a terrific compliment and looked forward to hearing the news when he returned.

The news was good: the 301 lived up to expectations, flew beautifully and expected to go straight into production. All we had to do was to take orders and await delivery.

*

I drove to Pretoria to obtain a South African licence to be able to fly demo flights for Hew. Botswana was a neighbouring country, with a similar climate, added to which I had flown on my Botswana licence for the past two years, therefore it was current, along with the various instrument and instructing ratings, so I was assuming a South African licence would only be a formality.

"Sorry lady," I was told politely, "we don't accept any other licence. The South African licence is the highest qualification in the world. I am afraid you will have to take the examinations and the various flight tests for the South African licence."

Not to be set back, I decided to buy all the necessary textbooks to study and booked a date when I could return for the exams. While the man looked for the next available date, I looked in my flight bag for my diary. As I took it out, my English CAA licence fell onto the counter. I was asked if it was mine.

When I said yes, a sudden smile broke out on the, until now, rather sour-looking official.

"But why didn't you say you had a British licence? Hold on a minute." He then disappeared for a couple of minutes.

When he returned, I was told I would need to take the air law written exam and a simple flight test at any flying school to validate the SA licence that he would then issue on the strength of the British one. He sold me the book I would need to study and wished me well.

I left the offices feeling on top of the world.

Chapter 13

NEARLY WHEELS UP

Working through some possible leads, I spoke to a farmer who showed an interest in purchasing a Mooney. After a few chats, he asked if I would bring a Mooney to his field so he could take a look at one. He gave me directions and with good-luck wishes from Hew, I set off for the field, ninety minutes west of Lansaria.

I was flying an old Mooney, designated an M20H, which was my first flight in that particular model. I was anxious to make a sale and concentrating hard on trying to find the correct field, which I had been warned was private and without a windsock, but was assured it was level, free of holes or obstructions and had been driven on in the last day or so.

Having located the correct field, using the compass heading and my wristwatch, I made the usual 'precautionary approach' to check the field was suitable for the Mooney, whose only fault was small ground clearance from the propeller. The aircraft was more suited to tarmac runways than rough field or bush strips.

On final approach I lowered the landing gear, which consisted of unlocking a catch, pulling the long undercarriage lever from the ground through an arc of 180 degrees, to throw it forward to lock under a wire catch in front of the panel. A red light always showed during transit and a green light when locked, to ensure a wheels-up landing was not made.

As the wind had been from the east, giving me a speedier trip, it also made the final approach easier with the sun behind me. I saw my 'green light' for the wheels as I went through the final checks before landing. As I rounded out for the last few feet, I heard the lovely sound of the stall-warner going off – always a welcome noise as a conventional training aircraft should be fully stalled prior to a good landing, accompanied by the stall-warner beeping.

Just before the final touchdown, I had a sudden cold feeling. The noise was not quite right. I looked down at my green light, and then saw the undercarriage lever was *not* under the catch. I slammed it forward with all my might while pulling the stick fully back. The stall-warner noise stopped as the Mooney gently settled onto the ground and the dim green landing light shone brightly.

I went cold with shock as I suddenly realised the stall-warning noise had been a 'gear not down' warning. I was puzzled as to why I had seen the green light, assuring all was in order. Out of curiosity, before turning into the sun, I turned off the master switch so no lights could show. Sure enough, with the sun behind me the green light glowed – enough to make me think a safe landing could be made.

There is a general saying among flying folk that there are two types of pilot. There are those who have landed with the wheels up, and those who are going to. I felt I had my 'wheels up' landing as sure as if it had been for real.

More annoying still was the absence of the farmer. I took a walk around, then after a further hour with no sign of anyone arriving, I set off to return to Lansaria.

Back at Lansaria, Hew told me that after I had left, the farmer had called up to cancel the meeting, but there was no way of getting in touch with me.

Well, the flight had been beautiful over lovely landscape and I had learned a truly invaluable lesson – although unproductive, sales-wise, it had been a lovely day.

I was not to know my first sale was just round the corner.

I called another farmer, Reg Vise, to explain the benefits of owning an aircraft and a Mooney in particular. Reg agreed owning an aircraft would be useful if he had a licence to fly. He owned large farms in South Africa and Botswana. Since he was a close friend of !re!ey, I offered to teach him to fly, should he buy a pleasant aircraft. Reg was a hard-working gentleman farmer who wore dark suits with a white shirt and black tie even in the heat of summer. He had started with nothing and built up his businesses of cattle farming to be among the most respected in Lobatse.

I had a lovely Mooney available at the right price, so Reg agreed to take a look at it, if I would bring it to Lobatse. While I was pre-flighting the Mooney on the ramp, an old friend from Botswana, called Trevor, came up and started chatting. He asked where I was going and if he could accompany me for the ride.

Pleased to have company, I agreed, asking if he had his passport.

"No, that's at home. Is it necessary, if I stay on the aircraft?"

Since he was not planning on leaving the aircraft and I saw the same friendly customs chap every day, I could not see a problem. Trevor put his bag in the aircraft while I finished checking out the Mooney.

We then went 'through customs' and on producing my passport, I asked if I could take an old friend with me, just for the trip, since he had no reason to exit the aircraft.

"No, that is not possible, at all – not without a passport. I am sorry. You may go; here is your passport back", was the unexpected reply.

I went out to the Mooney and Trevor arrived behind me to remove his bag. We chatted for a few minutes, and then I started the engine and asked the Tower for taxi clearance.

"CB confirm number on board?" came the non-standard query from the Control Tower.

I told him 'one' was given taxi clearance and took off, setting heading toward Lobatse. On changing frequency to Botswana's control, I was again asked how many souls were on board. With a normal approach and landing, I taxied down to the field entrance, where I had agreed to meet Reg Vise. However, after applying the brakes when parking, I saw several armed police holding machine guns, which were pointed toward me. They were approaching from police cars and more armed police were exiting the vehicles.

Wondering what was going on, I opened the door and started to get out.

"Don't move – stay where you are!" I heard a loud call through a cone. I stayed where I was and looked around, wondering what or who they were actually looking for.

One of the policemen came up to me, still with his gun pointing at me, which seemed somewhat unnecessary since there were plenty of others doing the same. He told me to get down slowly, which I did and was immediately held onto at either side by two further policemen.

One started toward the Mooney. I told him he must only walk on the walkway and to take care of the aircraft. Then I asked what he was looking for. Naturally by this time, I was beginning to think they were looking for drugs and getting terrified that perhaps someone may have planted some in the aircraft without my knowledge.

Obviously they could not be looking for a person – a Mooney's cockpit is similar to a small sports car; there is no room to conceal anything.

Finally, having looked at the small interior, the first policeman told me they understood a stowaway was on board – apparently someone had tried to sneak into this country without a passport, in my aircraft.

What a feeling of relief, after my worries of someone having planted drugs! I couldn't help laughing. With the tension dissolving, I explained that my friend Trevor wanted to come just for the ride and back, but was told he could not, so he had returned to the aircraft, removed his bag and went home.

There were orders now for everyone to stand down and profuse apologies given but it was explained that they had been alerted that I definitely had a stowaway without a passport on board.

After they had all gone, I went to the customs office to sign in and found Reg waiting when I came out. I explained what had happened. We had a good laugh: Reg told me he had decided to wait for everyone to go before coming up to say hello, and that he had seen me arrive, along with all the police cars and was also surprised that the possibility of someone arriving in the country without a passport could possibly call for such a large attendance of policemen.

I took Reg for a flight in the Mooney and encouraged him to try it for himself. He thought the aircraft would suit him but asked if I could take him on a longer trip before making up his mind. He agreed on a trip to Ghanzi, which was taken later on in the week. After returning from Ghanzi, he bought the aircraft.

Feeling encouraged, I approached more farmers about the advantages of owning an aircraft, since most fields were easily adapted into runways.

However, the rains were not as frequent as in most years and the first people to be badly affected by a drought are always farmers. Potentially interested customers were changing their minds about sales, even when one was almost agreed. Even our friendly 'rivals' at Cessna were feeling the effect of the drought.

The following week, when I arrived at my office, Hew told me that although he really did not want to give in, he had been forced to close down.

Sales were down everywhere, not just with us. So, in turn, the engineering business was down as fewer people were buying and flying aircraft. That meant there was not enough work for his engineers. I knew he had recently laid an engineer off, but had not realised it was a financial decision. He told me he had no choice but to give me my salary for the rest of the month but there was no need to come in, since there would not be an office as of the next day.

I was dumbstruck. Although I knew the company was struggling, I had not realised it had got this bad. I felt more sorry for Hew than for myself: this was his company and all his dreams, past work and many successes were now over.

I returned to my lodgings and saw Meggie as I got off my bike. She asked what was wrong. Not realising that it was so obvious, I told her I was suddenly and totally unexpectedly out of work. She was sympathetic and immediately told me not to worry about the rent until I managed to get work somewhere.

"I won't stay unemployed for long," I assured her, although inside I wanted to cry.

Chapter 14

THREE JOBS AT ONCE

It was a challenge. A new life had begun in a new country, but I had fallen in love with Africa and wanted to stay in an African country. My next job did not have to be connected with aircraft: I knew there were still no vacancies in the charter companies.

I thought about what to do next. Should I fly or continue in sales? Sales had a unique challenge about it: to make a successful sale felt similar to winning a contest.

Sales had opened up a new door. I found two companies in the phone book who I felt would be interesting to work for. The first was Camdons Real Estate, selling houses and the second was Ducati's Motorcycles, both in Downtown Jo'burg.

*

I visited Camdons first and was introduced to Duncan Groen who agreed I could start immediately. The salary was commission only, so he welcomed anyone who wanted to join. He insisted I attended every sales meeting, held every Monday morning; otherwise I could work in my own time.

The following Monday I attended the meeting at Camdons where I learned how to 'acquire' a house to sell for someone: simply to ask the people if they own the house they live in and would they think of selling it either now, or perhaps in six or seven months. Would they like to have it valued? I would then give my own estimate of what I thought the house was worth.

This last I thought somewhat strange, having someone like myself, completely new to the job, give a figure off the top of their head as to the value of the house. However, it seemed to work. There were no exams needed to start as an estate agent at that time.

When a house owner agreed, I would organise a 'Show House' for the following Saturday, where people would be attracted by signs directing them to the houses for sale, and if possible, be encouraged to make an offer on the house.

Two weeks later, on a Monday morning after leaving Camdons sales meeting, I went back to Lansaria airport for a sandwich at the café before visiting Ducati's Motorcycles. While eating, a man approached me. He was plain-looking, slightly balding and he had a slight paunch. He gave his name as Craig Woods, a photographer. He told me it had been suggested to ask me if I would like to work with him in flying and sales.

Excited, I said, 'yes' before he had even told me the plan.

My part of the teamwork would be to fly the rented aircraft, while Craig took photographs of houses from the air. After he had developed the photos, I would then approach the house owners and offer them an aerial view of their own house.

Craig told me the prices for the photos; I would take the orders and collect the 25%, deposit, which I could keep as commission.

Craig was happy to arrange and pay for the cost of the aircraft rental, identify the properties in terms of the roads or streets, organise delivery of the finished photos and collect the final payments.

This sounded brilliant, offering fun and simple work with immediate payment. The photos he showed me looked beautiful. I did not think it was likely there would be many refusals to buy an aerial photograph of the house someone owned. Craig planned on flying on Saturday mornings to take the shots and I could fit in whatever times I liked, to knock at doors. I agreed to start on Saturday.

Feeling much more cheerful, I drove down to Ducati and asked whether I could see the boss. Although I had always considered myself shy and a little introverted, I might have changed since being in the sales environment … or perhaps I was in an elated position of having accepted two jobs on the same day.

I introduced myself to Reuben Miller and asked him how his sales were going.

"Could do with improvement," he said, which I'd almost expected.

Reuben was tall and well-built with thick black hair and attractive brown eyes. He was dressed in a well-cut navy suit, white shirt, and a tie sporting an image of a Ducati.

I told him he could do with a high-powered, experienced, dynamic, salesforce to sell his bikes, to which he asked where that could be found.

I told him he was looking at his answer: that I could ride any bike well enough to show it off to advantage and had the sales background he needed, having just finished a year of selling aircraft. Co-incidentally I could start immediately and he could be looking at the stars as his goal.

Reuben smiled, leaned back in his chair and said,

"Well, I am a dreamer. Your offer sounds like a dream. Do you read your stars?"

To this day, I don't know what made me say, "the stars determine much in a person. You are obviously a Pisces, swimming against yourself. Pisces are my favourite people."

Shocked, Reuben sat bolt upright and said no one had ever guessed his star-sign. Then, after a long pause, he said,

"Yes, I have somewhere you could fit in with us. You can start Monday, but it will be on the smaller, messenger bikes to start with."

I was overjoyed. I would have happily taken any position, even selling goldfish. Selling motorbikes had been an attempted dream since I had started riding them, but whenever I approached companies, they were not interested unless I had sold before. Even telling Reuben I could not work on Monday mornings made no difference.

I planned to sell houses in the evenings and weekends, to fly with Craig on Saturday mornings and sell the photos while I was trying to 'collect' houses to sell. That left almost the entire week free to sell motorcycles.

Life was so good.

On Monday, after attending a meeting at Camdons, I drove home and then got a lift to a nearby bus stop, where I caught a bus to take me to the Ducati bike shop. The sales rep, Steve, had already told me there was no car-parking space on site – only for bikes. After being introduced to the other staff and mechanics, Reuben showed me to my office and said he wanted me to try to market one of the new products, the Cagiva 125cc, aimed at the messenger-boy market.

At first I was dismayed at being employed to sell a 125cc moped when my heart was set on the Ducatis. I looked at the brochure of the Cagiva, the specs and colours available and the price lists: the first Cagiva arrived later that day. I took it for a ride downtown and was pleasantly surprised to find not only was it a delight to ride, but the handling was light and the bike was beautifully balanced. Being a two-stroke, the standing start was impressive against the bigger four-strokes and the top speed was sufficient even for out-of-town work. On my first ride, whenever I saw a messenger bike, I rode up to it and easily overtook whoever was riding, even the average 400cc Honda.

I came back delighted with the bike and gave Reuben my verdict. He seemed pleased and gave me a list of the companies he wanted to supply with the new Cagiva. He also told me I could use one as my own company transport if there wasn't a spare Ducati to go home on. That was an unexpected bonus.

I took a Cagiva from choice for the first few days, partly to show willingness but mainly to find out more about the little bike.

The following day I called all the leads and managed to get dates booked for demos.

The biggest hurdle was that it was only 125cc. The messenger boys, all of whom were black, were paid very little and took the job to be 'someone important' riding an impressive bike. I noticed, depending on the size of the company and how many they employed, there was often an 'old boy' of about 60 who had been with the company since it started. The 'old boy' always had the biggest bike, usually a Honda CB 400. That was a lousy handling bike by anyone's standards, but economical and highly reliable. It didn't have much acceleration but it was big to look at, so my main task was to encourage the Honda riders to prefer the Cagiva. But when the messengers saw the Cagiva, the first question was always "How many ccs has it?" When I told them it was 125, they lost interest, and even if I could persuade them to try it, they rode it badly, slowly and saw no advantage in exchanging it for their bigger, more impressive-looking bike.

When I tried to bypass the messenger boys and market it to the managers, it was always the same story. The boys would leave if their bikes were changed; they did not want to be seen on a smaller bike.

I had to think of something, so I asked Reuben to remove the 125cc sticker from the Cagiva I used for a demo. I then approached the next company and told them I had a new fast bike on the market, which was lighter because the fuel tank was smaller – although it was actually bigger than most of the messenger bikes. When asked what size it was, I told them it was equivalent to a 500cc and I would happily demonstrate it against any of their top messenger riders on their largest fastest bikes.

The first time I tried this, I was put against an 'old boy' on a 400cc Honda. The short route was given and we set off together. I arrived back first and waited for the messenger, who shook my hand. I told him he was the better rider but the Cagiva was untouchable. Would he like to try it?

Of course he would. I told him to be careful of the throttle, as it would go much faster than the little Honda he was used to. He returned smiling. He liked the new, big bike and my first deal was done.

When I returned to the office, Reuben couldn't understand why just one sale had made me so happy – he was only paying me 25 Rand commission (about £25) on each bike. I told him I had found out how to sell it and from now on every lead would become a sale.

My strategy worked and sales were only slowed down by the lack of Cagivas available from the production line.

The first Saturday on the aerial photograph business also went well with Craig taking several rolls of film. Within a few days, he had developed the pictures and identified them on a map. On the first evening of knocking at doors, I was surprised at the ease of the sales. A pattern developed where a sale was almost guaranteed: it was just a question of which size and whether colour or black and white.

I soon settled into a comfortable routine. Monday mornings started with the Camden's meeting, then to Ducati. Leaving there, I would walk round 'my allotted area' trying to find people wishing to sell their house or look for another. A 'seller' usually became an automatic 'buyer'.

Saturday mornings were spent flying a little Cessna with Craig photographing houses, then for the remainder of Saturday and half of Sunday, I would usually plan a 'show house' for any house on my books to sell.

The show-house days were fun. The owners had to agree to vacate their house between 1pm and 5.30pm on Saturday and 11am to 5pm on Sunday. Naturally, the house was to be left in an immaculate state and then I would tell Camden's which day and time I planned a show-house day. The office crew would then put signs up everywhere to point people in the direction of the show house, with extra-large boards outside the house itself. All I had to do was occupy the property all day and remove the signs at the end of the day.

A trick I learned early on was to bring a bunch of flowers and put them on a table in the dining room or lounge and to put the oven on, at a low temperature with a couple of drops of vanilla essence inside, which gave the kitchen a lovely welcoming 'homely' aroma as you entered.

During my first week with Camdons, I managed to acquire a beautiful house in the outskirts of Randburg. The elderly couple were in no hurry to sell but agreed to put it on the market as they were planning to move into a smaller property at some time. The house was magnificent, with five bedrooms, a walled three-acre garden, and swimming pool and braai (barbeque) area at the top of the garden complete with a changing hut.

As this was my first week working, I suggested R180,000 for a price tag. The owner told me he had only paid R130, 000 for it some five years ago, and surely that was a trifle high. I told him it was exceptional and certainly worth R180,000. I then asked him if I could give a show house on the Sunday, to which he agreed.

During the show-house days, as anyone approached the house, I would first welcome them, then take down their contact details and whether they were looking to buy now, later or were 'just looking'. Also what their upper and lower limits were and then I would invite them to take a look round. This last instruction I felt uneasy with at first as it seemed possible for someone to make a living from swiping anything from every show house visited. The owners were always instructed to lock away or remove any valuables and I never heard of anything reported missing or to have vanished during a show-house day.

After my first show-house day, I welcomed the owners back and gave them the good news that from the dozen or so people who had looked over the house, there was one couple I hoped to get interested enough to make an offer.

A few days went by and I received a verbal offer for R165,000: the owners were happy to accept, especially as it was more than they thought the house was actually worth. I told them I thought they should get more, as the house was so beautiful and they agreed to wait longer as they were in no rush to move.

Every offer, accepted or rejected, had to be logged with Camdons, so I dropped into the office mentioning my suggestion of turning down the offer.

After that 'mistake' I nearly left the company. My boss told me in no uncertain terms that on no account should I ever turn an offer down. If necessary I must insist I overpriced the house and that the offer would probably be the best they'd get and make them see the wisdom of accepting it. I was then accused of costing the company thousands of Rands in the profit they and I would have got, had I allowed the deal to go through.

I left feeling furious and hurt. I waited a couple more days and then called the people who had made the original offer. I explained there was a good deal of interest in it and should they still be interested, they needed to improve their offer. They increased their offer to the original asking price of R180,000.

As it was only my second week at Camdons, I was hailed as a hero and hugged by all the management, who told me my destiny and fortune was secure with Camden's. My commission would be R3,700 (around £3,700).

I was amazed. It had all seemed so easy, effortless and enjoyable (apart from being nearly thrown out earlier), yet the figure was more than I had ever earned in one lump-sum in my life.

In the Ducati department, Steve had taken the most beautiful Ducati 900 SS in a part-exchange deal with a rather boring, new Ducati 900 Darmah. When I first saw the SS in the showroom, I fell in love with it. It had a striking customised paint job in purple and gold on the tank, side panels, tail-guard and fairing to match. Had I chosen the paintwork for a new bike, I doubt I could have selected a more attractive design. The price tag was R3,700. Suddenly I realised I could afford that bike when I received the commission. Never having spent what I hadn't actually got, I decided not to get a bridging loan but to wait until the commission came through.

Although I wasn't able to see !re!ey very often, I found being so busy hardly gave me time to think about anything apart from how to improve my sales technique.

A few months later, a man called Shane Nesbit came into my office to enquire about motorbikes. I cannot recall how the conversation turned to aircraft, but it transpired that Shane's brother Digby, who lived in Chiredzi, Zimbabwe, was thinking of buying an aircraft in a poor state. The idea was to spend a lot on the aircraft getting into immaculate condition, in Zimbabwe, and then sell it in South Africa, to get some funds out of the country.

I told Shane that I was still involved with aircraft sales and to give me a figure and I would find him an aircraft. He asked how he could get the aircraft to Chiredzi, to which I told him I would fly it there for him, if he bought it through me.

He returned the following day. I told him I had found what he was looking for: an old, tired Aztec, with high time on both engines and which could certainly do with a lick of paint. But it was airworthy and cheap, which made it a perfect project to work on. The aircraft was still on Hew's sales books and had not been sold.

After work next day, I took Shane to see the aircraft and he agreed it was the perfect project at a good price. Contact was made with Digby who asked if I would teach his wife to fly the twin, if he bought it. She already had a private pilot's licence.

I thought about the idea: to take a holiday in Zimbabwe and to teach someone to fly an Aztec, while staying as family in what sounded like a lovely property with a swimming pool and extensive grounds. There was a horse I was welcome to ride and a Cessna 150, which belonged to Digby. As Digby had not yet obtained his licence, I would be welcome to use it for transport.

It didn't need much time to think.

I agreed.

It was Friday evening, so I would need to ask Reuben for extended leave when Monday arrived. The weekend passed in a blur, flying the Cessna, selling more photographs, trying to take more houses onto my books and running a show-house day on Sunday, with an easily saleable, low-priced house.

After the weekly meeting at Camden's, I left on the Cagiva to deliver an ordered house photograph en route to Ducati. I did not arrive, and still have no recollection of what happened, apart from other peoples' theory of a hit-and-run. It was thought I was probably run into from behind and the driver had driven off.

Someone had found me – unconscious – and my little bike lying on either side of a dirt road. An ambulance delivered me to a hospital and the phone number (on the delivery box on the back of the Cagiva) was called to inform Ducati what had happened.

When I awoke, a couple of days later, I could not see anything except a complete blur. There were people round the bed: Reuben and Steve from Ducati, Craig the photographer and my boss Duncan from Camden's were all there. I was overwhelmed and embarrassed, since I was only dressed in a flimsy hospital gown and had no recollection of what had happened.

Reuben assured me the Cagiva was not hurt – just a bump from the back end is what he described. He was looking forward to seeing me back.

I felt a twinge of guilt, since I had vague memories of departing for Chiredzi.

Craig stayed until everyone else had gone and pressed an envelope into my hand, containing 200 Rands. He told me it was commission from the latest batch of photographs. I was grateful, although puzzled as I thought he owed me nothing. I had 'lost' the last few days completely.

The following day !re!ey appeared. I was delighted to see him but astounded as it didn't seem possible he could know that I was even in hospital. He told me he had heard through the grapevine I was hurt and had driven straight down. He never told me otherwise and I still wonder whether it was actually telepathy. There were no telephones in Ghanzi, although some people had radiophones and there was a weekly postal service.

After a brain-scan, I was diagnosed as having suffered brain-damage, associated with failing eyesight, which was gradually deteriorating with total loss of sight expected within six months. I was discharged within a couple of days, as they could offer me no more help.

Since I was discharged in late morning and feeling a bit depressed, I decided to go direct to Ducati rather than mope at home. Reuben greeted me warmly, as did all the other staff, but there was a changed atmosphere. Reuben had bad news, which he really didn't want to give me as soon as I was out of hospital but felt he had to. He was closing down Ducati in just three weeks' time.

I thanked him for his honesty and said I had already been torn with the temptation of flying out to Chiredzi. I was astounded to find that Reuben knew all about my offer to go out there and he thought I had accepted already. He was pleased for me as Ducati's closing would not affect me.

During the remaining weeks, my commission came through from Camden's, so I was able to buy my Ducati. Having not yet tried it, I had to go for a ride, which was dumb, as I still couldn't see much. Putting my foot down at a red light, I was unaware of a car coming up next to me. I was only wearing sandals and the car ran over my right foot: it was painful in the extreme and meant I would never forget my first ride on my beloved Ducati.

Since my sight was reducing by the day, I stopped riding any bikes and started going to work by bus. Even with the bus stationary, I could not make out the number so I had to flag down each one and ask the number, which was embarrassing and frustrating.

Having been told by the hospital there was nothing more that could be done to have my sight restored, I contacted the Guide Dog Centre to inquire about the possibility of a Guide Dog. I was asked for a doctor's note to say my eyesight was beyond saving, which was given by the hospital: I was then informed there was a 15-month wait for a dog.

Although I did not mind the wait, since I could still see a little, I begged if I could come and see the dog I might later be allocated. I was told, "No, but have no worries as you will soon learn to 'see' through your fingers."

I kept the Ducati: I would not accept defeat until I could see nothing at all.

It was probably the toughest period of my life. The daily rate of deterioration in my eyesight was noticeable. I suffered from depression for which the only 'cure' seemed to be to keep busy and ignore the truth ahead. I would not talk to anyone about my failing sight, although it was obvious to anyone who knew me.

Steve saw the rate of deterioration and through his girlfriend, Liz, who worked in the best eye specialist hospital in Johannesburg, managed to get an appointment for me to see the top eye specialist in Johannesburg. He organised a further brain scan and thoroughly tested my eyes. He told me not to worry about anything – it was only a straightforward bang on the skull resulting in loss of stereo vision, which although it deteriorates if left alone, could be corrected by taking some eye drops and swallowing some tablets. I left the hospital with the tablets and drops, feeling better than if someone had told me I had won the jackpot.

By the following day, I already noticed an improvement.

What perfect timing! There was now barely a week to the end of the month and I agreed to fly the Aztec the 300 nautical miles to Chiredzi, when Ducati had closed.

Chapter 15

A NEW LIFE IN CHIREDZI

A rriving at Buffalo Range airfield, I was greeted by Digby, who saw his Aztec for the first time.

Digby was a cheerful man with thinning brown hair and a large beer belly. We handed the aircraft over to the engineers who were to give it a complete new face-lift, along with reconditioned engines. He invited me back to meet his wife, Jesse, and to see his ranch where I was welcome to stay for as long as I liked.

Jesse had a beautiful radiant face and glistening shoulder-length fair hair. He told me Jesse was pregnant and perhaps I could delay her twin training, until she had their child, if I was not in too much of a hurry.

He then showed me his Cessna 150, telling me I could use it to fly or perhaps to start a flying club of my own. Since owning and running my own flying club had been a dream for a long time, I told him immediately that I'd like to do just that.

The following day I decided to go ahead on getting the club started. That meant flying the Cessna to Harare to pass a Zimbabwe medical, then have a Zimbabwe licence validated from my British one. The latter entailed taking an air law exam and showing the old licence and new medical to the Department of Civil Aviation. (DCA). I then needed to take a flight test to add an instructor rating to the commercial licence. That was booked for the following week, with the intervening period to be used to write a flying club manual to be submitted and accepted by the DCA.

Finally, the last hurdle to clear was to get the little Cessna approved for the Public Transport Certificate of Airworthiness, enabling me to use it to teach. This last hurdle was the hardest, as a rate of climb was needed to be witnessed as being at least 500 feet a minute, with two people aboard. The engineer who was trying to approve it for me accompanied me on each flight attempt to make the seemingly impossible rate of climb. We reduced the level of fuel to the minimum required, tried varying climb speeds in case any should prove more effective and even tried different places, hoping for more lift from hillier areas. As my weight was eight stone and the engineer barely 10 stone, there seemed little else to do short of increasing the engine size.

The problem was density altitude. Even by 9am, the sun was already burning at over 30 degrees, so a final attempt was to take off with minimum fuel at 6am. The instrument finally registered 500 feet per minute and held it long enough for the required tick in the last box.

The flying club became a reality. I called it 'N & B Flying Club', since Digby owned N & B Breweries, N & B Sugar Cane Refiners etc. All that was required now was students.

I took a walk down to the general store, where most of the population could be found and approached people asking if they had thought about learning to fly. The usual response was that they would love to, but couldn't afford to. So I offered a 15-minute trial flight for five dollars. Nearly everyone who took up the offer decided to go ahead and enlist in a full course of training for the private pilot licence. This might be because I told every student excitedly, after their trial flight, that they were a natural, gifted pilot and should take a licence.

I got round the local curfew – whereby any aircraft flying in Zimbabwe between 6pm and 6am would be automatically shot down by the local Zimbabwe Defence Force – by holding the first lesson at 6am, then 8am, 10am, 2pm and 4pm. (I imagine the curfew was for political reasons, but having no interest in politics at the time, I just accepted it). At noon, the intense heat of the day produced almost no climb rate from the poor little Cessna, ZS-WDI, so I used the period as a lunch break or to catch up with paperwork. There was even enough time during the midday break for me to cycle home and to swim 100 lengths before returning for the two o'clock lesson.

Within the second week of establishing my Club, every slot was filled, every day of the week. I socialised with many of those learning to fly, which resulted in being asked to join a band that was starting up that needed a drummer.

In South Africa, I had traded my XR500R Honda (worth very little because it had a seized engine) for an extra 12 pieces of drum kit from a man who had a 17-piece kit but couldn't even erect them to play, as he lived in a caravan. The new Tama drums were the same silver colour as my original Premier set and they were superb to play and even just to look at: I found them a total delight.

I joined the band, which we called PC and Company, although it was usually shortened to 'The Pisscats'. Band practice was every evening at

6pm, which fitted well with the night curfew closure of my club. Practice was held at Paul Warren's house, where we could leave our gear set up ready for the following day. Paul was a bank cashier who played lead and rhythm guitar in the band: he had a lovely voice and wrote most of the songs we played. Gradually we were invited to play at pubs and clubs and were always welcomed and treated well.

Life was so much fun and although working and playing hard, I was enjoying every minute of living. My relationship with !re!rey fizzled out, although neither of us ended it, or even planned to. But it was difficult to find time to see him, and our only meetings tended to be when I was in hospital, or when I was able to use someone's aircraft to take the owner for a long trip, to Ghanzi.

About this time I had a call from Terry Venter, who I'd known while he was working as an engineer for KASAC, and who was now living in South Africa. He asked if I would like to return to South Africa to fly an Aztec for Chobe Game Lodge. The job entailed flying from Jo'burg to Kasane, Northern Botswana, and staying in the remote wilderness for anything up to a week, then returning to South Africa to change passengers and return to the Bush. I told him I had settled happily in Zimbabwe and was running my own flying club, which I hoped to expand in time.

I was in regular communication with the DCA as to how my students could get tested in both the flight tests and ground exams. The main problem was being hours or miles from any test centre and the fact that I was the only person in charge of the flying club. I was given dispensation to invigilate the exams for my own students, which I was pleased about but more concerned about the final flight tests as the nearest flying school was Harare, some three hours by Cessna. Finally it was agreed I could test my own students at the end of their course, given the distance and impracticality of any other solution. I was overjoyed, as this had seemed the biggest hurdle since starting up.

Within a few months I had a few students approaching the end of their training. Three had already finished their written exams and were only a few hours from being ready for the final flight test.

Digby had a general manager called Rudi, who I was teaching to fly. He had gone solo and also flown a couple of solo cross-countries. He called me up one morning to ask if he could take the Cessna for a few circuits in my lunch period. As I intended to supervise the circuits, I took sandwiches to eat while Rudi flew. At lunchtime, Rudi appeared and asked for the keys, which I gave him, while I continued de-briefing the previous student. When I finished, I wondered where Rudi was, as there was no sign of activity by the little Cessna. Just as I was becoming concerned, the phone rang.

It was a humble, apologetic-sounding Rudi explaining that he was at his office with the keys of Digby's Cessna, but was sorry to inform me that I could not have the keys back; in other words, my flying club was finished.

I found this news impossible to comprehend. I told Rudi that not only could he not do this to me, since I had the aircraft booked at two and at four o'clock, but that I needed to know why Digby had changed his mind. Had I upset him in some way?

Rudi explained that Digby had bought the Cessna to use 'occasionally' round the farm. When I had appeared on the scene, he thought it was a good idea to keep the Cessna in use and looked after and perhaps turn a profit on the hours flown. Although Digby had happily taken the payments I had given him for the hours flown, he had not envisaged the amount of flying I would be doing every day. He also had not allowed for the engine overhaul to be done so soon. This cost in the region of £7,000 (much more in Zimbabwean dollars). Should I continue with my flying club, the engine hours would be finished and an overhaul needed in two weeks, but if my club ceased now, there would be enough hours to last Digby for a couple of years.

I was seething with anger, fury and helplessness. In desperation I asked Rudi, "surely he could have called me and asked for the keys with a couple of days' notice, not done it through you, like this?"

"No, Tizi, he only just noticed the problem with the hours and he honestly thought you would not have given him the keys to his aircraft. I'm only sorry I'm the one he used to take the keys."

I apologised to Rudi for my lack of manners and put the phone down. I thought about what to do. I had no aircraft, so the club was finished. Could I get another aircraft? To buy one was out of the question: I had no money. To attempt to borrow the amount for a replacement Cessna was equally impossible. I was not a resident in the country, nor a homeowner and I had nothing to put down as a deposit.

Still confused, with no way out, Paul Jones, my next student walked in and asked where the Cessna was. Paul was an attractive, practical, middle-aged farmer with a family in Chirezdi. I started telling him what had happened, then lost all my self-control and burst into tears; only the second time in my life that I had cried in public, the first being when my father died when I was eleven.

I asked Paul if he would finish his licence, either in Harare or at Buffalo Range. The latter was closer, but they only flew a few days a month as the instructors were all voluntary and each lesson had to be agreed with an instructor on a personal basis. He promised he would finish his licence and offered to take me for a drink. I declined the drink but he accepted a cup of tea, over which we put the world right and placed some heavy curses on Digby.

Strangely enough, after contacting all of my students, no one was unpleasant to me although most of them felt disgust with Digby. A couple of students even sympathised with me, saying it was to be expected from Digby.

At this time, I was staying in the spare room at the home of Colleen and John Smallpiece as their house was nearer to the airport than Digby's. John was learning to fly with me. They had both become like family. Colleen asked if the band might go full-time: I told her I would love nothing more, but we played mainly for charity functions and all the other members had full-time jobs.

Then I thought of Terry Venter with his offer of flying for Chobe Game Lodge. I called him up and asked if the position was still available and we agreed I'd start in a week. It gave me time to ensure most of the students had a chance to sit their ground exams, which gave me more peace of mind.

The evening before I left, my students gathered to thank me for giving them the chance to enter a new part of their lives. I was even presented with a beautiful copper coffee jug as a 'thank you' for the time and care I had given them. They all promised they would finish their licence.

When my last week in Zimbabwe was up, Colleen and John drove me to the station to catch the train to Jo'burg, complete with my 17-piece drumkit! A new life lay ahead in South Africa.

Chapter 16

IN THE FOOTSTEPS OF ELIZABETH TAYLOR

Terry Venter met me at Jo'burg station – surprised at my luggage – and told me more about my new job with Chobe. He said it was perfect for me as he knew I loved the Bush and didn't care for towns or concrete. The following day I was introduced to the little Piper Aztec, ZS JAN, which I was to fly solely for the next six months. The Aztec was an inexpensive aircraft to buy, economical to fly, and a reliable workhorse trainer. With gentle flying characteristics and no temptation to behave viciously, it performed well whether landing or taking off from short, rough tarmac, sand or gravel strips. It carried a very good load – basically whatever you could fit in, it would try to get airborne.

With this new job, it meant either flying the Aztec, usually to Chobe Game Lodge, or being on standby. I was issued with a beeper: when it beeped, I rode my bike (the Ducati retrieved from storage), to the nearest phone box ten kilometres away and called the Chobe office. I would then be given the time of departure and number of passengers to be taken to Chobe Game Lodge the following day. Initially I found that it was impossible to make a phone call, because all the phones were being used for hours by locals, mainly black women who were just chatting. So I hit on the idea of bringing along a six-foot Burmese python called Monty, who would sit around my neck while I rode my motorbike to the phones. As soon as I got off the bike, the phones would instantly be hung up or dropped, as most black people in Africa were terrified of snakes – even very friendly ones.

My routine settled to flying to Chobe, which could be for three to seven days, then returning to Jo'burg for three to four days.

My first visit to the Lodge was amazing: the fact that Elizabeth Taylor chose to re-marry Richard Burton at Chobe Game Lodge speaks volumes for the standard. All the chalets were individual, en-suite and immaculate.

There was a lovely pool, a fabulous restaurant with resident chef, Rex. Game drives were offered daily for residents as was an evening 'booze cruise', where people could take early 'sundowners' while cruising down the 'treacherous crocodile and hippo filled waters' of the Chobe River.

On my arrival, I was shown to a chalet and given a key. This was to be mine permanently and should I feel like it, I could keep anything there, rather than bring changes of clothing with me every trip. I was amazed at this generosity, especially when I heard the chalet rental costs. I had expected a tent, which was what most of the other safari camps offered, but this was luxury.

When I first flew to Chobe, I wandered around the Bush, taking photos of the elephants, lions and hippos, or writing long letters to friends in various countries.

The chef, Rex, told me I could use his canoe anytime I wanted as he never had time to take it out. He also offered to prepare me packed lunches whenever I went for a trip. I took him up on his offer and after a few sorties I found I spent nearly all the time I was in Chobe on the river. Rex was a lovely, gentle, quietly spoken man. With his interesting, lined and well-tanned face, I asked if he was born under the Cancer sign. He was amazed, asking how I had known. I told him he was like reading a book.

There were a few girls working as receptionists and hostesses with whom I got along really well. Sometimes we would go out for half a day on the Chobe rowing boat, or on occasions I would paddle in the canoe with just one of the girls, complete with packed lunches.

On one occasion, I paddled alone downriver and watched a cormorant dive into the water, then emerge carrying a fish. He (or she) flapped gently barely inches above the water for a considerable distance before taking off and flying into the distance, complete with the fish. I realised I was watching the effect of induced drag, which is least just above the surface of the ground/ water. The cormorant could not have left the water with the additional weight of the fish and entered a climb with the feathers still wet. By using the inbred knowledge that drag is reduced and lift is increased by flying as close as possible to the surface, until the feathers had dried, the bird was able to then continue to take off, once dried and fly to its destination.

Pilots had to be taught these little tricks at school!

Watching the little bird fly off with the fish took my attention from 'watching the water' ahead. Just ten feet in front of my tiny canoe, an enormous beautiful-but-ugly head of a hippo surfaced. The head looked like an oil painting, freshly painted on a canvas – still shining from the water, or the paints while drying. It was ugly because the proximity of the head spelt instant death.

In two amazing strokes of my paddle, I turned the canoe through a hundred-and-eighty degrees and continued paddling for my life, upstream. With the adrenalin pumping through my body, I am still sure I would have broken any speed record for the distance I covered in the following few seconds.

With enough distance covered, I dared to look behind and found I was not being pursued.

I knew there were more deaths attributed to hippos than to any other animal in Africa, even lions. Although the hippo is a vegetarian (so lone humans are of little interest, being inedible), the sight of a canoe will drive them into a killing frenzy. This is because crocodiles take and eat baby hippos – and from underneath, a canoe resembles a croc and therefore becomes an enemy. The immediate action for any hippo is to chomp the canoe in half, usually maiming or killing the occupants. Paddling to land and running is not wise, as a hippo can manage 40kms an hour over land, and they chase to kill.

My lucky hippo escape warned me not to lose concentration at any time while on or by a river.

Another 'close encounter' was while taking a swim across the Chobe River, having moored the canoe to the bank on an exceptionally hot afternoon. I had been told crocodiles only remained below the surface for seven minutes at a time. Whenever I wanted to take a swim in any part of the river, I watched the surface for about nine minutes to satisfy myself there were no crocs in the water. On one occasion, having watched the water and satisfied myself the water was safe, I swam across to the far side and later swam back. Halfway along the return trip, I felt something big and heavy brush against my leg.

With another adrenalin-filled superhuman effort in utter panic, I reached the side in seconds and got out. I could see no signs of anything splashing around, not even a 'log' in sight. It wasn't until many years later I discovered crocodiles could stay for hours underwater: had I have known earlier, I would have missed many swims.

On one flight to Chobe airstrip, my front-seat passenger introduced himself as Bill Johnson who told me he was a professional show jumper. I was surprised, as I hadn't heard his name (but why should I in a new country?), and we talked about horses for the entire three-and-a-half hour trip, which ended with Bill saying I could go over and ride his horses anytime I was free between charters.

My favourite horse of Bill's was the magnificent show-jumper Sword of Justice, who remains my favourite of all the horses I've ridden in my life. Bill's colours were green and white, but those colours didn't appear on the Sword's bridle and I asked him why that was. He said it wasn't possible to get leather in green and white. I rose to the challenge, found some green and white leather and made a unique hand-stitched bridle for the Sword.

Life was good.

I'd heard the Lippizaner stallions were giving displays every week in South Africa and was surprised to hear that they were only ridden by women. I went to watch a show and was amazed at how they did the same movements as the stallions in Austria, which were ridden only by men. Joining the show would fulfil a lifelong ambition, so I sought out the owner, Christiana, who invited me along. When I got there, she already had a horse, Capriano Magistra, saddled up ready for me. We went into the menage, which had mirrors right round its perimenter, so you can see how high the horse bring up his hooves in a 'piaffe' – an almost on-the-spot, controlled trot.

I felt I was in seventh heaven and to this day I still remember the feeling as a perfect horse went through his paces. I tried all the high school movements I had ridden on Kadett, then rode a perfect piaffe.

Christiana told me she would be keen to take me into the shows but I would need to be available every Sunday. She explained that the role was unpaid: women in South Africa were expected to be housewives, not needing to work, unlike in Austria, where the role was paid.

I was in a quandary. If I accepted, I'd lose my job at the Chobe Game Lodge, yet it was the offer of a lifetime. I told her I'd have to think about it: I never said 'no' but I never said 'yes' either. My heart was crying out to say 'yes' but my head reminded me that I had no savings, still had to pay rent, and would have to find a paying job that didn't need me on Sundays. To this day, 35 years later, it is still my one regret that I never said 'yes'.

*

Between trips to Chobe, I was called into the main office in Jo'burg and told I was to have a new aircraft, a Piper Navajo Chieftain, as they were getting busier and it would take more passengers. Would I be happy flying it?

I agreed it was a good move. I had flown many hours with KASAC in Chieftains and looked forward to the new aircraft. I was then asked if I could think of a suitable colour scheme for the new aircraft, as they wanted it to be appropriate for the company's image.

I dreamed up several colour schemes and then bought a couple of large model aircraft and painted the designs. I painted one with a purple background; purple was Chobe's main brochure colour, with a line of elephants, each one holding the preceding tail in its trunk. The second model I painted with an orange/red sunset in the background and trees at the back of the aircraft with a couple of lions beneath the trees and monkeys in the trees. Proud of my designs, I took them into the office, to give them an idea of how the aircraft could look. No comment was offered but I was asked if I would test fly the Chieftain.

I flew the test flight the following evening and found it a delight. Awaiting completion of the final paperwork I took the Aztec for its last flight to Chobe. When I returned, my friend Terry called me, asking me round. When I arrived, he seemed full of doom and misgivings and tried to warn me that someone fairly unpleasant and ruthless was trying to take my job, now that my aircraft had been changed to the Chieftain instead of the Aztec, which nobody else would fly.

"Tizi, please listen to me," he said. "No one wanted to fly that Aztec but there are still hundreds of pilots out of work that will do anything to take your job now you have a decent aircraft and I know one that is trying determinedly. He's called Trevor Arnold."

I ignored his warning, thinking it highly unlikely my trusted company would ditch their loyal pilot, just because someone else wanted my job. I was aware that I was popular with the passengers and all the staff at Chobe.

The following day, I was asked to go to the office. During my ride to downtown Jo'burg, I had a cold feeling I was to be fired. I kept thinking of what Terry had told me.

Arriving at the office, my boss said he was sorry to have to tell me my services were no longer needed. My world fell apart. I asked what had I done wrong – were they unhappy with my flying? I had never been even one minute late or taken a minute longer than necessary for any of the trips.

I was told my flying could not be faulted – but they did not feel I was the right person to take high-profile people around. Someone had told the office that I had strange hobbies, for a female. They quoted taming snakes and wild horses, riding whitewater marathons and mending saddlery. There was no mention of a boyfriend in my life and that was where they were becoming particularly uneasy.

In other words, someone had told Chobe I was gay.

I couldn't deny any of my hobbies but it seemed unfair to be fired for 'being queer' just because I was not seen to be actively dating. I had not seen !re!ey for a while. Although I still wore his engagement ring, I thought it would not be wise to show off my beautiful ring – of a cobra, its fangs open wide, hood spread, sporting diamond eyes – while explaining I was engaged to marry a Bushman in Ghanzi, Botswana. Since almost everyone in South Africa was very racist, this was a no-win situation.

Speechless for the first time I could remember, I took my paycheque and rode home in a depressed state of mind.

Shortly after arriving home, the phone rang. It was my friend Roni, girlfriend of another friend, Mike Zeltner. She asked how I was and I told her, "Miserable. I am jobless as of today. Chobe has turfed me out for being gay."

Roni laughed, to which I had a fairly hostile reaction, and then she said:

"Actually that's remarkably good news, right now. I was calling you to ask you to join Mike and myself in a celebration drink."

"I'm hardly in a mood to celebrate anything right now," I growled back.

"Bring a toothbrush and wear something pink. Bye." Roni hung up.

Snapping out of my mood and wondering what was going on, I changed into a pink dress and grabbed a bottle of Pink Lady I had bought long ago, in happier days, in case there anything to celebrate.

I jumped onto my purple Ducati, feeling it was almost pink, and shortly arrived at Mike and Roni's.

Roni heard the bike arrive. By the time I had reached the back door, she greeted me with a glass of pink champagne, with a pink cherry (well red...), also wearing a pink dress. I looked around for Mike, expecting him to be wearing pink, but was relieved to see he wasn't.

"What's the celebration?" I asked.

"We are drinking to our new pilot of Crocodile Safaris – you," said Mike with a smile.

I was stunned. It had to be a joke.

"Well you do want to fly, don't you? We need a full-time pilot-cum-sales-rep as of now and Roni told me the good news that you are done with Chobe."

I had to be dreaming. This sort of thing only happened in books – not in real life.

Mike told me he and Roni had decided to start Flying Crocodile Safaris, where people would be taken on a camping holiday, flying to the wilderness of the swamps in northern Botswana. The aircraft (Mike's own Cessna 310) and another leased one would be supplied, as would the tents, food and chefs (pilots!).

"Where do the holiday-makers come from?" I asked, curious.

"Well that's your job," said Mike, "which is where we need a pilot/ sales rep. I'll provide you with a portfolio which you can take door-to-door to interest people in the safari holiday of a lifetime. When you have signed up 10 people, we take an aircraft each to the swamps in Xaxaba, where we both land. Then we get into two or three Macorros, pick a suitable spot along the riverbanks and pitch our tents. We then get collected in seven to 10 days, flying back to Lansaria, to start again. Well, will you fly with me or must I look elsewhere?"

"When do I start?" was the only question left.

"Tomorrow. You can go out on the streets trying to interest enough people in a holiday. Just to fill two planes, then we can leave on Saturday."

He then showed me his portfolio, consisting of fabulous shots of the bush, wildlife, rivers, tented accommodation, Xaxaba airstrip and his twin Cessna 310.

"What's the second airplane and which do I fly?" I asked.

"There is a Cessna 207 which I can lease, which I will fly. You can fly my twin."

I was amazed at his generosity, being prepared to fly a single himself over the desert and swamps, yet offering me to fly his twin. I accepted to start the following day.

By lunchtime next day, I had ten people signed up to come the forthcoming weekend, with either a deposit or the full sum paid in advance. But one person was over 60 years old, which concerned Mike.

"Look, Tizi, we are *not* taking 'grannies'. Give her the money back. I am not taking the responsibility if anything goes wrong. She'll have to sleep in a tent and wash in the river, along with the rest of us."

No, I'm not giving her money back. She's coming and that's that. She can come in my plane – I will make sure she's OK."

The dispute went on for a while but our 'granny' came. She seemed to enjoy herself more than anyone and was less trouble than anyone else.

For the following trip, I went to the local snake park at Halfway House and encouraged 10 people to come.

The trip was amazing. After landing at Xaxaba, we split into three dugouts and headed a few hours up-river until we found a picturesque spot to camp. Everyone helped to pitch the tents, after which we had the traditional campfire dinner of sausages, eggs and smash with beer and tea. The following day was a snake-hunting expedition tracking and capturing various snakes, which were mostly released.

It was so much more fun than just walking and looking at the countryside, taking the odd snap of anything which moved, as on the previous trip.

Each day followed a similar theme … except one day a captive black mamba was brought back in a pillowcase at the end of the trip, to be housed in the Halfway House Snake Park. As we were checking customs from Botswana to return to South Africa, an official asked what was in the pillowcase. He was told it was a live black mamba – would he like to see it? He shrank back from the plane and wouldn't go near the second craft, bidding us to hurry on to South Africa, which we did.

The flights were as interesting and varied as the passengers we carried. I enjoyed the sales aspect prior to the trips as much as the flights and the trips themselves. With the onset of winter, however, people were more inclined to wait for the spring or summer to take a camping holiday, so I returned to teaching flying at the local club at Lansaria.

One of the students, John Lougher, had decided to learn to fly after joining Mike and myself on one of our Flying Crocodile Safaris. He was very knowledgeable about snakes and had a large collection of venomous ones, which he kept in fish-tanks in Durban. He invited me to see his collection. I was not only impressed with his tremendous assortment of beautiful cobras, adders, vipers and mambas but amazed that he employed a black 'girl' to not only keep his apartment tidy while he was away but to look after and feed all the 'lodgers'. Every black male and female I had ever met in Africa was terrified of snakes.

While I was teaching John to fly, he in turn taught me as much as he could about snakes. He taught me where to find the important information – such as how many different types of snakes there were in South Africa – and also insisted I learned the English and Latin names for every breed. Plus, more importantly, I had to learn which venom each snake possessed (if any); how poisonous they were; how long there was from bite to death and what could be used as anti-venom.

Despite John's interest in helping me, I was still surprised when he told me his long-term plans were to open a large snake park in Durban; he asked if I would be interested in being the joint curator for the new park.

I accepted immediately, asking when it would all happen. He told me within a couple of months, as he had already started the process by applying for permission for the snake park to be erected. He assured me he had the financial means and was only looking for someone to help him run it before he started getting the park built.

I went with him to Durban and he showed me the site: I was as excited as he was.

Chapter 17

WAITING FOR THE SNAKE PARK

I wrote to my parents, asking if they would like to visit Africa, since I was not especially busy at this time and told her of my new hopes for the future. I pointed out that it was winter, so the climate would suit them both better.

The reply was, "No, dear, neither of us would like the long trip. Even less keen on the idea of mosquitoes and of catching malaria and have an especial dislike of snakes." But she told me she would be happy to offer me a return ticket to visit them. About now would be ideal as they were not busy and summer was approaching, which suited me. Plus it would be cheaper for them to get a ticket from England, than the other way round.

How could I refuse? I agreed to visit almost immediately and my mother sent me an open return ticket.

I told John Lougher my plans and he said that the park should be almost up and ready by my return. We exchanged addresses and agreed to keep in touch and I agreed I would tie in my return with the park being ready to open.

The arrival at Heathrow was cold. I had already forgotten the British summer is so much cooler than the African winter.

There was hardly time for a cup of tea with my parents at 'home' when the phone rang. It was Nigel Harris, asking to speak with me. Nigel owned many aircraft and kept starting new flying businesses of all kinds. He was well-known for being an entrepreneur but also for being not especially honest.

"Hello Tizi, I heard you were in England," said Nigel. "How would you like a job taking a student or two from here to the south of France, teaching them for their private pilot's licence and returning in two weeks, when they can take their flight test and written exams?"

Somewhat taken aback, I asked, "When would I start? Where is 'here'? Which aircraft? And how in the heck did you know I was back in England?"

I had spoken to no one apart from my parents since arriving, and no one in South Africa apart from John, Mike and Roni knew I had come here.

"How about tomorrow? 'Here' is Stansted. The aircraft is a Cessna 172. Heard it through the bush vine. Say nine o'clock?"

"Hold on a cotton-pickin' moment. I've just come to England to see my folks. What on earth makes you think I want to disappear immediately to France with your students?"

Then I realised my English instructor rating was no longer current. I had a genuine 'out', so told Nigel the reason I could not do it.

"Well I figured your rating would have lapsed by now," he said. "so I have already booked you in to renew your rating tomorrow morning at Norwich, on a Slingsby. It's OK, I'm paying for the test, but I'll cancel it if you don't want to go to France."

I was dazed. I had planned to relax for a few days and catch up on everything, having been away a few years. I asked my mother if she would be offended if I went flying the following day.

It seemed dumb to let my English ratings lapse, apart from having a bunch of fun flying the Slingsby, to renew the rating with.

"Not at all," was her reply.

After renewing my lapsed rating, I found myself departing from Stansted the following day for a two-week 'PPL holiday'. It was hardly a holiday, since the poor students – brother and sister Mark and Gail Freeman – had to fly nearly four hours every day while there. Plus they had to absorb the ground studies, which I almost force-fed them up till midnight every day in the desperate attempt to cover the entire syllabus in two weeks.

I had deliberately squeezed the 14 days into 11, to allow for losing two or three days for poor weather. This turned out to be necessary; however, on the weathered-out days, both Gail and Mark elected to study rather than visit attractions within walking distance or a short taxi drive.

Mark and Gail were almost opposites. Gail was small-boned, petite and slim with shoulder-length dark brown hair and Mark was rounded with a heavy frame. Returning to Stansted, they both passed the final flight test and the ground exams on the same day. I was as delighted as they were. We all agreed it was extremely hard work all round, hardly a holiday.

Before I drove home, Nigel asked if I would like to pop over to South Africa if he gave me a ticket to go.

"Love to, but when?" I replied automatically, vaguely wondering about my 'visit to England', then added. "What's the catch?"

"There's no catch, you know me, but you might like to pick up an aircraft, a Mooney which I've just bought for a client, from Lansaria."

I stopped in my tracks, then assumed it was a joke. No, it needed collecting in ten days from Lansaria.

That was perfect timing. I could check with John Lougher how the snake park was progressing, fly the Mooney to England, take my promised 'time off' with my folks and then return home, on my ticket.

I now considered South Africa as my home, as I intended to retire there. It was October 1985 and I was 31 years old.

There were ten days before departing. Since Nigel was short of instructors, I agreed to help out over the next couple of days. The following day I was asked to fly with someone called Jim Bryant on a cross-country detail. I asked where he would like to go and he told me he would go wherever I suggested.

"How about you fly us to Redhill and I could take you up in a bi-plane, then you could fly us back here?" I proposed.

Jim approved of the idea. He plotted and planned, then flew us in a Cherokee to Redhill. On arrival, I asked if I could take Jim up in a Stampe. Someone suggested I follow the rules and fly the Tiger first, to get current. So I took CDC up for ten minutes, then took the Stampe – WEF – up for an aerobatic sequence practice over the airfield for five minutes, after which I was OK'd to take Jim up in anything we wanted to fly. Jim agreed on the Stampe.

While I was there, I was asked if I was taking part in the contest at Dunkeswell, Devon. I had not known that there was a contest the following day and agreed to take part.

We then returned in the Cherokee, which I'd carefully parked out of sight for fear of ribbing from the Tiger Club, about 'soiling their airfield with a nose-wheel aircraft.'

Jim admitted on the way back that he now only wanted to finish his licence so that he could join the Tiger Club. I was pleased to steer someone in a sensible direction. The Tiger Club was second to none in flying standards, piloting ability, discipline and airmanship.

Although not in the first three of the aerobatic contest, I had san enjoyable day and was so pleased to be reunited with my favourite Stampe. TKC gave me the best landing of my life, and Michael Jones, secretary of the Tiger Club, came up to congratulate me on my flying, saying he thought TKC and I were made for each other.

The following day I returned to normality, flying a Cessna with a student for Nigel before departing the next day for Lansaria courtesy of an airline to Jan Smuts then a small charter plane to Lansaria.

As I walked into the airport searching for the Mooney, someone from the Lansaria Flying Club came up to me to give me the message that the Mooney was just having the last finishing touches to its ferry tanks. It would be ready for a flight test that afternoon. Would I possibly have time to take a student for his PPL Flight Test, while I was waiting for the tanks to be installed?

I agreed, provided there was time for a cup of tea first.

During the flight test, the student Bruyns, was competent, careful, did not get lost or fly into controlled airspace and more importantly, didn't frighten me. We de-briefed his successful flight over another cup of tea (how can anyone live without it?). Then I took the Mooney for a cursory test flight, expecting to depart the following day for England.

The ferry tanks looked fine and checked out satisfactorily on the ground. However, once airborne, every time I tried selecting one of the two tanks, there was a cough and splutter, followed by silence as the engine stopped. Every attempt brought the same result, so I returned and explained the problem to the engineer preparing the aircraft for the flight. It was suggested I return the following day for a further flight test.

At least this gave me time to hunt down John Lougher, to find out news of the snake park and when I could aim to return. It was now the end of September: winter was approaching in England and summer about to arrive in South Africa. I preferred the latter in climate.

John found me at Lansaria. He was non-committal about the park, explaining there were more problems than he had anticipated with the buildings; perhaps it might take a few more months, not the weeks he had hoped. Meantime he decided to get his licence and was thinking of buying a Mooney when he qualified. Did I approve?

Of course I did, provided it didn't eat into the snake park funds. While we were chatting, I was given the message that a part was needed for the ferry tanks – perhaps I could pick it up from Carltonville? John told me we could use a Cessna 210, which he had at his disposal to rent, as transport.

After returning with the part, and while waiting for the repair, we discussed the park. I had assured him there was no hurry since there was plenty of work in England while I waited to return.

"But," I pointed out, "it is cold in winter over there."

John then dropped me off at Meggie's where I took my Cagiva and rode into the suburbs off Jo'burg to visit a friend, Sarah, whom I had promised to look up, should I have any spare time. Rockie her collie dog, thinking I was a messenger boy, bit my leg, which was equivalent to biting a postman – quite normal.

Sarah had told Rockie to let go, which he did and no more was said. However, Sarah's husband noticed a trail of blood to where I sat and asked if I was OK. I assured him I was but on request I pulled my trouser up. Quite surprisingly I found a steady flow of blood pouring out, so I apologised for the mess and offered to wipe it up. Sarah told me of course I could not, since it was Rockie's fault and found me a tin of Plastic Skin. I sprayed the substance over the hole, which stopped the blood from flowing.

The bite turned septic, so I visited a doctor before departing South Africa, who gave me antibiotics.

Finally, the following day, after lunch, the ferry tanks were proclaimed working. I was told it was working properly. There was no need for another flight test, if I wanted to get going: I should just take it up, try the tanks – which would work, -but if there was another problem, I should call it a flight test and return.

This seemed sensible if I was ever to get away. I filed a flight plan to Harare for the first leg and asked someone to notify Nigel in England that I had actually left, if I did not return within the hour.

The tanks worked fine. No coughs, splutters or dreaded 'silence' when I tried each tank in turn. Four hours later I landed at Harare and was amazed when someone called, "Hi Tizi, what are you doing here?" It was Toomba, a black engineer I had not seen for years. When I worked in Gaberone, Toomba had been stationed in Maun, but he had often used KASAC as an air taxi for his firm. Toomba was black as coal, well built, with an amazing smile. I remembered him as always being happy and this was no exception. He told me he was delighted to see me again. We chatted a short while and he insisted on driving me to a local hotel, to save me from waiting forever for a taxi.

The following day I started at first light, expecting a long flight to Wilson, Nharobi. It turned out a straightforward flight, apart from getting iced up in cloud at 15,000 feet. I had to descend as the pitot head had iced and the stall warning was wailing, with the airspeed dropping further and further. I called on the radio with my actions 'descending now – due ice' but received no reply. The cloud was thick: I had no idea how thick and I was aware that mount Killimanjaro was somewhere around, possibly beneath me, with the tops around 12 to 14,000 feet.

I thanked the Heavens that I had no passengers and that the aircraft was insured, since that removed the pressure. Naturally the chart had fallen onto the floor, beyond reach. I scrabbled around madly trying to keep the aircraft upright, but descending while reaching for the chart.

Having located the chart, I calculated by means of stopwatch, heading, last known position, and general whereabouts and found I was a good forty miles from the mountain. I broke cloud at 8,000 feet and the ice gradually melted. I elected to stay visual beneath the cloud, since I had not made contact with anyone since icing up. That was despite having filed an instrument flight plan and having remained in communication throughout the flight with an Air Traffic Controller during each phase of flight.

For the next few peaceful hours I appreciated the scenery with the radio turned off. There was no purpose in listening to meaningless squawks and static when the alternate was peace and the gentle purr of the engine.

With 50 miles to go, I tuned in to Wilson Airport and was surprised to receive a reply, requesting my details. In less than 20 minutes I was on the ground, after an eight-and-a-half hour flight. What I would have given for a cup of tea! Instead, the local customs official asked me for a General Declaration. I had none and remarked dryly that every other border I had crossed had supplied the necessary paperwork.

"Well you must supply your own, or the aircraft goes nowhere, and neither do you," came the vicious reply.

Tired and cross and feeling more like sleep than anything else, I asked if I could have a pen and paper and I would write the required information for them.

"No, the correct forms must be used. Call us when you have them filled in."

I was amazed, and even more so when someone told me I could probably get a form from the charter company on the other side of the airfield. A long walk would probably be good for me, but a long sleep would have been more welcome.

The form was found and completed, BMEK refuelled and the following day's Flight Plan submitted for the next stop, Abu Simnel. I then found a taxi and asked to be taken to the nearest cheap motel. There seemed no point wasting Nigel's money on a fancy hotel, when all I wanted was a tea, sandwich and a bed.

After I'd checked in, I asked if I could have a pot of tea and a sandwich sent to my room, figuring to have a deep, warm bath while I waited for dinner, then straight to bed.

"Sorry, no room service. There are plenty of restaurants a short walk away. I heard you are going early – could you pay now please, as there will be no one here at four in the morning."

I handed the money over, took my key and put my bag in the room. Then I walked out for something quick to eat and drink. Apart from a few restaurants (I would not trade waiting time for sleeping time), there only seemed a kebab hut and a chippy. I elected for the Chippy, ordering fish and chips and a cup of tea.

"Sorry. No tea." I was told.

"OK, anything at all to drink? Orange?" I pleaded, having been dehydrated for over nine hours.

"Orange, sure. Where is your bottle?" The woman held out her hand.

"I have no bottle. Could I have a can of something – anything?"

"No bottle, no drink. We have no cans."

I took my fish and walked through the village, stopping everywhere in the hope of a drink. Everywhere told the same story: no bottle, no drink. I finally found two extremely old tins of peach segments and returned to my room to eat the salted fish and chips, washed down with the peaches. Dying of thirst, but scared to drink the water, I ran a bath before retiring.

There was no bath plug, but no shower either, so with the greasy chip paper stemming the water, I continued to run the bath. No hot water either! Then on closer inspection there was no towel, nor sheets or a pillow for the bed.

This paled into insignificance as I skipped a few hundred times to dry off, then slid beneath the horrible smelling blanket to fall asleep instantly, only to be awakened a few minutes later by what sounded like an explosion. It was a noisy party with a full live rap band on the floor beneath. Despite everything, I must have fallen asleep as the alarm went off in what seemed a couple of minutes.

I got up and went outside. After a few minutes of panic, wondering if I was going to be trapped there, I saw my taxi arriving to rescue me from that hole.

After a cursory glance round BMEK (wild horses wouldn't have kept me in Wilson a moment longer), I took the weather forecast with me to read en route, then climbed aboard, started up and requested taxi for Abu Simnel.

"No, I'm sorry, you may *not* depart, you have no Diplomatic Clearance to fly over Egypt. You may not taxi. I repeat *not*."

"I don't care – I'll go without" I wanted to say, but instead closed down the engine, got out and limped to the control tower. I was furious since I knew Nigel had got the necessary clearance before I left England.

When I reached the control tower, I assured the controller I had seen the Dip Clearances before I had even left England, so please could I go?

"No, we have no record of them here. They have not arrived, so you must wait."

I couldn't believe it, neither could I take another night in this horrible country: I just wanted to get out. I turned and started to limp heavily away, toward BMEK. The controller walked after me and asked what I had done to my leg. He seemed genuinely concerned.

"A dog bit me some days ago." I rolled up my trouser leg. "It got infected, as you can see. I was told if I don't get to a hospital in England soon, I will have to have the leg amputated. It is painful already, but I am afraid if you don't let me depart now, I will hold you personally responsible for losing my leg. Can I take your name please?" I started writing his name he wore on his badge.

Luckily the leg had swollen up tremendously. It was a hideous dark purple, although due in part from a previous injury. I was not actually concerned in the least as I was halfway through the course of antibiotics.

The effect was tremendous. I was told I could depart immediately, so I hobbled as rapidly as I was able before he changed his mind. Starting up, requesting taxi and almost flying down the taxiway, I departed before it was too late, thanking dear Rockie for biting me.

I set heading immediately for Abu Simnel, where the chart said that fuel and customs were available. However, when I tried to call Abu Simnel there was no reply. I was now out of range for anyone behind me but unable to awaken Simnel ahead. Checking the chart, I decided to continue to Aswan.

I continued until I was overhead of Simnel and looked down to see if there was any activity at the airfield. I saw an unforgettably beautiful sight.

Abu Simnel was truly a 'one horse village', though there was no sign at all of a village, or indeed any habitation. There was a long, sand east-west runway and a small hut (perhaps containing a drum of Avgas-to-order). No sign of a control tower but I thought I imagined a hitching post. Perhaps there had been a horse, many years ago that died of isolation and loneliness. Perhaps there might be a bridle tied to the hitching post? I was tempted to fly lower and take a closer look at this beautiful spot of clean, inviting, empty desert strip but descending and circling would have wasted precious fuel and time, so I continued, determined to return one day, perhaps by camel.

When within radio range of Aswan, some hours after leaving the peace and beauty of Simnel, I called up, passed my details and requested landing permission, which I was granted. I then inquired if they had fuel and customs as I had departed from Wilson, Harare.

"Obviously we have fuel and customs. Which fuel do you want?" the controller replied.

It was a fairly dumb question. I had already told him I was flying a Mooney. I assumed air traffic controllers knew which types of fuel the various breeds of aircraft drank, even if not in what quantity.

"Avgas," I replied.

"No Avgas here, only Jet A1. Can you use Jet A1? We have plenty of that."

I tried asking the controller where I could get Avgas, customs and lights if I continued toward England.

"I do not know. You tell me where you want to go and I will tell you if it has what you require."

I studied the chart. Khartoum looked the next obvious stop: the airport was large and looked inviting, since there was a large town close to the airfield. But Nigel had told me on no account to land at Khartoum, as I would almost certainly be locked up and the aircraft impounded. His reasoning was that it was the probably the way Arabs would behave to a single white female if I landed there.

It seemed the next place was Luxor, Egypt – it had everything, so I changed course.

As I approached Khartoum, so beautifully illuminated it looked like a Christmas card scene, (it was only minus the wise men on camels), I had a strong desire to land. The controller I spoke to was so friendly, I felt sure it would be safe. I knew all the facilities were there and I was a little tired, but Nigel's warning echoed in my head, so I decided against it.

Flying toward and overhead the bright lights of the town and airfield of Khartoum had caused me to find some unexpected energy, but heading away into the black horizon with over an hour more to go, I had to concentrate to stay awake. I found myself nodding off, but each time my head dropped forward I awoke with a start.

Eventually Luxor came into view. BMEK gave me a lovely landing: the aircraft seemed to know I was tired. I was ready for a hot bath and a patch of grass, sand or a pile of blankets to curl up on.

However, as I taxied onto an allocated position, I saw two men awaiting my exit from the aircraft. I was 'accompanied' to an office where I was interrogated for over three hours. The same questions were asked over and over and then a different person would come in and ask the same questions.

Nigel had earlier briefed me not to let anyone in Egypt know I had started my flight from South Africa: I must remember the flight had started from Zimbabwe. My lack of interest in politics meant I had no idea why I had to keep quiet about coming from South Africa, but I'd been told that someone who had admitted to being from South Africa was still in jail in Egypt five years later. Every piece of South Africa identification had been removed from BMEK. I had even been granted a second passport from London, with which I had entered and departed South Africa. I had then had my new passport stamped in Harare, as initial point of departure.

The same questions: "where did you depart from?"

"*Harare.*"

"How did you get to Harare?"

"Commercial aircraft from Heathrow, London."

"Why were you asked to fly that little aircraft to England?"

"Because I worked in Africa before and have flown many Mooney aircraft."

"Where is your next stop?"

"I haven't checked the chart yet."

"Why did you stop here?"

Finally instead of the usual long explanation, I said: "I must have been mad. I just want to get the hell out of this horrible country and never return. I have been flying non-stop for well over twelve hours and I need to sleep. I'm getting out of here tomorrow regardless, with or without fuel."

That seemed to work. I was told to pay the landing fee of £100 and I could go. I felt sorry for Nigel. Under any other circumstances I would have queried, fought or refused to pay, but sleep was top priority. The landing fee should have been $10. I gave the wretched man his £100 and was directed to a taxi.

My taxi was four wheeled – almost unique among the donkey-carts. Reserved for airport personnel only, perhaps? The driver (wearing a long dress) drove slowly, at the same pace as the other transport on the tracks, which consisted mainly of donkeys in carts or being ridden. The ridden donkeys carried men riding in long dresses. I saw no women. The carts mostly displayed lighted lanterns, which looked striking against the pitch-blackness of the moonless night.

I saw some massive structures in the background, which I assumed were ancient pyramids: the sight was absolutely breathtaking and beautiful. This was surely the 'Golden City of Egypt'. I found myself thinking perhaps I was hasty in my earlier judgement. Maybe I should inquire whether anyone was looking for a pilot? I felt I could settle happily here. A honeymoon here would be perfect should I ever be lucky enough to get married. I still wore !re!rey's ring and would not have gone out with another man, yet it was tricky to stay in touch more than once or twice a year, depending on where I was. Ghanzi had no telephone connections and !re!rey did not write at all.

We drove up to a very impressive-looking hotel. I worried this wouldn't be cheap and I only wanted a wash, a lump of cheese and somewhere to sleep for six hours before departing again. Before getting out, I asked the taxi driver if there was anywhere smaller – a B&B would be fine. Then I discovered he spoke no English.

A room with tea, a sandwich and breakfast was less than £15. I paid in advance and was shown to a room the size of a ballroom, with a four-poster bed. While waiting for the sandwich and pot of tea to arrive, I slid into an enormous bath and relaxed for five minutes.

At the sound of a knock on the door, I put a dressing gown over my nightdress and opened the door. The servant entered, put the tray down on a table, then came up to me, put his arms round me and started trying to kiss me. Completely taken unawares, I was furious that someone could break the 'trance' I had fallen into since escaping the clutches of the airport. Due to the tired state I was in, without even thinking, I kneed the servant in the groin, then moved back and aimed a spinning back-kick at his stomach, but caught his side as he had already doubled over from the earlier kick.

I shouted "Out!" and pointed at the door. Taking the hint, he departed and after swallowing the sandwich and tea, I slept the few remaining hours only to awake in what seemed a few minutes to depart for France.

In daylight, even though it was the same route in reverse, it might as well have been a different country. Everything was shabby, dirty and derelict. The donkeys were filthy with dirty old carts, complete with battered and tatty old unlit lamps. All the people standing by the wayside wore tattered rags; even my fancied pyramids were just heaps of rubble, piled high. I just could not believe that the fantasy, magical world I had seen just the previous day had been a complete illusion. Or perhaps it appeared to be what I was really hoping to see, in a fairly exhausted state.

I went swiftly through the necessary paperwork, checked the weather and then departed for Nice. On landing, I was met by a fuel truck, filled BMEK then accepted a lift to the terminal to pay for the fuel and the landing fee. However, every time I asked an official where I could pay, I was sent on a long walk – to the wrong place. After walking what felt like several miles, I decided enough was enough and inquired where the control tower was. I told the controllers that no one wanted to take any money for the landing. On hearing from where I had departed they were all so helpful and agreed I could pay right there. After passing a receipt, I was asked if I would like a taxi into town, but I wanted to get away from the concrete, noise and bustle and to fly on to Montpelier.

BMEK sprang into the air, seeming as happy as I was to leave Nice. The short two-hour hop to Montpelier was smooth and peaceful as I had switched the radio off once clear of Nice. There was a friendly greeting and a taxi outside the airport. After a comfortable night's sleep, I popped over to Lezignan Corbieres to say hello to a few friends I had met during my training flights, then flew to Calais, then finally to Stansted.

I cleared customs and returned to Nigel's school where I was delighted to finally be able to relax for a day or so and spend time with my mother.

Chapter 18

ATLANTIC CROSSING

After a few more French 'holiday' trips, training people for their Private Pilot's Licence, Nigel asked me casually if I would like to take the Mooney over the pond to Florida.

"Of course, I'd love to but since I brought him from South Africa, is it fair I should also take him on to the US? You should really offer it to the other instructors first. If they all say no, then I'm hot-to-trot tomorrow," I replied eagerly.

I was worried about jumping in on a temporary basis and stealing all the cream.

"No, Tizi. First of all I have mentioned it to the others and we have all decided you should have first refusal, since you know that aircraft backwards. No one else has even flown a Mooney before, much less every Mooney ever produced. So you're ready to go tomorrow. I'm not sure about the forecast; the charts are in my office. Do you want to take a look at your route?"

I studied the route carefully. I never did find out that everyone, (including other professional 'Ferry Pilots') had refused the trip on the same grounds that I should have. To take a single-engined aircraft across the Atlantic in mid-winter is similar to playing Russian roulette. A failed engine not re-starting gave approximately between 15 seconds and 15 minutes of survival once you touched the water, due to the temperature. The planned departure was 14th November.

As it was, on that day, a hard overnight frost made it impossible to get into the aircraft, G-BMEK: both the lock and door were frozen and the entire aircraft was covered in a thick layer of ice.

My mother, who had driven me to the airport, helped to scrape the ice off. When it was finally de-iced, there was no life from the poor battery. I suggested the battery should be re-charged, I could put a 24-hour delay on the flight plan and shelter BMEK from the ice and cold in a hangar, somewhere on the airfield. Nigel agreed.

The following morning was still extremely cold, but everything was in order, apart from a fairly strong breeze forecasted further north.

My planned route was to fly to Reykjavik in Iceland, then Goose Bay then Montreal in Canada, then to Rochester, New York, where I was to have my ferry tanks removed at Batavia (a few minutes from Rochester). I'd then go south in a couple of hops to the final destination of Merritt Island, Florida, where BMEK was to live.

Merritt Island, although a long drive to the other side of Florida, was about a half-hour by Mooney, and Nigel was perfectly happy to let me visit my friend Cindy at Tampa before delivering BMEK finally to Merritt Island.

I set off from Stansted just before first light, en route to Reykjavik. Climbing through the damp thick dark clouds to FL100 (10,000 feet), I experienced a fair amount of ice on the wingtips and propeller. Ice could be heard flaking off the propeller and flying back against the airframe. As I levelled off, the sun was clearly visible and the sky bright, now that I was above the layer of cloud. I thought the ice was sure to melt with seven hours flying ahead of me in the brilliant sunshine.

My air speed had dropped considerably with the additional weight of the unwelcome ice, but there was no option but to wait for it to melt.

As I approached the British coastline, I was told to change frequencies. I checked in with the aircraft type, level, destination and expected time of arrival at Reykjavik. I was told to stand by, and then later informed that Reykjavik would not accept me, due to 70 knots of wind speed at their airport.

I requested the direction of the wind and found it was straight down the runway, so I asked again if there was a chance I could come in.

"Negative. You will not be accepted."

So I retraced my sky prints the way I had come, checked for an alternative and landed at Stornaway. To my surprise, even though the flight had only taken 4¼ hours since departing Stansted, and the last four hours in brilliant sunshine, the ice had not budged from the wingtips.

The following day, as the wind had dropped at Reykjavik, I was welcomed in.

After refuelling, I asked if there might be any space in a hangar for the night. The forecast was suggesting 50 to 70 knots of wind again, so I could not leave BMEK outside, even if it meant returning to Stornaway.

I was told the hangars were all full, but there was no harm in checking at each individual hangar to confirm this.

As I reached the last hangar, I was concerned I would have to return to Stornaway. Each hangar, so far, was full. With my request at the last hangar,

I was greeted with both good and bad news. Yes, there was space for one aircraft – because one 'went swimming' the day before.

I didn't need to ask if the pilot survived, having already been told there was minimal survival time if you went in during winter. Somewhat saddened, I accepted the empty space and tucked BMEK up snugly for the night.

I was booked into the Loftleidir Hotel where Nigel asked me to buy him an Icelandic sweater. They were magnificent but so were the prices.

While in the shop I got talking to someone called Per at the checkout. He spoke English quietly with an American accent. He wore smart brown trousers with a matching blazer and well-polished brown walking shoes. He was local and had never been away from Iceland. He asked me if he could show me round the town for the evening.

That seemed preferable to sitting in the room at the hotel, so I accepted with pleasure. He showed me the older buildings and told me the brief history of the airfield, then asked if he could take me to a bar for a drink. I told him I would rather not as I had no local currency, but he assured me that was not a problem for him.

What I had not realised was Iceland imports almost everything, including beer, spirits and wine. Everything is flown in, for practicality, and naturally it is reflected in the price. With a glass of wine or beer selling for around £8 a glass, the custom in Iceland seemed very different to an English bar, where a glass would have probably been less than 50p. The customer would come in and sit at a table, as is an option in Germany. The waiter would arrive with a mini credit-card terminal. He would take the credit card offered, make an imprint, which the customer would sign before delivery of the first drink (or round) and then write the total after the last drink. There was no skipping off without paying in that country. I was impressed with the system, if not with the prices. A noticeable difference was that no one seemed to get intoxicated. I was told by Per that most people would go to a bar perhaps on a Friday night and usually have one drink.

After the end of a lovely evening, Per returned me to the hotel and shook my hand, wishing me good luck for my flight over the pond. I was impressed by his lovely personality and beautiful manners and couldn't help wondering if most of the inhabitants were similar or had I met the nicest person on the island.

Something else that I couldn't fail to notice was all (not most) females were incredibly beautiful. I began to expect that every female I was likely to see would be tall and slender with blonde hair and blue eyes. I mentioned this to Per in the bar. He asked me, "Who won Miss World this year?"

It was Miss Iceland.

The following day the wind continued to blow at over fifty knots all day. I decided to get the charts from BMEK to study my route, even if I couldn't fly, but when I tried to leave the hotel I found it was impossible to walk on the solid ice.

However the wind died to about 40 knots westerly the following day and so I departed for Narsarsuaq, Greenland. To go direct to Goose Bay would have been over nine hours in zero wind, but with 40 knots on the nose, this would eat into my safety reserves. So I decided to play it safe and stop in Greenland.

As I approached Greenland, however, I was over an hour ahead of schedule. I rechecked my watch and the distance I'd travelled. With a rapid recalculation, I realised there was no necessity to stop at Greenland – there was enough fuel to go direct to Canada. The forecasted headwind had forgotten to blow.

However, to be safe, I decided to run the rear ferry tank fairly low before changing to the front ferry tank, then to finally switch to the aircraft's own tanks.

Having passed Greenland over two-and-half hours ago, with a good two-and-a-half hours of fuel remaining, the engine died. I wondered about the cause – there should have been another 20 minutes remaining on the rear ferry tank before I needed to change to the front one and the engine had sounded beautiful. (Silence is not golden but positively ugly in a single-engined aircraft over a large amount of freezing water).

My automatic action was to put the electric fuel pump on and switch the tank to the front ferry tank as I settled BMEK to the best glide speed. Still silence reigned. I looked down, praying there would be a ship in sight. At least if I ditched by a ship, there would be help at hand. As fate would determine, the entire Atlantic was isolated from ships or boats of any description. There was not even an iceberg to hold onto.

I had been cruising at 18,000 feet, which gave a further glide rate, if needed, although it was hardly applicable with around 450 miles to go. The extra altitude also gave a better radio range for communications, which so far had been useful, as I had been relaying messages for other aircraft transiting the Atlantic. It seemed fairly pointless to put out a Mayday call, since my time in the water would be minimal, but from earlier training I decided to let Oceanic Control know I was going for a swim, so they could tell Nigel.

Just as I pressed the transmit button, the engine fired. Not just a partial blip, but a full-blooded roar as it returned to life. I was relieved and amazed at the same time.

Assuming the fuel had died earlier than calculated, changing the tanks in a normally aspirated engine would have involved the usual 15 to 20 seconds of 'peace' while the engine started again. However, with a fuel-injected engine (as with a diesel engine), should the engine be starved of fuel, it should not re-start without being first drained from the airlock which would have occurred. BMEK was fuel-injected.

During those 16 silent seconds, I had been too busy to even become worried, but when the engine started, I found I had broken out into a heavy sweat and imagined my heart beating in front of my eyes, having fled from my body.

After the ten-hour flight, I arrived at Goose Bay, still with over two hours of fuel remaining, which confirmed the forecasted headwind all the way had definitely turned into a tail wind for the whole flight.

I thanked everyone above me who were obviously looking after me as I settled down to catch a few zzz's on a comfy sofa in the lounge, having refuelled and put in a flight plan for Rochester, the next stop.

Nothing eventful occurred on the next leg, except the earlier forecasted westerly headwind blew in full strength and slowed my progress. I stopped at Montreal after just six hours for additional fuel, which I didn't really need and a cup of tea, which I certainly did need. I then started BMEK and requested taxi clearance for Rochester, where I needed to stop for customs prior to flying on to Batavia.

"Sorry, we don't have an IFR flight plan for you. Are you going VFR or would you like to re-file your flight plan?" VFR stood for Visual Flying Rules, which meant you must be able to see ahead of you, plus all the aircraft around you. IFR (Instrument Flying Rules) assumed you are in cloud and had no visibility of anything around you. To fly IFR you had to have a current instrument rating and have set up a plan accepted by air traffic control before making a flight.

I tried to explain I had departed Goose Bay for Rochester and stopped here for fuel. All I intended was to continue the rest of the flight I had not finished but my route would be the same as on the original flight plan, so could I continue with the original plan?

"No, you need to either close down and re-file in the terminal or depart VFR."

I couldn't believe it: there was no one else talking on the radio, and at four o'clock in the morning there was not much likelihood of much happening, so I asked if I could give my details and route over the radio.

"No, that is not permissible, but you may continue VFR."

I agreed to fly under visual rules, to save an extra start in the freezing cold for the already cold aircraft and departed for Rochester. After a few minutes, I was told to call 'en-route frequencies' and Montreal switched me off.

I was irritated since, had I stuck to my Instrument Flight Plan, I would have been handed over to each frequency. Now I had to check which frequency I had to use, which varied with the direction and altitude being flown, with several options being shown on the chart. This needed careful scrutinising in the dim red glow of the cockpit.

When I was within ten miles of Rochester, I tried calling for entry clearance into their zone. Had I been on my original IFR plan, I would have been automatically handed over. The frequency was as busy as Heathrow, so I kept trying to get through.

"VFR traffic stand by – I am talking to IFR traffic," came the terse reply from the controller. There was no option but to commence an orbit until I could establish contact. After what seemed endless orbits, there was a five-second pause, which I grabbed and passed on my details. Again I was told they were busy with IFR traffic and to remain clear of controlled airspace.

While flying round and round and round in circles, I vowed I would never go on more than a local flight without filing a flight plan in Canada or America.

Eventually I was given approval to approach and land. The flight had been just under three hours, so I didn't bother with fuel – just cleared customs, tried to pay a landing fee and surprisingly found there was none, after which I departed rapidly for Batavia.

Although only 15 minutes away, Batavia was a wonderfully friendly airport.

There was no radio, so no one heard me approach or knew I was coming. I taxied up to the workshop to where the ferry tanks were to be removed and was greeted like a long-lost friend. I was given a cup of tea and biscuits and everyone was interested in the flight, the weather, everything. It was a refreshing change from the bureaucracy of Rochester International Airport.

After having the ferry tanks removed, I departed south, stopping at Knoxville to allow a Tornado to pass my southward track, then on to Vandenburg, having arranged to meet Cindy there. I arrived ahead of schedule, and as I was getting a cup of tea from the club's machine, someone walked in and exclaimed: "Tizi, what are you doing here?"

As he walked toward me and reached out a hand, he prompted me with his name: Tom Ferguson. It seemed amazing to meet one of the only people I knew in a remote far-flung airport in Tampa. Tom was checking up on a share of an aircraft for sale. Cindy walked in and was equally surprised: she had made her one and only parachute jump with Tom, when I first met her. We all went back to her house and chatted over a refreshing cup of tea before I departed finally for Merritt Island.

At Merritt Island I called Nigel to tell him his mission was complete, expecting to be told to return on an airline.

"Ah good. Since you've been gone, I've bought a Cherokee Archer at Merritt Island, to use here, for my school. Could you bring it back."

It was a statement, not a question. Nigel continued: "Stop off at Batavia and they will put in the ferry tanks from the Mooney, so you'll have the range for the pond."

"Delighted. Bye," I told him. Then I wondered why he had bought a Cherokee in the States. To be cheaper than one already in England, it would have to be well under half price, with the costs of the fuel, flight time on the engine and airframe and all the associated ferrying costs. Either it was a bargain, or a pile of junk. I just hoped the engine would last over the cold, wet water crossing.

I found the Cherokee and checked it over. Apart from being very old and tatty, it seemed reasonably sound. I took it for a flight test, to Vandenburg, as it made more sense to stay with Cindy rather than to find a hotel.

The following day, I flew the Cherokee, N21175, three hours to Columbia, then another three-hours to Shawnee Winchester and the final flight north to Batavia in under three hours.

There were a few days delay to fit the ferry tanks, which then had the problem of not working when I first tried them airborne. Since the tanks were from a completely different aircraft it would probably have been quicker to make new ones rather than make the existing ones fit. Eventually I was on my way to Bangor, Maine to clear customs and fly onto Moncton, Canada.

This stop was important to go through 'scrutineering' prior to be allowed to fly over the Atlantic. Everything was checked to be available and working, but in minute detail as to the required emergency equipment. The Cherokee and I failed the check abysmally. I was told the ferry tanks were not secured – they could come loose should I encounter turbulence and move forward, knocking me unconscious. I told the official, Tony, I was happy to take the risk and would avoid turbulence, but was told simply, "No it is not acceptable, and you do not have a choice."

Tony was only doing his job and he had my safety as his main interest. He was a tall powerful-looking man with short, dark hair wearing the Customs uniform, which made him look rather threatening.

He also informed me that a life jacket alone was of no use; I needed an immersion suit since, should I ditch, there was no chance of survival with just a life jacket. Plus there were many more 'survival items' required, some of which were strange, for example:

1. A snare to catch rabbits.

2. A fishing line and hook.

3. Matches.

4. A reflective (heat retaining) blanket.

5. Flares.

6. A dingy for the number of occupants.

7. A pan or container for water, to cook anything.

8. Tablets or means to purify salt water for drinking.

I told Tony I had just flown the Atlantic with no kit, no dingy or survival suit – just the same ferry tanks that I was now presenting him with. While I agreed a survival suit would be a pleasant luxury, over the water, I could not see any purpose in a rabbit snare or fishing hook.

Even if I was on land I would never be able to catch a rabbit with a snare, any more than a fish with a hook and line. Nor would I be able to make a fire with a few matches. Besides, where were the rabbits in the water?

"OK, calm down, Tizi. First there is a lot of hostile country you will fly over after leaving here, before starting over the water. Should you go down over the land or the water, we need to know you have at least a chance of survival. Our men here in Canada will conduct the Search and Rescue if you come down or fail to show up at your intended destination. When our guys come back with a body or with nothing found, it affects them very badly – sometimes it destroys their career."

Then he added: "I am not only concerned you may not get home OK, I am also concerned about my men. I'm sorry for the inconvenience but if you want to fly from Canada, it must be from here, at Moncton. This is the only 'scrutineering' base before the water. You will have to prove you have the necessary equipment and that everything is safe and secured before you may depart, since we obviously care more than you do about arriving alive."

I chuckled, thinking it was probably true, then asked if I could use his phone to call my boss in England. I told Nigel the expensive news.

While I had been waiting around Moncton airfield, I met a girl called Maryam, who was studying for her Private Pilot's Licence at the Flying Club at Moncton. Maryam was a young, fresh-faced student with long fair hair tied with a bow. When I told her I had to get all the equipment, she insisted on taking me shopping for it.

I found an engineer at Moncton prepared to improve the fittings of the ferry tanks. As this would take a day or so, Maryam took me shopping while the ferry tanks were re-fitted.

I then flew to Halifax and back to purchase a used survival kit (even a used one was over £100) and took Maryam with me on the trip. She happily put me up while I was waiting to depart and it seemed like a party atmosphere.

Finally the tanks were ready, but the weather had turned to low cloud and freezing conditions. I asked Tony if he would clear me to go, for when the weather improved. He checked the tanks and told me he would still not accept them, as they were not secure enough for the type of turbulence I could expect at this time of year. He added the weather was unlikely to clear for long enough to make a safe crossing.

He seemed to really be trying his utmost to prevent me from going. I felt tempted to tell him the English winter weather was not much better. Instead I called Nigel to update him. It was now 7th December, which was about the worst time and least amount of daylight, to make the crossing.

I offered to fly via Presque Isles, the most northern part of America and go via Greenland and then Iceland to England, since by going from the States, it was not necessary to get cleared on scrutineering. However, there was only a short window of four hours daylight in Greenland, to be able to make an approach to Narsarsuaq in marginal safety. I had already been warned about the perilous approach with high mountains either side of the final approach path: a couple of degrees off track and a wing could be gently removed by a large, unfeeling piece of granite.

Nigel considered my offer and chose the safer option, telling me to take the Cherokee back to Batavia and put it to bed, then get a commercial flight back to England.

I was disappointed not to be flying back myself since it had all been such a build-up. But part of me was relieved as it was filthy weather and there was no de-ice or anti-ice equipment on the Cherokee. Plus it wouldn't fly straight, but hung permanently to the right, heavily. That would have been hard enough work in daylight in summer, but fairly trying and uncomfortable in lousy conditions.

I bedded down the Cherokee at Batavia, some eight hours of flight, south of Moncton and returned home to England somewhat deflated, via a regular airline.

The day after I returned I was back in harness, flying a Twin Comanche to Newcastle and back in thick cloud, to collect some parts Nigel needed. During the next few days, I did some instrument instruction in singles, twins and also started flying the radio traffic reporting 'Jambuster' with Paul Hartley. That was terrific fun, as Paul was happy to go up in any weather, so long as he could make out the roads beneath him, to give a live radio broadcast of the traffic jams and queues.

A week after I had returned from Moncton, I received a telegram from Tony. He told me a Cessna 182 had departed from Moncton, with all the required survival equipment, the day after I had abandoned my attempt. The last received call from the aircraft was "icing up badly, 6,000 feet, attempting to climb." The search had now been called off. He had taken the same route I was to attempt.

Chapter 19

I JOIN THE UNIPART TEAM

During the next few weeks, I took a few more 'PPL holiday trips' to Carcassonne. After returning from one trip, a fellow instructor, Bic, told me there was a recruitment advertisement in *Flight* magazine: they were obviously looking for me.

Bic was a cheerful assistant flying instructor, who came from Pakistan and who worked for Nigel. He was keen to help everyone all the time ... but did not like flying upside-down. The ad stated that a Formation Aerobatic Pilot was required for the Unipart Aerobatic Team, so I applied, not really thinking it worth the effort as every pilot in the country would certainly be applying for the same position.

After a phone call followed by a flight test in his RF5 Fournier; then an unbearable wait of a few days I was told by John Taylor, – known as JT – that I had the job. JT was over six feet tall with an athletic build and was one of the best aerobatic pilots in the country.

At the news, I would have swung from my mother's chandeliers, had there been any. As there were none, my stepfather John opened an extra special bottle of wine to toast my success.

Toward spring of 1986, JT set out a training programme, where we flew down to Roanne, France from the base airfield of Biggin Hill. The plan was to fly as much as possible to practice before the season began. JT had also employed a man called Mike Dentith, so we could alternate shows with JT, plus being a back-up should anyone fall sick.

Before the week in Roanne, the RF4s were painted in matching livery: white background with a dark blue bottom, and with a blue and red stripe along the fuselage. The name of our sponsors, Unipart, was painted upside-down along both sides of the fuselage and we each had our name painted on our respective RF4. My allotted aircraft – G-AVWY – had 'Tizi Hodson' painted above the canopy, which made me feel really proud. I called my aircraft V-Wee.

Most French airfields did not charge for landings and the fuel was significantly cheaper. There was less controlled airspace and the hotel accommodation was better value than in the UK, hence the reason for training in France.

After returning home, the first air show was at Coventry Airfield. I was pleased with the display, which had always been very popular with the crowds and the air-show organisers. We flew a ten-minute display of basic formation flying, followed by synchronised loops and rolls, then flew towards and around each other in tight circles (the roulette), then synchronised stall turns, finishing with the mirror flight down the length of the display line.

The mirror meant one aircraft flew inverted, with the second aircraft keeping position beneath the aircraft above. It was much trickier than it sounds because, being inverted, the top aircraft suffered more drag than when erect. The engine stopped when inverted, so the aircraft was actually gliding steeply downward. The bottom aircraft had to use airbrake to stay in formation. Taking even a minute amount of airbrake made the little motor glider want to leap up in indignation: quite a large amount was needed to stay in place with the inverted aircraft above, which made it challenging.

At the end of the air show, JT and I walked toward our Fourniers. As I was to discover over the season, it was quite normal for a few of the participants to give an 'impromptu' display at the end of the day. Despite having flown their routine and been paid for it, there would always be a few pilots who would do a few manoeuvres overhead after taking off and before flying home.

JT and I watched this particular pilot doing a few manoeuvres, finishing with a loop at fairly low level. As the aircraft reached the top of the loop, JT said, "Oh no, he's too slow and too low." He grabbed my hand and held it firmly.

Within a few seconds the aircraft had, as predicted, stalled at the top of the loop, completed half a turn of a spin, collided with the ground and burst into a tremendous, instantaneous bonfire.

JT looked at me and said solemnly:

"There but for the grace of God, go you and I. Never show off to anyone, anywhere for whatever reason. Only ever fly rehearsed routines especially when it's to be flown at low level."

I knew I would take his advice.

*

When the season had started, we flew one or two shows in a weekend, or even two in a day. I always used any 'ferry flying' as an opportunity to improve my formation flying, tucking in close behind JT's right (or sometimes, left), wingtip.

One of the most memorable air shows was shortly after the season had started, when we were asked to give a display for the annual air-show at Roanne. Since they had provided us with the practice venue free of charge, this was a wonderful opportunity to return a favour.

The show started in a unique way. With some aircraft taxiing around and others airborne, there appeared a few horses with riders dressed as knights in armour. Two of them were carrying lances; another carried a large sword in one hand, controlling the horse with the other hand, despite the noise of aircraft all around them.

Two of the knights held a large banner on either side, with a message in French, which I could not see. The horses all wore highly decorative coats of bright colours matching the banners. They paraded around among the aircraft without seeming the least perturbed at the noise. With the parade and our own formation display over, we were able to enjoy the remainder of the show as we did not intend returning home until the following day.

A messenger came to JT and told him that a surprise presentation had been put on for all the pilots. Could we make our way to the bus in the car park, where we would be taken to our hotel? We would be given half an hour to bathe and change then the same bus would take us onward to our destination.

I was especially enthralled, as the whole air-show scene was still new and exciting to me. JT and I wandered over to the bus and found all the other air-show participants, including the Patrioulle de France team members – the French equivalent of the Red Arrows.

As we sat awaiting the last participant, we looked out to the completely blocked exit. Not only that, but the queue of cars could be seen stretching in the direction of our destination as far as the eye could see.

Someone voiced all our thoughts, saying, "We have no chance of making it to the show on time."

"Don't worry," said the driver. "We will have plenty of time."

Threading through the traffic to get outside the airfield took over twenty minutes; however, as soon as we were on the public road, there were two police cars and three police-motorcycles with blue lights flashing and the sirens wailing, waiting for us. The police drove in front of us, clearing the way, while the motorcycles moved ahead to control the traffic.

That way, we soon arrived at the hotel. After a quick bath and a change of clothes, we were collected by the same police escort who took us to our destination through the still heavy traffic, which parted like the waves for Moses.

The show was tremendous, starting with a horse and rider galloping down the length of the long arena, in front of us all. The rider jumped off the horse at full tilt, hit the ground and leapt back on, then repeated the trick, jumping off the opposite side and vaulting back on. I was highly impressed, having tried the same tricks on my ponies in earlier days but never having managed more than a steady canter.

The next part was seeing the jousting. Two mounted 'knights' at either end of the long, narrow field galloped straight for each other with their lances parallel. One knight was knocked off his horse and we all cheered the winner frantically. Another pair of knights did the same joust, again with one being knocked off. We all cheered wildly as the knights were jousting each 'survivor', until there was an overall winner. I still don't know if the jousting was arranged and the 'loser' threw himself off or whether they were actually knocked off by a blunt lance.

It was a memorable start to my season of display flying.

The shows continued and I was treated like royalty wherever I went with the Unipart Team. It was fortunate that I was the first professional female display pilot on the air-show scene, resulting in good publicity for Unipart on TV, radio stations, newspapers and magazines.

Another memorable occasion was when we flew a display over the races at Doncaster. The advantage of the quiet motor gliders meant even highly strung racehorses were not fazed by our appearance overhead. Having flown into Doncaster in the morning, we were asked if we would like to watch the racing from a box, as we were not flying until lunchtime. As neither the Queen Mother nor the Queen was expected, we were shown into the Royal Box and offered champagne and canapés as if *we* were royalty.

Most weekends were booked with Displays: I felt I was really beginning to learn how to fly. When the season came to an end, all too soon, it seemed to have 'flown by'.

JT packed the Fourniers away and told me to be in touch before spring if I wanted to fly the following year. It was a crazy question after the best year of my life and 86 displays behind me.

*

Summer was about to begin in South Africa, so I wrote to John Lougher to enquire how the snake park was going, since I could think of nothing better than to run the new Snake Park over the Southern African summer, which was our winter, then to return to the Unipart Team for the 1987 Season.

Receiving no reply, I rang him only to find the number disconnected, I finally made contact with his sister, Michelle, who told me he had spent the

275

snake park money on a new aircraft to fly charters himself: she was not sure the snake park was going ahead any more.

I was saddened and also angry. He shouldn't be taking chartered flights himself with only a private licence: it was illegal. If there were an accident, there would be no insurance or coverage for anyone. I expressed my feelings of guilt to Michelle, as I had introduced him to flying and had known very well he was a volatile character.

She agreed and told me both she and her husband had tried to persuade John to stick with the snake park plan, as they approved of him getting a real business going, instead of gambling. John had earlier told me that he had made all the snake park money by gambling in casinos, using a formula with which he always won. He had explained his simple formula to me, then took me to a casino in Durban. It worked, which frightened me, as I could see how it could be so tempting to live as a gambler. I had politely refused to go again. John had also told me that he was barred from almost every casino, since when you cashed in the winning chips, a photograph was taken and after too much continuous success, you were not welcomed back. I wondered if that was true, but on my visit with him, he had asked me to cash in his chips, with the winnings well over R2, 000. I had heard the camera click as I was asked for my name, which I gave as the first name I could think of.

Since the snake park seemed off the menu, I wondered what I would do for the winter. I had written regularly to Cindy and she had become a firm friend: she kept insisting I should emigrate to America and take a job flying, insisting I could stay with her as long as I liked, as she felt as if she was my sister.

Chapter 20

WILL YOU MARRY ME?

In early January 1987, just as the weather was cooling down, I departed England for Florida, where the weather is always either hot or warm.

At Cindy's house in Tampa, we had an early dinner and chatted for hours: she told me to make her house my home for as long as I wanted.

Life was good.

My first priority was to get an American flying licence and some transport. Cindy introduced me to her neighbours, Richard and Dorothy Kennedy, who could point me in the right direction to get whatever I needed: Richard was the local Sheriff.

The following day, Richard drove me to the office to get a driving licence. I took and passed the test in his patrol car, which was fun, and later he took me to a reputable dealer to buy a car. I bought a harmless, innocuous brown Dodge for less than $1,000. I had wanted a motorbike, of course, but Cindy refused to have a 'noisy, ugly' motorbike in her drive, so a car it had to be.

The next step was to find a flying school where I could take an American flying licence. I located one in Panama City and booked in for a weekend's training to pass the flight- and ground-school for the Airline Transport Rating. The course seemed frighteningly compressed, with an immense amount of information to be crammed into two days' study. Yet since, in America, you are trained to pass the written tests, rather than to thoroughly understand the subject (as in England), it was not even hard work.

After two nights in a hired trailer I emerged victorious with a brand new ATR (Airline Transport Rating.) I should have felt proud, but I didn't. I had worked so hard, studying every spare hour in the day for six months to pass my English Commercial Pilots Licence, then, in just two days, I had taken and passed the highest flight test America offered.

Back at Tampa, I telephoned several companies, offering them my valuable services, as a pilot. Every time came the same question. Having told me I sounded English, the interviewer asked for my social security number. No number, no work – simple.

Cindy did not know how I could get a number, short of marrying someone, so I asked Richard what he could suggest: he didn't know anyone available to help out.

So I checked the local newspaper for 'non-flying' jobs for immediate cash and found someone advertising for a groom/exercise rider for a small racing yard. I called up and was told to come in the following day.

It was only after a week that I discovered the job was expected to be voluntary, despite working twelve-hour days. The work was tremendous fun and I would have stayed if I'd had a separate income.

While I was sitting on the bonnet of my car reading the job ads in the newspaper, I was offered to buy a bottle of perfume from a local sales rep who introduced himself as Phil. He was six feet tall with a fit physique and was slim and attractive. I told Phil that I had no money to buy his perfume … and no job, come to that. It resulted in my starting work selling perfumes the following day for Phil and his buddy, Steve. Steve was the quieter of the two, a plump man with short brown hair.

After a couple of weeks selling perfumes, I asked Phil if he would do me the favour of marrying me, so I could return to flying as that was where I belonged – in the sky. He and Steve argued and finally tossed a coin as to who should marry me.

Steve lost. "OK then," he said to Phil, "but only if you are my Best Man", to which Phil agreed happily.

Monday morning found Steve and I at the Public Notary's office where we bought and signed the marriage licence. Directly after signing the certificate, we all went upstairs to the Commissioner of Oaths, where Steve and I were pronounced Man and Wife.

I shook Steve's hand and said, "Thank you very much, Steve."

Phil did point out that it would have been more appropriate had we both exchanged a kiss, instead of shaking hands. Ignoring his remark, I asked Steve if he would come with me to get my social security number, as I felt it might be quicker with 'my husband' there.

Coming down in the elevator after being allocated my precious number, I was ecstatic and told Steve I felt so happy, I could kiss him right then, for his help. He told me not to bring feelings into it; he had only married me to help out – and for the money (I'd promised him fifty percent of my earnings).

The following day, I walked into the office of Top Flight Air Services for employment that afternoon. I did get around to mentioning to my parents that I'd got married, but they both understood my need to fly and my lack of interest in being a wife or mother to anyone.

A few weeks earlier I'd been for an interview with Top Flight Air Services, as a potential cheque pilot, flying cancelled cheques around Florida. The Chief Pilot, Jim Harvard, told me he would definitely employ me when I managed to get a work permit. So when I returned to Top Flight after getting married, I asked for Jim Harvard. He told me that he remembered the interview. I showed him my social security number and asked if he had meant what he had said.

After asking how I had got it and hearing the answer, he said: "Heck, you must have been desperate. Yes, you can start right away." He then showed me the aircraft and the paperwork and suggested I buy myself a uniform and return the following day, where he could take me for a check flight.

After the check flight with Jim, I flew one of Top Flight's twin-engined aircraft, a Piper Aerostar, with an examiner to validate my American ATR licence for multi-engined work. I had used a single-engined aircraft for the initial test, to keep costs at a minimum.

The 'line training' followed, where I flew a few routes with Jim as training Captain, while he showed me the way the routes and cargo were handled. Then I was allowed on my own.

My first trip was from Tampa International to Sarasota, Palm Beach, Miami and Orlando and back to Tampa. The Aerostar was a fast ship cruising at 210 knots. It was a favourite among cheque-flying operations as it was one of the faster twins, capable of carrying a large amount of cargo and not having an uneconomical appetite for fuel.

Top Flight operated mainly Piper Aerostar aircraft, plus a Piper Navajo and a Beechcraft Baron. The latter two flew considerably slower at 170 and 180 knots respectively and carried less of a load, so were used as back-up aircraft.

The routes flown were always the same and mostly flown through the night. Cancelled cheques were delivered to bank personnel who met the pilot at a specified airport, then drove to the respective banks to pay in the cheques before the banks opened for business in the morning. Thus, meeting deadlines on every flight became the name of the game.

There was not even a minute to spare for pre-flight checks or take-off checks – these were all done at a fast taxi speed en route to the take-off point. Once airborne, the aircraft was turned onto the required heading and maximum flight speed, using the most efficient flight level, which gave either the best tail wind or the least head wind to enable the deadline to be reached.

Should the deadline be missed by even 60 seconds, the entire flight and the fuel were wasted.

Many companies would put in a tender to get the bank contracts, at the lowest price at which they could operate, in order to secure the business. The lowest tender would usually win the contract, but that was no use for any pilot who could not operate fast enough to meet the deadlines. The pilot would receive the salary regardless, but the company would not be paid for any late deliveries. It was cutthroat, but an exciting, challenging and demanding job.

On one of the routes, sympathising with the hard-working Aerostar, I put my feelings on a piece of paper.

I named it: *The Forgotten Mail Plane.*

Struggling, fighting, pushing
Against the unseen forces
Everything fire walled
Yet no forward speed

Deadlines to meet but no way round or through
This treacherous WIND

Dropping the nose to gain a knot
Then turbulence arrives
And rears its ugly head
No hope now on the deadline
And no choice but to reduce that power

The power of airspeed, safety and height
Of altitude and time
Waiting sadly, helplessly
For the turbulence to cease
Deadlines already lost
But the mail must get through
Engine noise has died to a whisper
No longer pressing, vibrating, fighting
Now almost lost and lifeless

Yet still forcing through
The waves of air
The eddies of turbulence
Of violence
Still trying
The noble airplane won't give in

Then cloud is broken
Turbulence gone
A last gallant effort from Man and Machine
The deadline is made – two seconds to spare
Now bustle and motion as packages shift
Are sorted and gone

But...
Not a thought to the poor tired, battle-scarred
Mail plane
Not a word of thanks
Forlorn, forgotten on the ramp
Just another day
Just another night
One more flight
A night in the life of the little mail plane.

The routes were always 'put up for bid' every six months to the pilots in the company where the most senior pilot had first pick of the routes, going down in seniority.

When I joined Top Flight, a fairly senior pilot had just left and Jim Harvard was flying his route. I was naturally given the 'spare route', which was a lovely comfortable life and suited me completely. I took off at 5am every morning and returned home by 10am with the day's work done, having only flown to Miami and back.

On Saturdays I departed in the evening for Miami, to night-stop there, then picked up the huge bags of cheques the following afternoon, returning late Sunday. All pay was based on duty hours, which was one hour before scheduled take-off time to 30 minutes after landing time. The hours flown were immaterial to the salaries, which were taken into account when bidding for a route.

However, after a month, the routes were all put up for auction again and I lost my route to end up with scraps: a 7.30pm departure, to finish at 3am. After riding home and in bed by 4am, it was a requirement to call the office at 8am to say whether or not I had made the connection.

Despite not being able to adjust to working by night and sleeping by day, I did enjoy the type of flying.

The advantages of flying through the quiet night skies were many. On occasions, tremendous firework or laser displays could be seen from an elevated position. By flying the same routes with the same call sign (my own was 'Check Air 215'), the controllers became friends on the otherwise silent flights with short conversations, continuing each night. It reminded me of playing postal chess.

As with most comfortable lifestyles, everything comes to an end and Top Flight eventually closed down. I decided to return to the UK as it was a time of feast for any qualified pilot and famine for any flying operation in England.

This had always happened on a five-year cycle for any pilots seeking work and probably always will.

Back in England, a company delivering newspapers through the night took me on, flying Bandeirantes and King Airs. This was easier work than flying cancelled cheques in America. The airport staff accomplished the newspaper loading and unloading.

However, the company was very keen to cut every corner, to ensure a worthwhile profit. Although I did not know before joining, I soon discovered that three aircraft laden with papers had recently crashed while flying through the night, after picking up ice and being unable to dislodge it.

After one flight where light ice was forecast, although I did not fly into any, I could not get the de-icing equipment to function and reported it after landing as not working.

The following evening, I was allocated the same aircraft. I saw the tech log had been signed off, stating the malfunctioning de-ice equipment had been repaired.

Nothing in the de-ice department functioned and with heavy ice forecast, I decided it was time to part from the company rather than take an early departure from the world.

An old friend, Glen Fricker, suggested I should join the airline, Air UK as a First Officer. He had started with the company six months previously and assured me it was an easy lifestyle, well-paid with plenty of free time.

It seemed something completely different to any other flying, so I joined Air UK and for the next ten years I was grossly overpaid and under-worked. The fun had completely disappeared from flying, along with the challenges presented to the average pilot flying in any other work.

Gone were the days of preparing a flight log and a flight plan for a new destination. When you're flying for an airline, everything is prepared for you, even the tracks to fly and the distances and the time it will take. The office staff, who were told the number of passengers and the fuel ordered, prepared the weight and balance calculations and then the load-sheet was produced by computer.

With the weather forecast obtained, there was a 'Go' or 'No Go', with the limits carefully laid down. Should a pilot attempt to land when the weather was below the recommended limits, even if the landing was good and everyone arrived at the destination, the pilot would be questioned as to why the approach was made and probably fired.

There were many good sides to flying for an airline: the salary was excellent and the hours were minimal. I told all my friends that the best part of the job was the view from the office window. Flying, for example at 31,000 feet over the Alps on a beautiful day, can be spectacular: however many times you see the view, it is always slightly different with the different weather conditions.

There was plenty of free time, which gave me the chance to gain a black belt in the Choi Kwang Do, style of martial arts, and to reach advanced level of scuba diving and to gain a Category 9 level in skydiving, in my spare time. Plus to obtain, train and fly my three hawks, who were Xraysay, the Kestrel; Buzz, the Ferruginous Hawk and Xarra, the Golden Eagle.

When there were 'slot delays' I made good use of them by writing a chapter, or a part of one, for my first book 'A True Partnership'. The book described how I had obtained, trained and hunted the hawks. A slot delay occurred frequently. When a passenger checked a bag into the airport, the bags were all loaded and checked against the number of passengers. However, there was many an occasion when a passenger would check their bag in and then NOT board the aircraft. Should there be one bag too many for the number of passengers who had boarded, the aircraft could not depart. It was possible a terrorist had planted a bomb on board with no intention of accompanying the bomb.

The passengers would all be asked to exit the aircraft, personally identify their own baggage and return to their seats. The remaining bag or bags left on the tarmac would be disposed of and the aircraft was free to go.

Each departing aircraft was allocated a departure slot, obtained by the office personnel, from Air Traffic and given to the pilot. Should there be an unusual delay, like a 'baggage check', almost invariably the departure slot would be missed and another would have to be applied for. The next slot could be anything from ten minutes to a few hours.

There was always a debate of whether to allow the seated passengers to leave the aircraft and take a walk round or do some last-minute shopping, but the obvious reason to not allow them to depart, was that they might not ALL return.

I felt exceedingly sorry for the cabin crew, who had absolutely nothing to do with making the slots. Sometimes a pilot could chivvy people along or beg for an earlier slot from Air Traffic, yet the passengers always vented their frustrations on the poor overworked but underpaid cabin crew. The pilots were safely tucked away behind a locked door.

After a few years operating similar routes from Stansted to either Charles de Gaulle, Brussels, Florence, Jersey, Guernsey, Southampton, Heathrow or wherever, I volunteered for a company move to Scotland, based in Edinburgh. The move was really for the benefit of Xarra, the golden eagle I had recently acquired and was hunting and flying in small fields around Duxford. With the empty skies and large farms in Scotland, there was more room to stretch her wings. The aircraft flying routes were less varied, but it was a change of scenery.

On one trip, while I was driving south to visit my parents, I got stuck in a traffic jam on the M6. In my car was Aski, my dog; Xraysay, the kestrel, sitting on the front handle by the windscreen; and Xarra, the golden eagle, who was sitting on a large perch in the back of the car. Buzz, the ferruginous hawk, was also in the back, but she was in a box as she preferred to travel in the darkness and safety of her box.

It was a hot day in August, and I had the windows open. I looked to my left and saw a car pulling a glider-shaped box behind it. I asked if it was a glider and the driver, who was named Chris Rollings, agreed it was. He then asked if the bird in front was a kestrel or a merlin, looking at Xraysay.

I was quite impressed, as most of the British public do not recognise any of the indigenous birds of prey, and told him it was a kestrel.

He then noticed Xarra and asked what she was. After explaining it was a golden eagle, we started a conversation that lasted nearly half an hour, as the traffic was at a standstill. Before the traffic moved, Chris passed me a piece of paper with his name and number on it with the offer of taking me for a glider flight where I could see an eagle whilst gliding.

A few weeks later, having made contact again, Chris took me for an amazing flight in one of his company gliders, the DG 500, and a few days later, I took Chris hunting with Xarra and Buzz, with the offer of dinner afterwards with whatever the hawks caught.

Luckily Xarra caught a pheasant and Buzz caught a rabbit on that afternoon, so dinner was pheasant starters and rabbit steak for the main course.

It was only much later that Chris had admitted how worried he was about what the dinner would consist of, with visions of rat or squirrel.

*

After two of the coldest years in my life, in Scotland, I thought there had to be a more interesting way of making a living in aviation.

In earlier years I had enjoyed instructing, so I decided to return to full-time instructing, flying for OATS – Oxford Air Training Services, based at Gloucestershire Airport. I naturally nicknamed it Goats, which did not go down well with the Head Office when they called up to be told "Hello, Goats, Tizi speaking, can I help you?"

The following year-and-a-half were spent teaching private pilots to further their skills to enable them to take the necessary commercial and instrument flying exams, which would enable them to become an airline pilot.

The flying was interesting, challenging and satisfying once again and I thought I would retire with GOATS when unexpectedly, we were all given two weeks' notice to leave the premises. The Big Bosses had pulled out of Gloucester Airport and decided to continue with the original base, which was already established at Oxford. The instructors who wished to do so could relocate to Oxford or take employment elsewhere. The students could finish their training at Oxford or anywhere of their choice.

It was tough on the students to have to learn new routes all over again having paid a semi-fortune on their training to date. By persevering, I encouraged my students to finish their remaining training and pass the flight tests in the remaining two weeks and I decided to move on.

I had bought a house in Gloucestershire, with the original intention of retiring with OATS in the future. I preferred to make a living flying from Gloucestershire Airport, but I was not particularly tempted to fly the basic trainer, such as the Cherokee, Cessna or Tomahawk. So I offered my flying services to James Black, who operated Tiger Moth bi-planes based at Manchester, Barton and at Syerston, Leeds. James accepted immediately and I started teaching people to fly in Tiger Moths.

The old bi-planes were so much more fun than the BAe 146, which required operating, as opposed to flying. The only drawback was the drive to either Barton or Syerston, which could take from two to five hours, depending on traffic.

It became routine to drive up to one of the bases, fly perhaps a dozen short flights and then, after cleaning the Moth, I would stay in a B&B and fly another dozen or so flights the following day. Although the flying was fantastic fun, the travelling was exhausting.

At this stage Chris Rollings was instructing on gliders for the Mile High Gliding Corporation, in Colorado, USA, but with the terrorist attacks on September 11th, all flying and gliding in the US ceased immediately.

Chris returned to England at the same time that James Black closed the Tiger Moth flying for the winter months. When I met Chris, we got on really well and it didn't take him long to persuade me to start a new venture for airshows, with him flying a glider and me flying an aeroplane. We'd fly in formation, which was the first time this had been done: we called ourselves The SweetHawks.

While we were working on this, Chris took a job in Australia, which is somewhere I'd always wanted to go. He suggested I go too and, although I didn't manage to get a job there, we both had a holiday on the east coast for a couple of weeks. At Rockhampton, there was a bull-riding rodeo which I was determined to see. It looked so much fun to try and stay on the bull while it was bucking its head off. The idea was to stay on until the eight-second bell, but to get off before 12 seconds had passed, as the idea was to encourage the bull to buck harder each time and not be tamed. Naturally, I wanted to try it and I found out there was a training session the following week.

To prepare for this, I bought a new black felt bull-riding hat, of the style that all the cowboys were wearing. It set me back about a month's salary, but I thought it was worth it, so I was disappointed to find that rookies had to wear crash-helmets instead. Chris was nervous and someone asked him what he'd do if I got trampled to death.

"I'll find myself another Sheila," he said, which I thought was fantastic.

As it was, I managed to stay aboard ET, the bull, until the eight-second bell, then lost face by falling over as I dismounted. It was still one of the proudest moments of my life.

After riding the bull, we went to the beach where we saw an advertisement for camel rides. It looked boring because all the camels were part of a camel-train, with each camel tied to the one in front by its nose. I asked about the prospects of riding one by myself, perhaps galloping along the beach, and the owner agreed as long as I didn't press charges if I got hurt. Ginger would be my camel.

"Ginger used to be a racing camel," said Jonny, the owner, "but he's now used to being in a train. I've no idea whether he'll just stop, or will lie down, or will only walk. Do you want to take the chance?"

Of course I did. The camel-train had left Ginger behind and by now was off at the end of the beach. I gave Ginger some encouragement to set off in the direction of the train: he thought about it, went into an interesting series of bucks and then started galloping. This was as exciting as riding ET! It felt much faster than being on a racehorse, but maybe that was because I was much higher up.

*

Chris and I decided to start our own Tiger Moth operation and borrowed the Tiger I had flown during the summer. By testing the waters, or rather skies, with a borrowed airplane during the winter, we had the option of buying an airplane if the company was successful, or returning it to Syerston should the idea fail.

With one rented Moth, the company was started in the winter of 2001. We called it Tiger Airways.

At first, there were not too many flights – one or two a day as we got started. The people who came to fly were a lovely mixture of people who had never flown an aircraft through to pilots who had flown in WW2 and were being given a Special Birthday Flight as a gift to bring back memories. People were soon asking me to fly aerobatic displays for weddings and funerals: dropping ashes for people's recently deceased relatives we called 'The Ashes Flights'. As word spread, we added another

biplane, this time a Stampe SV4, to the fleet, and another pilot.

We were to run Tiger Airways for another 17 years and I considered myself to be the luckiest person in the world. Sadly, Chris died from bone marrow cancer in 2017 and, soon after this, the CAA closed down Tiger Airways. As they explained, we had run it together so, without Chris, there was no Tiger Airways.

Heartbroken, I sold all the aircraft for a pittance and the prices I got didn't even cover the mortgages still outstanding on the six biplanes, the RF6 and the Firefly. Sadly, I had no option as the hanger cost £3,000 a month to keep aeroplanes that were no longer going to fly and were worth less as they got older.

My flying days were over: I had fallen off my bicycle returning from work in June 2016 and sustained a blood clot to the brain. So my commercial flying licence was temporarily removed.

With no reason to stay in Gloucester, I looked to move for a new start and a new life elsewhere. Initially I tried to move south, to be nearer my mother and sister, but the house prices were well above anything I could afford. A friend, Julie Angell, hunted for homes for me further north, using Rightmove on the computer. Embarrassingly I couldn't and still cannot use a computer with any success. I sold my house in Gloucester and then bought a house in Gedney Hill, Lincolnshire. It was the best move possible as it rarely rains here and seems to have more sunshine than in any other county in the UK. The garden at Gedney Hill is three times the size of my house in Gloucester, so I have taken up gardening with unexpected passion. My dog, Tiger, moved with me. I'd bought him as a rescue pup in Gloucester while flying for Tiger Airways (hence the name). He and Chris had become close friends and at Chris' memorial service, I played the saxophone while Tiger 'sang' Morning Has Broken. Tiger kept me alive during the worst months of my life, with Chris' death and the closure of Tiger Airways.

Tiger is an exceptional dog. He gained his bronze, silver and gold certificates from the Kennel Club all within one month and three days: it's usual to wait six months between each certificate. I trained him in agility and he rapidly gained championship status. Then I enrolled him as a therapy dog, where he visited care homes in Gloucester, brightening their lives.

A friend, Randal Carey, offered me Solar – a Harris Hawk – as he was retiring from being a professional falconer, due to his health. He had flown with me previously, both in a biplane and with my Golden Eagle, Xarra. Solar then joined me and Tiger and I taught her to hunt, with Tiger's help. He would demonstrate to her how to chase a rabbit; she would follow him and a few months later she became a brilliant hunting hawk providing most meals for us all. I now take Tiger to visit care homes in Lincolnshire on a regular basis to help the elderly living there: he's been my soulmate for 12 years now.

Although my aircraft flying days are behind me, flying continues to rule my life, albeit with a hawk and not an aircraft. Flying Solar with Tiger as back-up is fabulous: Tiger surpasses himself by always finding Solar when she has caught a rabbit or bird in thick crop or at the bottom of a deep ditch and I have no idea where she is.

I still believe that life is good.

FLYING

To live is to fly
To fly is to live
Some live to fly
Others fly to live

Flying......
Above an overcast
Beneath layered cloud
A narrow tunnel of light
Of life, of hope
Eerie quiet
But for the purr of the engine
Is this seventh Heaven
Or beyond?

Only an airplane
Can give this magic feeling
Of life within life
Of life after life
Or is this a glimpse
Of the afterlife?

A cloud appears
The spell is lost
But the feeling of peace remains
Tranquillity, smooth skies
Stillness

Here above in the skies
Looking up always higher
Never down never lower

Can happiness really be found
There below on Mother Earth?
There's no reality below
Lies, mistrust, cheating
Dishonesty, hatred, deceiving
Unhappiness, sorrow abounds

While up up in the skies
The calling clear blue skies
They're beckoning, reaching
To draw you higher

Peace and love are found
Friendliness and trust
Bad thoughts scatter like dust
Honesty and calmness remain

To fly is to live
To live is to fly.

Milton Keynes UK
Ingram Content Group UK Ltd.
UKHW041837121024
449535UK00001B/139